NATURAL PENNSYLVANIA

NATURAL
PENNSYLVANIA

*Exploring the
State Forest
Natural Areas*

CHARLES
FERGUS

STACKPOLE
BOOKS

Published by
STACKPOLE BOOKS
5067 Ritter Road
Mechanicsburg, PA 17055
www.stackpolebooks.com

10 9 8 7 6 5 4 3 2 1

First edition

Printed in the United States of America

Cover design by Caroline Stover
Cover photographs by the author

Library of Congress Cataloging-in-Publication Data

Fergus, Charles
    Natural Pennsylvania : exploring the state forest natural areas / Charles Fergus.— 1st ed.
    p. cm.
  ISBN 0-8117-2038-1
    1. Forest reserves—Pennsylvania—Guidebooks. 2. Pennsylvania—Guidebooks. I. Title.

SD428.A2 P44 2002
333.78'2'09748—dc21   2001034865

For Will, my good helper,
who kept me from walking too fast and missing the frogs

CONTENTS

INTRODUCTION

Centuries-old hemlocks whose trunks grow thick and straight, red-brown pillars sidelit by the dawn.

A chain of ponds: the remains of ice hillocks that rose when glaciers lay on the land, when musk oxen roamed a windswept tundra where today an oak forest dominates.

A canyon with waterfalls tumbling down its rocky slopes, groves of red pine, and nesting bald eagles.

A creeping shrub thought to be twelve hundred years old.

Bogs with plants that trap and eat insects.

A pure stand of paper birch.

Islands that echo with the squawks of nesting egrets, a gap cut by a stream through a sandstone mountain, a pocket of pin oaks near a bustling city.

Otters and warblers and salamanders and dragonflies. Plants ranging from tiny spring beauties to towering pines that make you stop and listen to the breeze murmuring a hundred feet above your head.

All of these can be found in the little-known complex of natural areas set aside within Pennsylvania's state-owned forests. The natural areas protect and showcase rare plants, unusual animals, striking geological formations, and special forest types and ecosystems. Sixty-one such places exist, from an island in the Delaware River near Philadelphia to Pike County's jut toward New Jersey in the Poconos; from the highest point in the commonwealth, in Somerset County just north of the Mason-Dixon line, to Warren County near the New York border. Pennsylvania has over two million acres of state forest lands open to the public for hiking, sightseeing, and nature appreciation. The state forests are accessible through a network of dirt and gravel roads, many of them built by the Civilian Conservation Corps in the 1930s. The natural areas, which total more than sixty-nine thousand acres, are managed by the Bureau of Forestry, an arm of the Pennsylvania Department of Conservation and Natural Resources.

Before writing this book, I began planning for a long and challenging season in the field. I waxed my hiking boots and made sure my compass, binoculars, and camera were in good order. I bought several new field guides to fill gaps in my library, as well as a new daypack to carry them in. In February, on cross-country skis and snowshoes, I made my first visits to natural areas still deep in snow. I planned a canoe trip that had to be postponed when rain turned a river into a muddy roller coaster, and a forecast of snow and fifty-mile-an-hour winds suggested that, in mid-April, it was not yet time to float through a certain natural area in northern Pennsylvania.

I also contacted Jim Nelson, retired chief forester for the state of Pennsylvania and one of the architects of the natural area system. We met in late April at the Hemlocks in Perry County, between Nelson's home in East Berlin and mine in Centre County. Nelson showed up driving a forest green Dodge Dakota pickup truck with a personalized license plate that read "4STRY." He was of medium height, with combed-back gray hair and merry blue eyes set in a weather-pinked face. He had brought his dog Toby, a spaniel of mixed ancestry who, Nelson said, was "seventeen years old and still going strong." We sat on a log with the grove of virgin hemlocks filling the valley before us like a deep-green lake. The hammering of a pileated woodpecker rang out from Rising Mountain, and around us the buds of striped maple and black birch swelled a clear, pale green, ready to send out leaves.

According to Nelson, the first special sites in the state forests were set aside informally during the early 1900s. Most of them were scraps of the old-growth woods that had once covered much of Pennsylvania—remnants that, for one reason or another, usually a boundary dispute or surveying error, had escaped the widespread logging that had temporarily made Pennsylvania the lumber capital of the nation while badly despoiling the land. At that time, the Bureau of Forestry was a fledgling organization set up by conservation-minded foresters such as Joseph T. Rothrock, the state's first commissioner of forestry. The agency was charged with buying logged-over land (the going rate was two dollars an acre), laying the groundwork for the new second-growth forests that, the early conservationists foresaw, would once again make Pennsylvania a productive, sylvan place.

In 1921, the state legislature authorized the Bureau of Forestry to protect groves of trees deemed "unique and unusual"; the sites were called forest monuments. In 1970, the name for such lands was changed to natural areas. Foresters were instructed to look for old-growth stands that had been missed during earlier surveys and to identify distinctive plant communities, such as those in bogs, as well as the best examples of typical forest types—northern hardwood, mixed oak, hardwood swamp, and the like—that occur in present-day Pennsylvania. People from outside the agency also proposed places that were exceptionally scenic or had special biological, historical, or geological significance. Some natural areas were envisioned to be prime sites for scientific research; others for their educational value. Several areas were set aside partly because they had been badly abused, such as Carbaugh Run in Adams County. There, Nelson told me, the woods were cut three and four times for the making of charcoal, then swept by repeated wildfires. Today Carbaugh Run Natural Area is growing back as healthy woodland, demonstrating the resilience that the eastern deciduous forest often seems able to muster.

As Nelson and I sat on our log at the Hemlocks, he emphasized that the natural areas are not managed for commercial timber sales, still a major part of the Bureau of Forestry's mission, as Pennsylvania's hardwoods are some of the most valuable forest resources in the nation. Biological and physical processes will operate without human interference, giving scientists a chance to document the cycling of natural systems and the effects on forests of fire, insect infestations, and normal aging and decline of dominant tree and plant types. In old-growth stands, foresters will take no heroic measures to save trees that are, in fact, nearing the end of their life span; instead, smaller trees will grow to fill gaps in the forest canopy created when mature trees die. Regarding the pure stand of paper birches in the Marion Brooks Natural Area in Elk County, Nelson said, "Birches are not trees of the climax forest. We recognize that some day we'll lose them. It will be fascinating to see how long the stand lasts and what kinds of trees replace the birches."

Nelson went over the list of natural areas, pointing out unique qualities of each: I wanted to know when a given area could be seen in its best light before planning my days afield. When we were done, we hiked down into the Hemlocks—Nelson, his old dog Toby, and I. Ferns cloaked the slopes from which rose the mammoth trees, their boles innocent of branches for many feet, trees that had been seedlings a century before the United States came into existence.

We followed the trail toward Patterson Run, gurgling in its rocky bed. I spotted a pair of hermit thrushes, their rumps reddish and their pale breasts marked with dark speckles. They bobbed their tails nervously before flitting off into the deep shade of the hemlocks. Perhaps they had stopped off in this cool mountain valley on their migration; maybe I'd see them in the northern tier, in Lycoming or Tioga County, come summer. Or maybe they would stay and nest in the ferns at the base of a wind-thrown giant, or in a shrubby hemlock that stood waiting for its chance to surge upward toward the sun.

· · ·

I hope this book appeals to armchair travelers who enjoy reading about nature. I hope even more that it inspires people to go exploring in Pennsylvania's natural places. I love to hike in the Rocky Mountains, paddle and portage through the canoe country of Minnesota, and explore the rugged coast of Iceland—but I also thrill to the considerable charms of Penn's Woods. Where possible, I tried to visit natural areas in the company of experts—biologists, botanists, archaeologists, birders, naturalists—who possessed special knowledge of the sites and their unique features.

I have organized *Natural Pennsylvania* to be a companion work to a booklet published by the Bureau of Forestry, *Pennsylvania State Forest Natural Areas & Wild Areas,* which numbers and briefly describes the natural areas and arranges them by state forest district. (The booklet also covers sixteen wild areas, which are larger, more remote tracts of land.) The twenty-four-page publication is available free from the Bureau of Forestry, Pennsylvania Department of Conservation and Natural Resources, P.O. Box 8552, Harrisburg, PA 17105-8552.

Anyone intending to visit a natural area should first obtain a public-use map for the forest district in which it is found. The maps are free and can be requested from the Bureau of Forestry at the address above. They are also available, either on-site or by mail, from each state forest district office. A list of the twenty district offices, with addresses and telephone numbers, appears as an appendix to this book. I found the state foresters to be very helpful in suggesting hiking routes and things to see and do.

The Bureau of Forestry publishes maps or brochures for a number of the natural areas, and I've indicated these resources in the text. At times, the publications may be temporarily out of print and unavailable from the Bureau headquarters in Harrisburg. A prospective visitor can, however, request a district forester to make a photocopy of an old brochure. Foresters also told me of plans to issue new brochures for some of the natural areas.

I include directions on how to drive to each natural area. Note that many of the areas are reached via unimproved roads that can become dangerous or impassable in winter. Always check with the local state forest district office before making a winter visit. The Pennsylvania Official Transportation and Tourism Map depicts the natural areas with a special symbol, a small circle with contrasting panels of black and white. The map is available at state welcome centers and interstate rest areas; as part of a *Pennsylvania Visitors Guide* obtainable by telephoning (800) VISIT PA or through the Internet website www.state.pa.us/visit; or by contacting the Pennsylvania Department of Transportation, Distribution Services Unit, 6th Floor Forum Place, 555 Walnut Street, Harrisburg, PA 17101, telephone (717) 787-6746. The *Pennsylvania Atlas and Gazetteer*, published by DeLorme Mapping and available in bookstores, is useful for negotiating back roads and finding natural areas and other outdoor attractions.

Some natural areas can be safely explored by using the state forest public-use maps. Where appropriate, I list the U.S. Geological Survey 7.5-minute topographic quadrangles that cover a given area. You can buy these maps from the federal government, from map dealers (try an Internet search), and from local outfitting stores. All of the natural areas can be visited during day trips, although several, such as Kettle Creek Gorge in the Kettle Creek Wild Area in Sullivan County, require a long and strenuous hike. For many of the natural areas, particularly the more isolated ones, it is best to have a compass and know how to use it. I also always carried a survival kit—space blanket, matches in a waterproof container, first-aid supplies, whistle, and knife—which I fortunately never needed to use. Some of the natural areas aren't necessarily intended to be visited by many people. (Though there will always be those admirable diehards who insist on struggling into each and every buggy, humid, slippery, distant place.)

At times during my year in the field, as I strolled along well-trodden paths or hopped from hummock to hummock in swamps or stood on rocks overlooking forested valleys—or, a rather more difficult task, sat at my desk writing about the plants and animals I had seen and the people who had informed me—I wondered if I'd bitten off more than I could chew. *Sixty-one* natural areas. Each one unique, beautiful, and complex. It's hard to characterize a place after having spent a day or perhaps only a morning or an afternoon there, keeping to the safe and predictable trail instead of striking out across the landscape. But invariably I would brighten at the thought that I could go back in the future—and repeated visits during different seasons are certainly the best, and perhaps the only, way to gain a true feeling for a place.

It also felt good knowing that these green places will be protected forever; that the trees will mature; that many years after we are gone, old-growth forests will stand in all their diversity and complexity, rare plants will blossom and scatter seeds, animals will succeed in their generations—and that these habitats and life forms will remain present for our descendants who are willing to seek out, observe, and contemplate.

NATURAL AREA
DEFINITIONS AND
GUIDELINES

1. No human habitation is permitted except primitive-type backpack camping in designated areas only.
2. Access for all but essential administrative activities is restricted to foot trails and non-motorized watercraft, except in designated areas.
3. Buildings and other improvements are restricted to the minimum required for public health, safety, and interpretive aids.
4. Timber harvesting is not permitted except to maintain public safety.
5. Leases and mineral development are prohibited. However, subsurface oil and gas rights may be leased where no surface use or disturbance of any kind will take place on the natural area. New rights-of-way are prohibited except for designated utility corridors in the Bucktail Natural Area.

_____

from *Pennsylvania State Forest Natural Areas & Wild Areas*

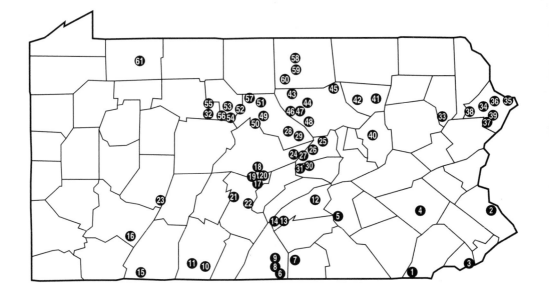

PENNSYLVANIA'S STATE NATURAL AREAS

1. Goat Hill
   Serpentine Barrens
2. David R. Johnson
3. Little Tinicum Island
4. Ruth Zimmerman
5. Sheets Island
   Archipelago
6. Beartown Woods
7. Carbaugh Run
8. Meeting of the Pines
9. Mt. Cydonia Ponds
10. Pine Ridge
11. Sweet Root
12. Box Huckleberry
13. Frank E. Masland, Jr.
14. Hemlocks
15. Mt. Davis
16. Roaring Run
17. Alan Seeger
18. Bear Meadows
19. Big Flat Laurel
20. Detweiler Run

21. Little Juniata
    Water Gap
22. Rocky Ridge
23. Charles F. Lewis
24. Bear Run
25. Halfway Run
26. The Hook
27. Joyce Kilmer
28. Mt. Logan
29. Rosecrans Bog
30. Snyder-Middle-
    swarth
31. Tall Timbers
32. Marion Brooks
33. Spruce Swamp
34. Bruce Lake
35. Buckhorn
36. Little Mud Pond
    Swamp
37. Pennel Run
38. Pine Lake
39. Stillwater

40. Jakey Hollow
41. Tamarack Run
42. Kettle Creek Gorge
43. Algerine Swamp
44. Bark Cabin
45. Devil's Elbow
46. Lebo Red Pine
47. Miller Run
48. Torbert Island
49. Cranberry Swamp
50. East Branch Swamp
51. Tamarack Swamp
52. Bucktail
53. Johnson Run
54. Lower Jerry Run
55. Pine Tree Trail
56. Wycoff Run
57. Forrest H. Dutlinger
58. Black Ash Swamp
59. Pine Creek Gorge
60. Reynolds Spring
61. Anders Run

1   GOAT HILL SERPENTINE BARRENS

602 ACRES, VALLEY FORGE STATE FOREST, CHESTER COUNTY

Fog filled the swales. It drifted down slopes that slanted off in different, confusing directions. It gave the pitch pines—hunched over, twisted—a spooky, surreal aspect, as if they might suddenly rise up, pluck their roots from the ground, and walk off across the land. But of course, plants don't have that kind of mobility.

Dew beaded the autumn-tan grasses in openings between the pines. Spiderwebs looked spun out of silver. From above the fog came the hoarse honking of a flock of Canada geese, and from a nearby redcedar tree, a mockingbird slurred out its string of borrowed birdcalls.

Ed Dix checked his compass before leading the way downhill. "I've been to Goat Hill five or six times," he told me, "but I still find it easy to get turned around here." Dix is a botanist for the Pennsylvania Bureau of Forestry and the author of the booklet *Pennsylvania State Forest Natural Areas & Wild Areas*. It was late October when I met him at Goat Hill Serpentine Barrens. Not a prime time of the year to see plants in flower or to watch for breeding birds, but at least the ticks, those parasitic pests for which Goat Hill is famous, weren't out, and the air was cool. (In summer, the low-lying, unshaded barrens can get stiflingly hot.)

The unmarked path wound between patches of breast-high greenbrier, whose thorny stems sprawled across the ground like tangles of barbed wire. The trail sidestepped around thickets of scrub oak. The shrubby trees were no taller than the greenbriers, and their twisted, springy branches were covered with leaves now turning a dull coppery brown.

"According to the old accounts," said Dix, "Goat Hill Barrens used to be more open, probably because of fires set by the Indians to improve the area for hunting, and fires caused by lightning. But now the trees are starting to close in." The trees include red maple, sassafras, juneberry, black gum, and several species of oaks—post oak, blackjack oak, basket oak, and southern red oak—found only in Pennsylvania's southeast corner.

Goat Hill Serpentine Barrens is set amid fertile farms, well-stocked woodlots, and suburban homes. Its scrubby, marginal character comes from its soil, weathered from deposits of serpentine rock. Geologists believe that serpentine formed tens of miles beneath the earth's surface under extremely high temperatures and pressures, then was squeezed upward through fault zones during eras of mountain building. In the East, serpentine pokes up through the crust in only a few places, most of them in southeastern Pennsylvania and adjacent Maryland. Serpentine is often grayish green in color, and the soil at Goat Hill Barrens shows that same odd tint. The soil is thin, highly erodable, acidic, and not able to hold much moisture. It is low in elements that most plants need, such as potassium, nitrogen, calcium, and phosphorus, and it bears substances toxic to many plants: magnesium, nickel, and chromium. The plants that do grow on serpentine soils are often stunted. And they include many rare species adapted to the inhospitable environment.

Dix and I passed a slumped-in pit where, a century and a half earlier, miners had extracted serpentine ore, perhaps for magnesia, used to produce epsom salts, or chromite, an ingredient in paint. After 1900, much of Pennsylvania's remaining serpentine was carted away for highway fill. I picked up some chips; their telltale dull gray-green was shot through with white veins, and the rocks had a slick, soapy feel.

We scrambled up a slope to a brittle outcropping. "Look." With his fingertips Dix ruffled the tiny, pointed leaves of a small plant growing out of a crack in the rocks. "Fameflower. In summer, it has a beautiful deep pink flower." He showed me maidenhair fern and field chickweed: "The chickweed is an early bloomer; I'm afraid we've missed it, and you need the flower to positively identify the plant." A variety of field chickweed at Goat Hill has not been found anywhere else in the world; dense hairs on the leaves of this ground-hugging plant protect it from drying winds and insulate it against the sun.

I spotted a dainty white bloom among the rocks and knew it for an aster. "Great!" said Dix, leaning in. "I love asters." He identified it as *Aster depauperatus,* the serpentine aster, known from only three counties in Pennsylvania and one county in Maryland.

Botanists list more than two hundred plants as characteristic of the serpentine barrens ecosystem. Sixteen of these plants are endemic, or confined to serpentine sites. Others, like little bluestem and northern dropseed, are prairie grasses stranded far from their current range. Around seven thousand years ago, during an era known as the postglacial hypsithermal period, prairie extended eastward into Pennsylvania; at that time, the climate was warmer and drier than it is today—conditions that still exist in modern serpentine

Grayish green serpentine rock juts from the soil at Goat Hill Serpentine Barrens.

Pitch pine and prairie grasses are key components of the vegetation at serpentine barrens sites.

barrens. Goat Hill hosts the most diverse plant assemblage in all twelve of the serpentine barrens in Chester County, most of which have been destroyed or fragmented by mining and suburban sprawl.

Not only must barrens plants draw nourishment from poor soil and resist drought, winds, and sun, they must also withstand the fires that periodically sweep through these dry lowlands. The thick, plated bark of the pitch pine, the main conifer found at serpentine barrens, protects the tree's vital inner cambium layer against fire. Pitch pines actually benefit from fire: the heat melts a waxy substance in the cones so that the seeds are more easily released.

The fog was lifting as Dix and I followed a powerline right-of-way on a southwesterly heading. The map implied that we briefly crossed the Mason-Dixon line into Maryland. Soon, however, we left the powerline and worked our way north on faint trails into a wooded area. There the pines were low and spectacularly gnarled, almost like high-altitude conifers. In open areas, our boots shushed through broom sedge, a common grass of rough, dry terrain. We heard catbirds mewling and chickadees chittering; a red-bellied woodpecker scolded us with its rattling call, and a cardinal flashed past. Song sparrows scratched for seeds on the ground and plucked the round blue berries from the greenbrier vines.

In spring and summer, Goat Hill Barrens resounds with the singing of birds, including some that are unusual in southeastern Pennsylvania. Whip-poor-wills breed among the severe hills, calling loudly and repeatedly at night. Barred owls nest in woodlands near the northern edge of the natural area, where steep slopes fall away to pretty Octoraro Creek, part of the Pennsylvania scenic rivers system. Breeding warblers include the yellow-throated, pine, worm-eating, black-and-white, chestnut-sided, prairie, Kentucky, hooded, cerulean, and parula species, as well as the yellow-breasted chat and American redstart.

Dix and I looked up as a praying mantis, brown and almost six inches long, went clattering overhead like some Rube Goldberg flying machine. An angle wing butterfly sailed past, its orangish, brown-spotted wings edged with filigrees and angular scallops. The unique plant community at Goat Hill supports a host of butterflies and moths, including fifteen species deemed rare. One of these rarities is the barrens buck moth, known from only a handful of locations across Pennsylvania. In September and early October, adult buck moths fly about in daylight looking for mates. Their wings, spanning two to three inches, are sooty black with white bands; the males have red-tipped abdomens. Females lay their eggs on the stunted oak species. In spring, the spine-studded caterpillars eat the emerging leaves.

The rough green snake is another denizen of serpentine barrens. This shy serpent is classified as a threatened species in Pennsylvania. It has a vivid green back, a pale yellow belly, and a purple-black lining to its mouth, which it may open suddenly in a bizarre grin evolved to startle predators.

Before 1979, Goat Hill Barrens was itself a threatened place. An excavating company proposed quarrying serpentine rock for road-base material. Local citizens banded together to fight the mining. Scientists, personnel from government agencies, and representatives of the Nature Conservancy, a private national organization dedicated to buying and preserving important natural lands, persuaded the commonwealth of Pennsylvania to buy the barrens. Today, the Bureau of Forestry owns 602 acres at Goat Hill and the Nature Conservancy owns 93 adjoining acres; about 300 acres remain in private hands. The National Park Service has designated Goat Hill Barrens as a national natural landmark.

The Nature Conservancy purchased and now manages the 225-acre Chrome Serpentine Barrens, also in Chester County; there, ecologists are experimenting with controlled burning, in which small fires are set to kill off invading brush and trees that, over time, otherwise would shade or crowd out serpentine plants. Such "prescribed burns" may someday be used to maintain the prairies and savannas at Goat Hill. Nearby Nottingham Serpentine Barrens, also preserved through Nature Conservancy efforts, is now a county park with developed trails, picnic and camping areas, fishing ponds, and playgrounds.

No such niceties beckon at Goat Hill.

Ed Dix and I wandered among the pitch pines. We heard a red-tailed hawk screaming high overhead and focused our binoculars on a small band of migrating warblers foraging in the underbrush. We identified the new (to me) trees: blackjack oak, with leathery, triangular leaves; post oak, with cross-shaped leaves; and umbrella magnolia, its lanceolate leaves more than a foot in length, a southern species whose range barely reaches north into Pennsylvania. On the floor of the dwarf forest, we found a clump of American holly, the familiar Christmas plant with its shiny evergreen leaves and red berries. My field guide listed American holly as a shrub or a tree of "moist woods," which Goat Hill Barrens decidedly is not.

I shared the entry with Dix. He smiled and quoted a colleague of his, a botanist with the Nature Conservancy, who says of plants, "They grow where t. y can, not where they should."

TO GET THERE. Head south out of Chester County on U.S. Route 1. After crossing the Mason-Dixon line, continue 2 miles into Maryland. Turn right on Red Pump Road (watch for a sign announcing the Horseshoe Scout Reservation) and drive 1.5 miles, coming back into Pennsylvania, to a small parking area on the left with a sign for the natural area.

From the parking lot, follow the beaten trail to the left toward the powerline right-of-way and several mobile homes. Turn right on the powerline or take the unmarked trail that parallels it. Other paths break off to the right (northeast), forming a maze in the greenbrier-infested woods. Staying within sight of the powerline, the visitor will find serpentine outcrops, evidence of old mining, and many barrens plants. Hikers should wear long trousers to protect against briers, take precautions against ticks, carry ample drinking water, and have a compass and a copy of the Rising Sun, Maryland, topographic quadrangle.

2   DAVID R. JOHNSON

56 ACRES, VALLEY FORGE STATE FOREST, BUCKS COUNTY

Some natural areas are expansive, wild, and imposing. Others are small, calling not for expeditionary outings, but for slow, contemplative rambles. Such a place is David R. Johnson Natural Area, near New Hope in eastern Bucks County, around twenty miles north of Philadelphia and fifteen miles northwest of where the Pennsylvania border thrusts eastward near Trenton, New Jersey.

The area's fifty-six wooded acres surround a small, unnamed brook that was almost dry when I visited in late October; the stream drains into the Delaware River less than a mile to the east. It was a cool and blustery day, and the wind was plucking the last golden leaves from the tuliptrees, whose crowns swung back and forth against a cobalt blue sky. The tuliptree is named for tulip-shaped flowers that appear high in the branches in spring. In the southern Appalachians, where the species attains its greatest growth, tuliptrees can be 200 feet tall. Although considerably shorter than that, the tuliptrees at David R. Johnson were nevertheless the most impressive trees at the natural area: tall, perfectly straight, and with thick, tight-barked trunks.

I saw little in the way of wildlife on my midday walk. A hawk screamed somewhere above the forest canopy, and I was scolded—*chur, chur, chur*—by a red-bellied woodpecker that flew from tree to tree preceding me up the ravine. A wide variety of trees grow in the rich soil of the hollow, including several large hackberries; white ash, sugar maple, and American beech, found more frequently in northern Pennsylvania than in the southeastern part of the state, also graced the site. Leaning against a large beech with a deep cavity in its trunk, I found myself face-to-face with a pair of deer mice. Their pointed noses actively sampled the air as their whiskers twitched and their huge, dark eyes blinked. The rodents kept popping their heads out to look about, then ducking back inside. Deer and raccoon tracks marked the soil near the stream. Undoubtedly the ravine serves as a stopping-off place for migrating songbirds in the fall, although I didn't see any during my brief visit; it would also be an excellent nesting habitat for forest birds in spring and summer.

All too soon, the informal footpath met a line of No Trespassing signs. To stay within the natural area, I angled downslope and to the left, crossing the brook (a trickle under flat stones), and ascending to gravel-surfaced Laurel Road. Open hardwood forest covered the slope above me. A leisurely walk downhill brought me back to the car.

The natural area is named for a former owner of the site.

TO GET THERE. From the intersection of PA Routes 32 and 179 in New Hope, drive north on Route 32 for 3.8 miles to Laurel Road on the left, which continues up the small, narrow valley occupied by the natural area. After parking at a wide spot on the berm along Route 32, hike uphill on the nearby gated woods road on a southwesterly heading.

---

3   LITTLE TINICUM ISLAND

200 ACRES, VALLEY FORGE STATE FOREST, DELAWARE COUNTY

We think of Pennsylvania as a place of mountains, forests, farms—not of the sea in any way. Yet one small part of our state is directly influenced by the Atlantic Ocean: lands fringing the lower Delaware River, which rises and falls twice a day with the tide.

Little Tinicum Island is a welt of sand and silt in the river about twelve miles downstream from the center of Philadelphia and a few score miles north of Delaware Bay, which opens to the Atlantic between Cape May, New Jersey, and Cape Henlopen, Delaware. The island lies on an east-west orientation. It is 2.2 miles long and about 200 yards wide. Apparently, it is eroding from the upstream end (it was reported to be 2.6 miles long in 1862).

I saw the island on a clear day in late October. I had been planning to canoe to it, and indeed, I now realized that I could have done so, despite the many warnings I had gotten regarding tidal currents and wind, as well as boat-swamping wakes from passing freighters, tugboats, oil tankers, and ocean liners, as a dredged, forty-foot-deep shipping channel leading to the ports of Philadelphia and Camden, New Jersey, lies south of the island. But I hadn't brought my canoe, not wanting to haul it on top of my truck through southeastern Pennsylvania while visiting other natural areas, or leave it parked outside a friend's center city apartment.

So I found myself in a motorboat, with Mike Silvestri of South Philadelphia at the controls, cruising across five hundred yards of quiet, olive green water between the town of Essington, Pennsylvania, and Little Tinicum Island. From the boat, the island appeared as a long, narrow strip of sandy shoreline backed up by brush and trees. Silvestri steered the boat east and ran along the island's north shore. Overhead, an airliner descended toward the Philadelphia International Airport with a screaming, thundering din. The plane flew so low that I could see the hydraulic lines in its wheel wells and the rivets on its silver skin.

When Europeans arrived in the New World, an estimated 5,700 acres of freshwater tidal marsh bordered the Delaware in southeastern Pennsylvania, fingering back into shallows, coves, and tributary streams. Today, only around two hundred acres of the original marshland remain in our state, protected by the John Heinz National Wildlife Refuge, a federal property on the mainland across from Little Tinicum Island. In the boat with Silvestri and me were Mike McMenamin, law enforcement officer at the refuge, who had arranged the ride, and Valley Forge assistant district forester Jeff Stuffle, whose district includes Little Tinicum Island Natural Area. Across the river, oil refineries jutted up against the hazy sky. Docks, marinas, petrochemical plants, and the looming gray walls of factories and warehouses made the shoreline inhospitable to wildlife.

With so much of the surrounding habitat extinguished, Little Tinicum Island is a particularly important resting area for birds during their spring and fall migrations along the Atlantic Flyway. Waterfowl, wading birds, and perching birds all descend on this tiny oasis. The best time to spot spring migrants and breeding species is from late April through early June. Most autumn migrants pass down the river between September and early November.

John Miller is an ardent birder who works for Northwest Airlines at the Philadelphia Airport. He keeps a list of the species he has spotted on and near Little Tinicum. Birding from a small motorboat, he has seen bald eagles, ospreys, cormorants, common and red-throated loons, brants, whistling swans, and a variety of grebes, herons, sandpipers, gulls, terns, ducks, and perching birds. According to Miller, the peregrine falcons nesting on Philadelphia's highway bridges sometimes hunt for waterfowl on small ponds at the island's east end. Many species nest on the island, including green herons, mallards, black ducks, ring-necked pheasants, tree swallows, house wrens, warblers, and flycatchers.

Little Tinicum Island, in the Delaware River south of Philadelphia, provides nesting and resting habitats for birds ranging from green herons to warblers.

In the Delaware estuary, wildlife and plants must cope with changing salinity as ocean water flows up the river on the rising tide, mixes with fresh water, then ebbs away again. Fifty years ago, the Delaware was little more than an open sewer, poisoned with sewage and industrial waste. But antipollution efforts in the late twentieth century helped the Delaware flush itself toward cleanliness, and ocean fish such as herring, anchovies, bluefish, flounder, and needlefish now venture far up the waterway. The tidal waters also support fishes that spend most of their adult lives in salt water and migrate into fresh water to spawn, including American shad and striped bass, both favorites of anglers. Atlantic sturgeon, once abundant in the Delaware, may be coming back—biologists spotted a six- to eight-foot specimen in 1997 near Easton, far above Philadelphia—and the smaller shortnose sturgeon, a state and federally designated endangered species, are rapidly increasing in the river. Then there are the nondescript smaller fishes, many of them rare or endangered in Pennsylvania, with outlandish and unfamiliar titles: striped killifish, mummichog, pipefish, hogchoker.

In the estuary, botanists have found nearly twenty species of plants growing in the intertidal zone, the area between high and low tides—rare plants with odd names such as awl-shaped mudwort and sensitive joint-vetch. A brief survey of Little Tinicum Island in August 1983 turned up seventeen different trees and shrubs and thirty-four plants. Three of the plants were extremely rare for Pennsylvania: water hemp, Walter's barnyard grass, and wild rice. Other plants are more common, including exotics such as Japanese knotweed, purple loosestrife, Norway maple, and tree of heaven, aggressive invaders that can choke out native plants and alter natural ecosystems.

A few mammals haunt Little Tinicum Island. Visitors may find tracks of red foxes, opossums, raccoons, muskrats, and Norway rats on the beach at low tide. Gray squirrels live in the trees.

Silvestri guided the boat into the shallows near the island's east end. Stuffle and I, wearing hipboots, eased over the side and waded ashore. In 1640, Swedish explorers occupied Little Tinicum Island and the near shoreline, where they established the first permanent European settlement in what is now Pennsylvania, thirty-nine years before William Penn started his colony. In 1643, the first royal governor of New Sweden, Johan Printz (he weighed three hundred pounds, and the local Indians dubbed him "Big Tub"), constructed the Printzhoff, a combined home and government office building, on the site where today Governor Printz Park stands on the mainland in Essington. In 1655, Dutch troops led by Peter Stuyvesant, governor of New Netherland, seized the Swedish colony. After the British wrested control from the Dutch, settlers built dikes on Little Tinicum Island and grew crops and pastured livestock there. Either British or American forces breached the dikes during the Revolutionary War. Modern dredging operations to maintain and deepen the Delaware shipping channel have dumped tons of spoil on Little Tinicum Island, obliterating all traces of past occupations.

Stuffle and I kicked through vast quantities of trash that had washed up on the island—plastic bottles of all colors, shapes, and sizes, old tar-stained dock pilings and rubber boots and rusting steel drums and frayed ropes and used cocaine vials. There weren't any birds about, so we checked out the trees, which included silver maple, box elder, green ash, Devil's club, sweetgum, black gum, tuliptree, dogwood, sumac, mulberry, catalpa, aspen, alder, willow, red maple, cottonwood, black cherry, sycamore—all in about two acres of sandy soil. Most of the trees had dropped their leaves, although some, including the orange-and-maroon gums, remained in glorious color. A summertime foray would have been less comfortable, with blackberry canes and poison ivy barring the way, and hordes of mosquitoes and biting flies.

Stuffle and I hiked around the eastern prow of the island on the thin band of sand. Big jets screamed over one after another. The wake from a freighter slapped against our boots. The tide had turned, the ebb had begun, and fresh water was flowing against salt water, washing it back out to sea. The difference between high and low tides in the estuary is nearly six feet. Little Tinicum Island changes size with the tide, from around 200 acres at high tide to 250 acres at low tide. During low tide, a person can walk around the island fifty to seventy-five feet out from shore.

We didn't have much time; Silvestri needed to get back to his yacht club, where homemade ravioli were being prepared. Stuffle and I splashed through the shallows to the boat, and soon the wooded island receded in our wake.

TO GET THERE. Take the exit for Wanamaker Avenue and PA Route 420 off I-95. Drive south toward the Delaware River for 0.5 mile to Second Street in Essington. Turn right and continue about 100 yards to Governor Printz Park. Here the grassy riverbank affords a good view of Little Tinicum Island. You can also see the island when flying into or out of the Philadelphia airport.

Little Tinicum Island is accessible by canoe, rowboat, or light motorized boat; pull any watercraft well above the high-tide line, and tie it up with slack. Do not try to swim to the island. There are no trails, marked or otherwise. Primitive camping is permitted, and waterfowl hunting and fishing are allowed, except in posted areas.

To learn more about freshwater tidal marsh ecology, visit the 1,200-acre John Heinz National Wildlife Refuge at Tinicum. The refuge, open daily from 8:30 A.M. to sunset, has trails, wildlife observation platforms, and a 145-acre impoundment that attracts migrating waterfowl. The main entrance at 86th Street and Lindbergh Boulevard leads to a visitor contact station open from 9 A.M. to 4 P.M. every day. On weekends, staff members and volunteers give programs and lead nature walks for the public. For more information, call (215) 365-3118. Request a map with directions to the refuge.

---

4   RUTH ZIMMERMAN

33 ACRES, VALLEY FORGE STATE FOREST, BERKS COUNTY

While exploring Ruth Zimmerman Natural Area, I concluded that the place needs a tree trail—a footpath to take visitors past markers denoting the burly pin oaks and behemoth red oaks and classically straight tuliptrees and rough-trunked shagbark hickories and smooth-barked white ash trees that dominate the site. I went there with Maurice Hobaugh, now

Many different types of trees, including large pin oaks, greet the visitor at Ruth Zimmerman Natural Area.

retired, who had been chief forester in the Valley Forge district when Ruth Zimmerman, a widow, donated her property to the state in 1989. "We didn't know what to do with it," Hobaugh admitted to me, "so we made it into a natural area, set it aside as an example of forest succession." I had learned elsewhere that Mrs. Zimmerman did not want to see her property developed—it's in an area where many new homes now stand—and for that reason had given it to the state.

The natural area, which is just east of Reading, lies far from other Bureau of Forestry holdings. It is made up of two tracts separated by the paved Mexico Road. In the natural area grow American beech, black gum, chestnut oak, white oak, red maple, yellow birch, and bigtooth aspen trees. Hobaugh pointed out a good-size American chestnut, a tree that was once common in Pennsylvania but has been driven near to extinction by a blight caused by a fungus. He identified a slippery elm: "If the leaf feels rough, it's slippery elm, and if it feels smooth, it's American elm, which is the opposite of what you'd expect after hearing the trees' names." Beneath the big trees, understory trees and shrubs prospered: black haw, maple-leaf viburnum, hawthorn, spicebush, witch hazel, and ironwood, whose smooth gray trunk has a rippled, sinewy look to it, earning it the common name "musclewood."

Narrow Antietam Creek winds through the 17.7-acre tract on the south side of Mexico Road; that parcel has the larger trees and the greater species diversity. The tract north of Mexico Road, 15.8 acres, has wetter soil and grows mainly red maple, sassafras, and swamp white oak. Along the eastern border of the smaller parcel stands a lightning-blasted red oak with a ten-inch-wide strip of bark blown off its side from ground level to forty feet up.

Although the soil is fairly rocky, Hobaugh pronounced the larger south parcel as "site one" in quality. "To a forester, that means it grows big, tall trees." Hobaugh is no stranger to big, tall trees: he is listed as the nominator of twenty-six champion and cochampion trees—the largest of their species known in the state—in the most recent edition of *Big Trees of Pennsylvania*, sponsored and published by the Pennsylvania Forestry Association. None of Hobaugh's champions are at Ruth Zimmerman, but I noticed the old forester casting critical glances at the height and crown spread of several trees there. He looked up at one particularly majestic red oak—with a straight, thick trunk, heavy limbs, and a broad, robust crown—and estimated that it was ninety feet tall: "Almost makes you want to stand at attention and salute," he said.

TO GET THERE. From the village of Oley, where PA Routes 662 and 73 intersect and run concurrently, drive west. After 1.8 miles, Route 662 veers off to the right; immediately after, exit left off Route 73 onto Oley Road. Go 0.2 mile on Oley Road, and turn left on Basket Road. After 1.9 miles, turn right on Mexico Road. Continue 0.7 mile and park on the left in an informal parking area, the old driveway of the Zimmerman residence, adjacent to the concrete slab foundation, all that remains of the house.

5   SHEETS ISLAND ARCHIPELAGO

70 ACRES, WEISER STATE FOREST, DAUPHIN COUNTY

The Susquehanna ran full and olive green. Merlin Benner motored the flat-bottomed boat against the river's flow, guiding it in close to the island, under overhanging trees whose crowns were festooned with stick-built nests. A stale chicken-house smell tainted the air, despite the drizzle and the breeze on this raw April morning. Benner, a biologist for the Bureau of Forestry, asked me to throw the anchor overboard. He grinned while offering advice on behavior beneath an egret rookery: "Don't look up with your mouth open. Always wear a hat."

The great egret, *Ardea alba,* breeds in just one place in Pennsylvania: Wade Island, in the middle of the mile-wide Susquehanna within the city limits of Harrisburg.

An egret, pure white against the leaden sky, came sailing in to the island. It extended its black legs and, with a flurry of wing flapping, slowed itself sufficiently to grab hold of a branch, upon which it teetered back and forth. It held a stick crosswise in its bill. It added the stick to a half-built nest. At another nest ten feet away, an egret straightened out its long neck, pointed its bill upward, gave a hoarse call, *rowk,* and fluffed up its feathers. Delicate white plumes rose above the bird's back like fountains of spray.

Those spectacular plumes—or, rather, human greed for them—nearly caused the species' extinction in the early twentieth century.

In *Birds of America,* published in 1917, T. Gilbert Pearson wrote that egret plumes "have long been sought as adornments for women's headwear. The only way to get these 'aigrettes' is to shoot the bird, and shoot it at the time it is engaged in the care of its nestlings. . . . The plume-hunter must be content to wait until the young appear, and the instinct of parental care is so aroused that the old birds will return again and again despite the fact that they see their companions falling all about them before the guns of the inhuman hunters."

In 1886, feather dealers in New York were paying ninety cents for the plumes of a single egret. In 1902, over twenty-eight hundred pounds of plumes were sold in London, commanding almost twice their weight in gold. Pearson and other conservationists reckoned that market hunting would ultimately wipe out the great egret. But laws and educational campaigns—and, in 1905, nationwide outrage over the murder of a warden employed by the Audubon Society at the hands of Florida plume hunters—helped bring the egret back. Today *Ardea alba* breeds widely in the South and along the Mississippi River. Great egrets have nested in Pennsylvania since 1975. Approximately 150 pairs nest on Wade Island.

During the spring, when egrets and herons are courting and laying eggs, and in summer, when adult birds are feeding their young, Wade Island is off-limits to the public, although people are allowed to float past and anchor to watch the birds. I'm sure I wouldn't want to spend much time beneath the colony, based on what Benner has found on the guano-spattered ground: dead creatures that the parent birds caught, swallowed, and then regurgitated to feed their nestlings, including baby wood ducks, frogs, crayfish (the staple in summer), and various fishes, such as bass, sunfish, minnows, and catfish.

Wade Island is part of the Sheets Island Archipelago, a natural area that encompasses around four dozen islands scattered in the Susquehanna, over seven miles from the Rockville train bridge near Marysville to the Harvey Taylor Bridge linking downtown Harrisburg with the west shore. On Wade Island, the densely grown trees were not fully leafed out when we visited, giving us an excellent view of the nests of the egrets, as well as those of black-crowned night-herons, crow-size birds with long, white plumes hanging down like tassels from the backs of their black-capped heads and eyes as red as rubies. Wade Island is the largest black-crowned night-heron rookery in the state, with one hundred to three hundred nesting pairs.

A double-crested cormorant flew over our boat and landed on the far side of the island. It, too, held a stick in its beak. Accomplished divers, cormorants are fish-eating waterbirds whose population has expanded throughout the Northeast since the banning of the pesticide DDT in the 1970s. In 1996, birders found cormorants nesting on Wade Island, the first such site in Pennsylvania. Now, all along the lower Susquehanna, cormorants can be seen perched on rocks and snags, holding their wings out to dry, looking like huge grounded bats.

Grackles, glossy black with yellow eyes, repeated their squeaky *creeek* calls. The *ha-ronk* of a Canada goose signaled that a pair of this ground-nesting species had set up housekeeping on Wade. Fish crows gave their nasal caws; two blue-winged teal flashed past. Red-winged blackbirds sang a liquid *ook-a-lee.* But it was the great egrets that held our attention.

"Look closely at their bills," Benner said.

I focused my binoculars on an egret. The base of its bill was a brilliant lime green. "They take on that color during the breeding season," Benner told me. The eye was yellow with a black iris. The white aigrettes rose airily above the bird's back, and its fluffy head looked like a ball of cotton. Throughout the colony, egrets were displaying to their mates and calling loudly.

When we had seen enough, we weighed anchor and drifted downstream. Mist softened the lines of the capitol and the tall buildings in the city. Floating in the Susquehanna were wood ducks, common mergansers, horned grebes, buffleheads, and half a dozen loons, big birds in their striking black-and-white breeding plumage. The loons sat low in the water like submarines and kept diving and popping back up again. Above the river flew a belted kingfisher, along with mixed flocks of northern rough-winged swallows, tree swallows, and barn swallows. A large tern sent us scrambling for our field guides. Long wings, forked tail, a black-topped head, and a huge scissors-shaped scarlet bill identified it as a Caspian tern, a species that migrates through Pennsylvania.

On the fringe of a wooded island, a great blue heron stood like a lanky statue. A smaller green heron shuffled and then froze, crouching, on a limb. A snowy egret hunted in the shallows. At the head of Sheets Island itself, blackbirds scolded a big, shadowy bird skulking in the brush; probably it was a hawk, and perhaps it had taken a blackbird as prey, and it quite refused to give us a look.

Farther along, we beached the boat and climbed the steep, muddy bank onto Sheets, at thirty-four acres the largest island in the natural area. The rich alluvial soil supported river birch, silver maple, sycamore, oak, and, according to Benner, papaw trees, the last a southern species that is rare in Pennsylvania. In summer, the island would be covered with herbaceous plants, including trout lily, false Solomon's seal, and jack-in-the-pulpit. Elderberry, buttonbush, and viburnum grew in clumps. Poison ivy, just sending forth its glossy pernicious leaves, thicketed the ground and climbed up tree trunks; the plants had hairy stalks as thick as my thigh.

If inhospitable to humans, the islands are a welcoming habitat for wildlife. On Sheets, we spotted many migrating songbirds, including yellow-rumped warblers, yellow warblers, blue-gray gnatcatchers, a least flycatcher, and a ruby-crowned kinglet. The Pennsylvania Audubon Society has designated the Sheets Island Archipelago as an Important Bird Area. A brochure published by the Bureau of Forestry lists 217 avian species—including 21 considered threatened or endangered in Pennsylvania—that use the islands for breeding, feeding, or resting during migration. Some of the rarer species are American bitterns, yellow-crowned night-herons, ospreys, bald eagles, and peregrine falcons. On Sheets, Benner has found signs of river otters: droppings filled with fish scales; slides, steep banks down which the otters skid when entering into the water; and a probable nest cavity, a hole in the bank that, when we checked it, did not show signs of recent use. "We think otters are working their way up the Susquehanna from Chesapeake Bay," Benner said.

We got back into the boat and pushed off. The current caught hold and hurried us along. The breeze blew the drizzle into our faces. We sat snugged down into our life vests, gloved hands ready to bring binoculars to bear should anything offer. The boat drifted quietly between the newly greening islands.

Twenty-five years ago, I lived for a while in Harrisburg. From the shore, I had often gazed on the islands and found them beautiful, but I'd had no idea how productive they were, and I had never taken the time to visit them. I vowed to bring my family back for a float trip.

"It's a great stretch for canoeing during the summer," said Benner. "You can stop and wade in many places. A breeze often springs up during the day, coming upriver, so sometimes you have to paddle just to get downstream; you can use the islands to break the wind.

"You forget you're in the city. When you get a little farther down, you don't even hear the cars and trucks."

TO GET THERE. To canoe through the Sheets Island Archipelago, put in at the Pennsylvania Fish and Boat Commission launching site at Fort Hunter (make sure your boat registration is current), just off U.S. Route 322 north of Harrisburg. An unhurried day's float will get you to another Fish and Boat Commission launch site at West Fairview, on the west shore at the mouth of Conodoguinet Creek. An alternate takeout farther downriver is City Island, accessible via the Market Street Bridge. The Susquehanna is a powerful river. Do not attempt this trip during high water. Every passenger should wear a life jacket at all times.

6   BEARTOWN WOODS

27 ACRES, MICHAUX STATE FOREST, FRANKLIN COUNTY

Michaux State Forest straddles South Mountain, the northernmost extension of the famous Blue Ridge. This rocky arm of the Appalachian Mountain system runs from North Carolina's Great Smoky Mountains to just south of Carlisle, Pennsylvania, where it sinks into the fertile floor of the Great Valley. Of four natural areas in Michaux State Forest, Beartown Woods is the smallest and least exceptional. It lies less than two miles from the Maryland border along Pennsylvania Route 16.

The natural area surrounds a small pocket of northern hardwoods. The sugar maple, yellow birch, and American beech trees are much more common in northern Pennsylvania, New England, and Canada, although they also show up in microhabitats—including damp, north-facing slopes, such as the one at Beartown Woods—as far south as Georgia. In the natural area, many of the trees are straight, tall, and impressively large. American basswood, white pine, eastern hemlock (including many dead specimens, still standing), and tuliptrees grow near pretty Red Run. A short interpretive trail has signposts giving attributes of the various trees and listing products for which their wood is used.

When I visited, many of the signs had been defaced or stolen. The plaintive calling of a wood thrush and the rush of Red Run were all but drowned out by the roar of passing cars and trucks. The Appalachian Trail crosses Route 16 at Beartown Woods, and you can get away from the motor drone by hiking north on the footpath, which ascends into drier oak forest. If Beartown Woods were tucked away in some hollow, arrived at after a healthy walk, it would be a lovely spot for a picnic or an hour of meditation.

TO GET THERE. You have to look sharp, and watch in your rearview mirror for tailgaters, to arrive safely. Beartown Woods lies about 5 miles east of Waynesboro and a mile and a half west of Blue Ridge Summit on PA Route 16. Look for a picnic table on the south side of the road.

7   CARBAUGH RUN

780 ACRES, MICHAUX STATE FOREST, ADAMS COUNTY

"People have probably been using this trail for twelve thousand years." Kurt Carr, an archaeologist for the Pennsylvania Historical and Museum Commission, paused on the path next to Carbaugh Run; he bent, picked up a small stone, looked closely at it. "Rhyolite," he said, flipping it back onto the ground, "but not cultural."

On our left, the clean waters of Carbaugh Run chuckled between rocky banks. Mountain laurel hedged us in, and the deep green boughs of hemlocks and the paler green needles of white pines cast their shade on the stream and the trail—a trail beaten down over the millennia by Native Americans drawn to this narrow valley by deposits of rhyolite, a mineral they mined and fashioned into what archaeologists call "cultural objects": scrapers, knives, drills, awls, and spear and arrow points.

Twelve thousand years ago, Carr told me, the people here hunted caribou. "The forests were spruce and pine, with lots of open areas. There were mammoths and mastodons, bison, wild horses, camels, sabertooth tigers—the whole late Pleistocene suite of North American mammals."

We stepped off of the trail into a shady level area. A mat of decomposing hemlock needles covered the ground. Carr zeroed in on a fallen hemlock. Where the tree's roots had heaved up the soil, there lay scores of stone chips and flakes. "This is all cultural stuff," Carr said, squatting and sorting through the flakes. The fragments were thin, an inch or two wide, several inches long, and sharp-edged. "This was a camp. They were actually shaping the tools and spear points right here."

Carr is in his fifties, blue-eyed and gray-bearded, a bandanna tied over his pate against the sun on this bright May day. A friendly, energetic man, he had offered to guide me at Carbaugh Run and to show me the camps and mining sites to which Indians from all over the Mid-Atlantic region had once journeyed.

Rhyolite had its genesis long before humans appeared on the earth. During the Precambrian Era over 600 million years ago, volcanoes laid down beds of lava. An ancient sea submerged the lava, and sediments buried it to great depths. The continents of North America and Africa came grinding together, folding the rock layers. Heat and pressure altered, or metamorphosed, the rocks, changing their physical properties. The collision of continents uplifted the land, forming the ancestral Appalachians. Over many eons, rain and wind and freezing and thawing wore the mountains down to their basal layers, so that the much-altered volcanic rocks once again showed on the surface of the land.

Rhyolite (technically "metarhyolite," or metamorphosed rhyolite) is fairly hard to flake, but once worked, it takes on a sharp edge that makes for an excellent cutting tool. On Snaggy Ridge, five hundred feet above Carbaugh Run, the rhyolite is blue-black, weathering to dull gray. Building on work done by archaeologists in the nineteenth century, Carr and Tennessean Robert Winters, a lithic technologist (read: flint knapper), worked out details of the mining and the processing of rhyolite by the people at Carbaugh Run.

A side trail left the run and angled up toward Snaggy Ridge; Carr led the way up it. As we climbed, I listened to a yellow-billed cuckoo calling, and the incessant noontime prating of red-eyed vireos. From somewhere to the west came a distant rumble of thunder.

On Snaggy Ridge, rhyolite stuck out of the ground like old bones. The Indians, Carr said, had ignored the emergent formations. He gestured at several depressions, each about two feet deep, three feet wide, and a dozen feet long. "They dug the rhyolite out of these little quarries." Similar depressions were strung out all along the ridge, beneath a modern forest of chestnut oaks, black gums, and red maples.

A tattered blue plastic tarp on a wooden framework sagged over a slumped-in trench. Carr and Winters had done a dig there, excavating a one- by seven-meter trench through a quarry pit. Judging from the size and shape of the flakes they found, Carr and Winters concluded that the ancients had dug down to the buried rhyolite and then used hefty stone hammers to knock large blocks free. They carried the cores, perhaps in woven fabric bags or wooden baskets, down to Carbaugh Run. "We don't think they camped on the ridge because there's no water source," Carr said. When Winters conducted knapping tests, he found that freshly dug, groundwater-impregnated rhyolite works into tools and points much more easily than does exposed, dried-out rhyolite, which tends to shatter.

In the trench, Carr and Winters found two classes of artifacts that puzzled them: remnants of two small fires built at the bottom of the pit, and finished spear points. Carbon 14 dating of the burnt wood yielded dates of

7,550 years and 7,970 years before present. The finishing of projectile points hadn't taken place on the ridge (many more broken points would have been found), and the archaeologists concluded that the points they had uncovered had not been accidentally lost. "The people were taking the rhyolite out of the earth," Carr said. "Maybe they returned the spear points as ceremonial offerings."

We hiked to the northern point of Snaggy Ridge, passing ore pits and a rock shelter. Some of the sites had been looted, turned upside down by people hunting for artifacts. One of the reasons Carbaugh Run had been made a natural area was to try to prevent illegal digging.

We scrambled down the steep slope back to the flat along the run, where the natives had camped while chipping the rhyolite cores into tools and points. The fragments, which Carr called *debitage,* still had edges that looked sharp enough to cut leather. Carr showed me how the toolmakers had worked: squatting down, they held the cores against the sides of their thighs, then used blows from clubs of hardwood, such as hickory, or antler (Winters tried moose and caribou antler in his experiments) to knap off flakes. Over the centuries, over the millennia, the flakes had built up to depths of eight and ten inches in some places.

As near as archaeologists can tell, Native Americans began fashioning rhyolite into tools and points 11,500 years before present. Around 9,300 years ago, its use increased greatly. "People were coming here, mining the rhyolite, making objects, and carrying them back to their homes," Carr said. "Carbaugh Run rhyolite has turned up on islands in the Susquehanna, along the Upper Delaware River and the Potomac, along the Shenandoah River near present-day Front Royal, Virginia, and in the Genesee and Mohawk Valleys in New York."

After this burst of activity, the use of rhyolite waned for several thousand years, with native peoples turning to local stone sources and apparently traveling and trading little. Then, starting around 4,500 years ago, rhyolite was traded, said Carr, "by the ton." Archaeologists have found it all over the Delmarva Peninsula.

"We don't know much about the waves of activity or the trading systems that evolved," he added. "Maybe the tribes and bands also traded beans, or wooden artifacts, or people. But those aspects of a society tend to vanish over time, especially in a humid climate like Pennsylvania's. What we see today is the preserved part of that culture. Only the rhyolite survives."

> **TO GET THERE.** Carbaugh Run Natural Area lies south of U.S. Route 30. The best way to reach it is to drive south on PA Route 233 for 1.6 miles, then turn left (east) onto District Road (see the Michaux State Forest public-use map). After 2.1 miles, you come to a sign for the natural area and a small parking lot, with a trail leading north, down into the Carbaugh Run drainage. The area is on the Caledonia Park, Pennsylvania, topographic quadrangle.

8   MEETING OF THE PINES

611 ACRES, MICHAUX STATE FOREST, FRANKLIN COUNTY

Black oaks grew straight and tall from the hummocky earth. Thick black cherry trees stood nearby, along with a butternut, a scattering of black locusts, several black birches, and a sycamore. Mike Kusko, district forester in the Michaux State Forest, and I were having a tough time finding pines at Meeting of the Pines Natural Area. I began thinking that the name should be changed to Dwindling of the Pines—because, according to Kusko, that's precisely what is happening with at least two of the five pine species around which the natural area, on the west flank of South Mountain between Gettysburg and Chambersburg, was originally formed.

In 1974, when the Bureau of Forestry created Meeting of the Pines Natural Area, it was not as difficult to find white pine, pitch pine, Table Mountain pine, shortleaf pine, and Virginia pine—five of the six pines native to Pennsylvania. (The sixth, red pine, is found in northern Pennsylvania.) Today, the shortleaf and Virginia pines—short-lived trees intolerant of the shade produced by hardwood trees that have overtopped them—have begun dying out.

But no matter. One of the reasons for setting aside a natural area is to let natural processes occur without human intervention—in this case, the succession of forest tree species on an environmentally damaged site.

We had parked nearby at Penn State University's Mont Alto campus and, on foot, followed grass-grown Brickers Clearing Road into the adjacent natural area. Turning east off the road put us in an old mining area where small and large pits interrupted the slope of the land.

From the mid-1700s until the early 1900s, the South Mountain region sustained a prosperous iron-producing industry. Workers dug ore from open pits and transported it to furnaces, one of which stood at Mont Alto. The charcoal-fueled furnaces smelted the ore into "pig iron," so called because the resulting ingots resembled lines of nursing piglets. The pigs were forged into tools, stoves, kettles—even cannonballs used by the Continental Army during the Revolutionary War.

To keep the furnaces in blast, iron companies needed huge quantities of wood. They bought up forested tracts, and workers cut down the trees, stacked the logs on level hearths, covered the stacks with soil, and, through the use of slow fires, converted the wood to charcoal. South Mountain— most of it now managed by the Bureau of Forestry as the Michaux State Forest—was cut over, or "charcoaled," at least once and in many places two and three times. When the forests came back in brush, uncontrolled fires repeatedly swept across South Mountain.

So it was, too, on Mont Alto Mountain, as this ridge of South Mountain is locally known, and on whose slope lies Meeting of the Pines.

We found some impressive black oaks: tall, straight trees that caused Kusko to put his hands on his hips and stand there craning his neck. A century earlier, the ground here would have been bare soil cauterized by wildfires. Now the earth was covered with leaf litter and blanketed with shrubs and low plants.

In 1896, Joseph Rothrock, the state's first forestry commissioner, wrote that the loss of the state's trees "each year from forest fires is enormous . . . but the destruction of young timber, of leaf mold and of good soil from the same cause is, if possible, a vastly greater calamity." Rothrock supervised the purchasing of many cut-over tracts, which became the core of today's two million acres of state forest. In 1903, he founded the Pennsylvania State Forest Academy at Mont Alto to train professional foresters. (Penn State merged the school into its statewide campus system in 1937.)

The foresters-in-training planted some of the pines that grew to cover the ravaged land around Mont Alto, and also several non-native conifers, including Scotch pine, Norway spruce, European larch, and Port Orford cedar. Other pines seeded in naturally, and hardwoods resprouted from stumps.

The onslaught on the forest was not finished. The American chestnut, *Castanea dentata,* was one of the most common trees in Pennsylvania and the Northeast. Humans and wildlife relished its sweet-tasting nuts, and people used the beautiful, durable wood for products ranging from fence posts to house trim. Around 1900, a fungus from Asia entered North America and proceeded to destroy the continent's chestnuts. The blight struck South Mountain around 1911; by the 1920s, it had reduced the region's chestnut trees to gray, barkless snags. The forest remained open and sun-drenched: perfect for pines.

Kusko and I kept walking, looking for the darker green of conifers in a forest swimming with new, pale green hardwood leaves. Finally we found a pine: a white pine, *Pinus strobus,* an abundant species in Pennsylvania and throughout the Northeast. White pine has soft, flexible needles that grow in bundles of five. This tree was tall and healthy, its lofty crown held high above the hardwoods, in no danger of being shaded out any time soon.

Another pine: this one unfamiliar to me, with plated bark showing an orangish tint. Kusko pointed out tiny holes in the bark. Some of the holes oozed drops of golden resin. The tree was a shortleaf pine, *Pinus echinata.* A southern species, shortleaf pine grows from Florida to southern Pennsylvania and New Jersey in the east. Also called old-field pine, it often seeds itself on land no longer being farmed. The shortleaf pines at Meeting of the Pines probably had been planted during reforestation.

We came upon some Table Mountain pines—wiry-looking trees whose sparse tops supported huge cones. I found one on the ground. It was about the size of an orange, and heavy in the hand; each cone scale was tipped with a small, sharp spur. No seedlings on the shaded ground: it was too shady, too dark, for them to grow. Table Mountain pine, *Pinus pungens,* benefits from fires that open the cones and disperse their seeds while clearing the forest canopy and letting in sunlight. Table Mountain pine is another southern species that just ranges into Pennsylvania. According to Joseph Illick, in his 1914 book, *Pennsylvania Trees,* "table mountain pine occurs in pure stands on mountains in Franklin County"; Meeting of the Pines Natural Area is of course in Franklin County. Table Mountain pine likes dry, rocky slopes. Rarely does it grow more than forty feet tall.

Kusko pointed out yet another sort of pine: pitch pine, *Pinus rigida.* The mature trees had thick, rough, ashy brown bark. The needles, about three inches long, grew in bundles of three. I am partial to pitch pine; or, rather, to pine knots, the rock-hard, resin-filled branch stubs that remain on the forest floor long after the fallen tree has rotted into dust. Put a pitch pine knot in a campfire, and smell its fragrance while staring, mesmerized, at its pale dancing flames.

It took another half hour of searching before we found a Virginia pine, *Pinus virginiana,* identifiable by short needles, two to a bundle, and small, sharp prickles on its cones. Virginia pine colonizes dry rocky sites and poor, sandy soils. It is another short-lived tree, another southern species that barely drifts into Pennsylvania. This specimen, in the shade of the oaks, looked sickly; its crown had dead branches, and its needles were few.

We had found all five pine species—something Kusko had doubted could still be done. He had duties back at the office, so I wandered on alone into the natural area. A gas line right-of-way climbs Mont Alto Mountain, and I followed it uphill. As I climbed, I found many places where all-terrain vehicles had gouged the soil. Illegally, the drivers had made new trails off into the woods. As if in defiance of the machines, rattlesnake-weed grew between the wheel ruts, pretty plants with maroon veins on the upper surfaces of their leaves, and long stalks supporting bright, dandelionlike flowers. The surrounding forest was dominated by chestnut oaks, which have largely replaced the American chestnut on dry uplands in Pennsylvania.

On the top of the mountain, a grassy trail led through patches of mountain laurel. On the path, stargrass and cinquefoil raised their yellow blooms. A male scarlet tanager landed in the green crown of a chestnut oak; on the ground beneath the oak, an eastern towhee scuffed noisily, searching for insects in the leaves. Gray squirrels sounded their hollow, knocking calls throughout the woods. A crow landed in a snag above my head, looked about, failed to remark me, cawed three times, and flew off.

South Mountain is a long, wild island jutting into the sky, a different place from the valley below, with its tended fields and frenetic traffic and commercial sprawl—fragmented views of which I could make out through the scrawny, needle-clad branches of a Table Mountain pine. I sat on a rock ledge beneath the pine. The evening's first wood thrushes began to sing. The wind came sifting through the needles of the pine.

TO GET THERE. From the village of Mont Alto, drive north on PA Route 233. A little less than a mile brings you to the entrance to Penn State's Mont Alto campus. Turn left and drive across a bridge onto the campus grounds. In summer and between academic sessions, you will probably find parking in the visitor lots indicated by a sign. When classes are in session, ask campus security, in Weistling Hall, where to park.

Circle the small campus counterclockwise on a one-way road, keeping alert for a yellow gate on the right. Beyond the gate is Brickers Clearing Road. In the woods to the right of Brickers Clearing Road are the different species of pine; take along a good tree identification book. It's easiest to find the pines during winter, when the hardwoods have shed their leaves.

Walk on Brickers Clearing Road to a pipeline right-of-way angling up the mountain. Climb partway up to an illegal ATV trail, on the left, which makes for easy walking, and explore the woods; or go all the way to the top. A grassy trail runs along the ridge on a northeast-to-southwest heading; this trail marks the eastern boundary of the natural area. Stands of Table Mountain pine and pitch pine occur just below the ridge on the mountain's west-facing slope.

Meeting of the Pines Natural Area is on the Waynesboro, Pennsylvania, topographic quadrangle.

9 MT. CYDONIA PONDS

183 ACRES, MICHAUX STATE FOREST, FRANKLIN COUNTY

Tim Maret, an ecologist at Shippensburg University, stuck his collecting net into the brown-tinted water. He poked the net's outer rim into the bottom of the pond, then jigged the net upward; he did that three or four times while slowly wading forward. We both wore hipboots. Mosquitoes buzzed around our heads. A yellow-billed cuckoo called *gowk gowk gowk* from the surrounding woods. Maret made a final upward swoop with the net and brought it out, gushing water through its mesh. Clasping its handle between his arm and side, he sorted through the muck and rotting leaves in the netting.

"Here's one." He cupped a small, squirming animal in his hands. The larval salamander was muddy brown, an inch and a half long. No legs and a long tail: it looked vaguely like a fish, a tadpole, a snake. Maret bent over and filled his hands with water, and the immature salamander stopped thrashing. On each side of its blunt head, gills spread out like reddish brown feathers.

"A marbled salamander, *Ambystoma opacum*. His mother laid her eggs in the pond basin in the fall and then crawled back into the woods. Rain filled the pond, the eggs hatched, and the larvae lived under the ice all winter." Maret moved his hands into a shaft of sunlight. The salamander glistened. Pale flecks marked its sides. When it became an adult, it would be a stocky four-incher, with black and white bands from head to tail.

"Right now, the marbled salamanders have a huge jump on the other amphibians in the ponds," said Maret. "This guy's in no hurry—he'll definitely get out before the pond dries up."

Mt. Cydonia Ponds Natural Area includes about sixty vernal ponds in English Valley, which lies between Mt. Cydonia and Little Mountain in eastern Franklin County. Most of the ponds are an acre in size or smaller; some are only ten feet across. During most years, the ponds dry up by late summer, which means that fish cannot live in them. And without fish present as top predators, an assortment of amphibians—as well as many other life forms—flourish in the pocket wetlands.

The gilled larvae of salamanders, toads, and frogs live in Mt. Cydonia's ponds. Ecologist Tim Maret displays, top to bottom, a Jefferson salamander, spotted salamander, and marbled salamander.

On a day in May, Maret showed me the ponds where he and his graduate students conduct research. With his net, he introduced me to the pond dwellers: Caddisfly larvae, which build protective shelters by snipping off plant parts and gluing them together into a chimneylike cell. Dragonfly naiads, segmented, mud-colored insects that prey on other aquatic invertebrates and on immature salamanders and frogs. Backswimmers, insects that inject a proteolytic enzyme that basically turns their prey into mush. Predaceous diving beetles: "They eat lots of tadpoles," Maret said. A damselfly naiad: "Those feathers on its tail? They're gills." Midge larvae, tiny worms that looked like squirming bits of red thread. Tadpoles of wood frogs, green frogs, and toads, pollywogs that propel themselves with their tails while using their mouths to scrape up or filter out algae and bacteria suspended in the water.

Vernal ponds are crucial habitats for salamanders and frogs, which gather there to mate and lay eggs. The marbled salamanders show up in autumn. Early in the spring, Jefferson salamanders and then spotted salamanders congregate. Wood frogs home in on the ponds in late February or early March, particularly during warm rains. Spring peepers convene in mid–March, and American toads arrive in May. Red-spotted newts breed in the deeper, weedier ponds during spring and summer. The competition is fierce and, as Maret and other ecologists have discovered, complex. The goal of each hatchling is to grow quickly and leave the pond before it dries up. To do so, an amphibian must change from an aquatic mode of existence to a land-based one. A salamander sprouts limbs and feet. A frog absorbs its tail, grows limbs, and develops lungs and a digestive system that can process insect food rather than plant food.

"When a pond goes dry," Maret said, "some of the larvae may be able to survive in mud and damp leaves at the bottom of the basin. But if the pond *really* dries up, it's all over. You can smell it when the larvae die. Sometimes it's just a mass of maggots."

At another pond, Maret dredged up a Jefferson salamander, a spotted salamander, and a marbled salamander. "This guy," Maret said, pointing at the stout, two-inch-long Jefferson, by far the largest of the three, "will eat that guy"—he indicated the slender, inch-long spotted salamander larva. "Salamanders are gape-limited predators, which means they'll eat anything they can fit into their mouths. The Jeffersons are the sharks of the ponds. Right now, the spotted salamanders are hiding in the shallows, avoiding the open water where the Jeffersons lurk.

"Look at that Jeff," he said with a grin. "Doesn't he look evil?"

I got out my hand lens. Round unblinking eyes stared back at me. The mouth was a lipless slash.

Definitely ominous, but I would have called him "determined" rather than "evil."

Maret has found two types, or morphs, of Jefferson salamanders: narrow-headed ones and fat-headed ones. The ecologist believes that soon after

In early spring, wood frogs breed in the vernal ponds at Mt. Cydonia Natural Area.

Dozens of shallow ponds dot the landscape at Mt. Cydonia, providing breeding habitat for many species of amphibians.

they hatch, the larvae make a "developmental decision" to prey on verte-brates—spotted salamanders, wood frog tadpoles, spring peeper tadpoles, and even smaller Jefferson salamander larvae—instead of insects and zoo-plankton. Eating the larger, higher-protein prey lets the Jeffersons grow faster, upping the odds that they'll be able to metamorphose before their habitat vanishes. Maret admits he does not know the precise stimulus dri-ving the larval Jeffersons' "decision."

It's one of the mysteries of Mt. Cydonia's ponds.

Another mystery, recently solved, is the ponds' origin. In the past, peo-ple believed the wetlands were old pits left after iron ore was mined in the mid-1800s. A scientist with the Nature Conservancy studied pollen in the ponds' nine-foot-thick sediments. In the lowest depths, she found large quantities of spruce pollen. Spruce, a tree of boreal forests, hasn't grown widely in southern Pennsylvania since the last ice age, more than 10,000 years ago. Radiocarbon dating of organic matter in a similar pond five miles northeast of the Mt. Cydonia complex yielded dates of 15,210 years before present. It seems that most of the ponds are natural, and only a few are flooded ore pits.

Maret and I flushed a pair of mallards and, later, two wood ducks from ponds. We stole up on another pond and spotted three painted turtles basking on a half-submerged log. Through my binoculars, I could see the turtles' flattened carapaces, the bright yellow markings on the sides of their heads, and their red shell margins. The colorful reptiles slipped into the water at our approach. On a floating bed of sphagnum moss, Maret caught a northern cricket frog, an inch-long treefrog with spectacular neon green markings on its back.

I had planned to visit the Mt. Cydonia ponds in early spring, when the wood frogs and spring peepers call vociferously. The wood frogs make a quacking sound, like ducks, and the peepers' vocalizations are high-pitched and penetrating, resembling the jingling of sleigh bells from a distance. When my trip didn't come together, Maret assured me I'd find plenty of natural marvels later in the spring.

"From an ecological research perspective, the adults are a pain," he said. "Only once a year can you reliably find them: when they come to the pond to breed. Then they disappear for another year." The large salamanders spend most of their lives hidden in damp places such as cracks and crevices beneath rocks and logs. "That's why I concentrate on the larvae."

He agreed that the ponds are a special place in early March, when the frogs and salamanders are stirred by ancient instincts to gather and mate. "Afternoon and evenings are good times to visit," Maret said. "A warm, drizzly night is just phenomenal."

TO GET THERE. From the Michaux State Forest district office near Fayetteville, go west on U.S. Route 30, the Lincoln Highway. After 2.3 miles, opposite an automobile junkyard, turn left (south) at a sign reading "Mt. Cydonia Sand." You are now on Mt. Cydonia Road. Follow it past Stump Run Road on the left. The roadway turns to sand; keep going straight past the quarry on your left. (Watch out for dump trucks.) After slightly more than 1 mile, Mt. Cydonia Road bends to the left; continue straight on Irishtown Road. After another 0.6 mile, park at a wide spot opposite a grassy clearing set off from Irishtown Road by a row of large stones.

The natural area is on the west side of Irishtown Road. (There are also many vernal ponds on state forest lands to the east, in a logged-over area.) Muck Pond Trail follows the western boundary of Mt. Cydonia Natural Area past several ponds; the trail takes off from the right-hand side of the grassy clearing across from the parking spot. It's a confusing footpath, because it branches in several places where people on all-terrain vehicles have illegally carved out other routes. Visitors should carry a Scotland, Pennsylvania, topographic quadrangle and a compass. Should you get disoriented in this heavily wooded, relatively flat area, return to Irishtown Road by heading southeast.

10 PINE RIDGE

568 ACRES, BUCHANAN STATE FOREST, BEDFORD COUNTY

In 1681, when William Penn founded Pennsylvania, forests stretched westward as far as the eye could see. Gradually, settlers arrived and began clearing the land. By 1900, more than two hundred thousand farms and nineteen million acres of farmland covered two-thirds of the state. Today, around seven and a half million acres remain as agricultural land. Much of the rest—including many acres that probably never should have been farmed in the first place—has slowly reverted to trees.

In Pine Ridge Natural Area, in southern Bedford County six miles north of the Mason-Dixon line, pines and oaks have reforested a territory of worn-out, hilly farms. During the Depression Era of the 1930s, the Resettlement Administration—part of Franklin Delano Roosevelt's "New Deal"—offered farmers in the area a chance to sell their land to the government and move to towns or cities or buy new farms elsewhere. Over thirteen thousand acres passed into federal ownership in the region. Later, the land was transferred to the state of Pennsylvania. The Bureau of Forestry in 1970 established Pine Ridge Natural Area to demonstrate early plant succession following "man's occupancy, misuse, and abandonment of the land," according to the Buchanan State Forest public-use map.

I visited Pine Ridge on a warm day in early September. On the Jasper Trail I hiked through open woods, mainly white and chestnut oaks, along with white and Virginia pines, the trees growing on soil so thin that slabs of shale poked through it in many places.

Virginia pine—also known as Jersey pine and scrub pine—is a hardy tree that colonizes dry sites and poor soil, particularly abandoned fields. The species ranges from northern Alabama to southern Pennsylvania and west-central New Jersey; the famous New Jersey pine barrens include many Virginia pine stands. The tree's wood is light, soft, and brittle, little used save for paper pulp. At maturity, Virginia pine is not an imposing tree: thirty or forty feet, bristling and ragged looking, with irregular spreading branches and shaggy reddish bark. Even the needles seem lacking in grace; they come two to a bundle and are short and twisted. I picked up a cone from the ground. It was about two inches long. A spine tipped each cone scale, and the compact, tapering fruit prickled my skin as I rolled it about in my palm.

An excellent quality of Virginia pine is that it stabilizes exposed soil and then yields to more valuable, slower-growing tree species. On Pine Ridge, in what were once fields, hardwoods were now eclipsing the Virginia pines, with red maple and black cherry surging upward in openings where pines lay fallen and decaying.

In a clearing, grasses and goldenrod thrust up around bushy apple trees. Judging from the weathered locust fenceposts nearby, the trees were farmstead plantings, but it had been years since anyone had pruned them to encourage fruiting. Feeding wells excavated by yellow-bellied sapsuckers stitched lines across the trees' scaly-barked trunks. Yellow jackets fed on meager windfall apples that lay rotting on the ground.

Evidence of abandoned settlements, including old grave markers, is scattered throughout the woods now reclaiming Pine Ridge Natural Area.

Jasper Trail passed a red pine plantation, and the differences between the red and Virginia species caught my eye. The red pines were tall and straight, their needles long, slender, and soft looking. Red pine is longer-lived than Virginia pine, and the red pines had not been invaded by hardwoods. Beneath the big pines spread extensive beds of ground pine, not a tree but a type of club moss. Club mosses are low evergreen shrubs that creep across the soil, often growing in nutrient-poor, acidic places. Above their shining green leaves, the plants held up branching clusters of candle-like, spore-bearing cones. Walking among ground pine in October leaves a hiker's boots dusted with pale yellow pollen.

At a signpost, I turned left onto blue-blazed Buxton Trail, which at one time was a wagon road. On my right grew a line of sassafras trees, including one of the largest I've ever seen in Pennsylvania: more than eighteen inches in diameter at breast height and well over fifty feet tall. (In the U.S. South, sassafras regularly gets this big and often grows even larger.) I passed some excellent black oaks, plus black walnut, tuliptree, red and sugar maple, black locust, and black cherry trees—even a hillside infested with ailanthus, also known as tree of heaven, an Asian import that grows more like a weed than a tree, identifiable by its compound leaves and many small leaflets and by the stinking, acrid smell produced when breaking off a twig.

I was brought to a standstill by a beautiful plant, downy rattlesnake plantain, with dark green, oval-shaped leaves broken up into a checkered pattern by bold, china white veins. Downy rattlesnake plantain is an orchid, a ground-hugging plant that, in favorable years, sends up a stalk of white flowers in late summer. Farther along, I met with another striking plant, spotted wintergreen, whose tapering leaves are dark green with a pale green, almost white, pattern centering on the midrib and extending out toward the toothed leaf margin.

Walking quietly, I scared a nice fat doe, who wasn't sure where or what I was and stood looking about among the pines, her ears flicking and her nose twitching. Overhead, two pairs of pileated woodpeckers were having some sort of a territorial dust-up, with much screaming, scrabbling about on tree trunks, and windmilling black-and-white wings.

A wood turtle sat on the path. It had a sheath of skin around its neck, gray and marked with reddish orange. The turtle lay on the ground with all four legs tucked inside its shell and only its blackish beaked head protruding, fixing one yellow-and-black eye on me. I sat down next to it. I wondered how a turtle conceives of time. We waited, the turtle and I, until a fly landed on the reptile's head and trod across its eye, and only then did the turtle blink.

I came to a truly huge tree. The oak had a thick, leaning trunk and a broken crown. Its bark was rough and ridged like that of a chestnut oak, but the wide-spreading boughs bore the distinctive bristle-tipped leaves of a red or a black oak. The tree's roots had dug down deep at the bottom of a ravine, where they must have found a reliable source of water.

The clearing of the land and the withdrawal of its native inhabitants, the seasons and the strivings of settlers, the wagons that crept past carrying crops and supplies and the quick and the dead, the eventual abandonment of the fields and the reassertion of the woods—the tree had seen it all.

TO GET THERE. From the stop sign at the intersection in the village of Chaneysville (south of Bedford), head east on Ragged Mountain Road. The road passes a white church on the left, then begins to climb, and soon reaches state forest land. After 1.5 miles, where the road makes a sharp bend to the left near a sign for Pine Ridge Natural Area, turn right onto gravel Abey Road, which forms the western boundary of the natural area. After driving 1.3 miles on Abey Road, cross the Georgetown Branch on a one-lane bridge and park just past the bridge on the left.

  The natural area is crisscrossed by paths and old roads. A hiker can bushwhack, following trails and using a compass and the Buchanan State Forest public-use map. Or, a good overview can be had by taking red-blazed Jasper Trail as it climbs northeast from the parking area, then turning left (west) onto blue-blazed Buxton Trail, which descends to Georgetown Branch and then leads back to the parking area.

11   SWEET ROOT

1,403 ACRES, BUCHANAN STATE FOREST, BEDFORD COUNTY

The destruction was as incredible as the trees themselves: tall, straight old-growth hemlocks, all of them dead. Most of the trees remained standing, stripped of their foliage, a haze of gray-brown twigs at the ends of their massive branches. It was not just the old hemlocks that had died, but their potential successors as well, the smaller hemlocks growing in the once-shaded understory. The upright corpses filled the steep-sided, boulder-choked gap in Tussey Mountain from which Sweet Root Run issued. The stream, gurgling between rocks, was the only sound I heard, where before the breeze would have gossiped in feathery green crowns overhead.

  Sweet Root Gap is a rugged place, which is why loggers passed over the big hemlocks when the region was timbered around 1900. A century later, an insect pest with a cartoonish name, the hemlock woolly adelgid, has destroyed the great trees. Someday, during a summer downpour or a winter ice storm, or when winds follow a long spell of rain, the trees' shallow roots will let go. They will come thundering down, choking the gorge, there to slowly rot.

  Marcia Bonta, in her book *More Outbound Journeys in Pennsylvania,* published in 1995, notes that "Sweet Root Natural Area is not a place for

At Sweet Root, black birch and basswood seedlings cluster beneath old-growth hemlocks destroyed by an insect pest.

hikers," because of fallen trees—and Bonta visited before the hemlocks were stricken. Today conditions are more difficult yet. Determined to penetrate to the old-growth stand, estimated at seventy acres, I worked my way directly up Sweet Root Run. I crawled over fallen trunks. Twisted to get through layered limbs. Balanced on wet rocks patched with moss. Boots with good soles, and a stout hiking staff, helped me keep my balance. I was alone, but it would be wiser to enter Sweet Root with a partner; you wouldn't want to break an ankle in such a thick, inaccessible place.

Rock formations slanted out of the mountain, sheer faces of pale sandstone above sloping fields of slabs. The Allegheny woodrat, an endangered species in Pennsylvania, lives in crevices and caves among the rocks at Sweet Root. Bobcats, timber rattlesnakes, and northern copperheads hunt for mice, voles, squirrels, and chipmunks. While approaching the gap, I had listened to a pair of barred owls calling back and forth—haunting, hollow, nine-syllable calls, *Who cooks for you, who cooks for youall?,* the male's voice pitched higher than the female's booming bass—and had flushed one of the birds from the ground next to the trail.

In the gap, deer and raccoon tracks marked the sand in the infrequent open stretches between fallen trees. Ten-foot-tall black birches and basswoods grew in thickets; I wedged myself sideways between the two-inch trunks. Stopping to rest, I dipped a hand into Sweet Root Run. The water tasted pure and sweet, which had prompted settlers to give the creek its name. Joseph Powell, an early resident, ran a trading post along Sweet Root

Run starting around 1734. His brother George discovered saltpeter in a cave in the gap. Elisha Huff mined the saltpeter, used to make gunpowder during the American Revolution. In the early 1800s, runaway slaves heading north to freedom walked the long adjacent farm valleys in the night; by day, they hid in the forested mountains, in spots like Sweet Root Gap.

Sweat was dripping off my nose when I made it to the heart of the old-growth stand. Through the naked limbs of dead hemlocks, I could see high up on the hundred-foot walls of the cliffs forming the northeast side of the gap. According to a Bureau of Forestry survey, virgin chestnut oaks grow along the rocky top, and Table Mountain pines cling to the ledges.

But my eyes were on the dead hemlocks. It was disheartening to see so many blasted, irreplaceable (in my lifetime, anyway) old-growth trees. The size, beauty, and rarity of the hemlocks, and their ability to recall for visitors what the primeval eastern forest had once looked like, prompted the State Forest Commission in 1921 to name Sweet Root as one of thirteen state forest monuments, which later became the core of our current natural area system. The Sweet Root hemlocks were not as large as some I have seen, because the soil is thin. Most of the trees were about two feet in diameter at breast height, with a few exceeding three feet. Many had lost their bark; their trunks were pale gray, their branches broken-off stubs.

The hemlock woolly adelgid is the size of those diaphanous-winged aphids clinging to the stems of your tomato plants. The insect arrived on the West Coast of North America from Asia in the early 1900s, perhaps hitchhiking on imported trees or shrubs; it was first found in the East in Virginia in 1956. Western hemlocks showed some resistance to the adelgid, but eastern hemlocks have not fared as well.

Adult female adelgids winter among the hemlock needles. They secrete a white, waxy substance that looks like the fake snow people spray on Christmas trees. After hatching, the adelgid nymphs feed by inserting a narrow stylet into a twig and sucking out sap. Millions of nymphs can infest a single tree. Their feeding causes needles to die and fall off prematurely. Adelgids produce two generations of sap-sucking nymphs each year.

On a hemlock in someone's yard, insecticidal soaps can wipe out invading adelgids. But aerial spraying, the only practical way to treat hemlocks in the forest, does not adequately drench the trees' needles. The woolly adelgid is destroying hemlocks from Virginia's Smoky Mountains north to New England. In Pennsylvania, foresters have found the pest in thirty-two counties, mainly in the northeastern, southeastern, and south-central parts of the state.

Adelgids can kill a tree in as few as four years. Old-growth hemlocks are nearing the ends of their natural lives, and old trees—especially those on marginal sites like Sweet Root Gap—may lack the vigor and resilience of younger trees on better soil. In some places, trees seem able to hang on and survive an adelgid infestation, which may be relieved when bitter winter temperatures freeze the pests or drenching rains wash them away. Scientists are searching in Asia for parasites and predators to fight the adelgid. But no one knows if these natural controls will halt the invasion, or which or how many of the state's hemlocks will perish.

A hemlock stand—whether of old-growth or younger trees—is a special place, not simply because of its cathedral beauty. The dense evergreen crowns provide nesting cover for golden-crowned kinglets, several warbler species, dark-eyed juncos, and sharp-shinned hawks. The near-complete shade cast by the interlocking boughs keeps streams cool even on the sunniest summer days; cold-water aquatic life, from tiny invertebrates to brook trout, require chill waters. Other species of wildlife, about whose life cycles we know little, may depend on cool, shady habitats; one is the rare small-footed bat, which prefers to hibernate in caves and mine shafts in hemlock forests.

As I retraced my steps, I wondered what would happen now at Sweet Root Gap. Other trees that thrive in damp ravines may someday stand as tall as the hemlocks: species such as yellow birch, tuliptree, and the basswoods that would spring from the crowded seedlings through which I was making such tedious progress.

It struck me that Sweet Root represents an opportunity as well as a tragedy. Not often is a stand of old-growth trees suddenly wiped out. A university forestry department, a team of state biologists and botanists, a group of professional ecologists—or a consortium of all of these—should intensively study the natural area over many years. They should document this unwelcome event, charting the changes in plant and animal populations that follow.

TO GET THERE. Sweet Root Picnic Area is on PA Route 326, 0.75 mile north of the Bureau of Forestry office just west of Chaneysville. A sign notes that the picnic area is on the site of a Civilian Conservation Corps camp that was active from 1933 to 1935.

Hike west from the picnic area on the gated forest road, noting the old CCC foundations on your right. The road extends along a tongue of state land, then crosses a short stretch of private land, before entering the gap in Tussey Mountain. The owner of the private tract does not mind hikers crossing his property to view the natural area, although visitors should not use the route during the autumn hunting season. On the private land, the road forks in a logged-over area; take the right fork, paralleling Sweet Root Run. The gap is about a mile from the picnic area.

Sweet Root Natural Area also includes an upland basin—known locally as a "cove"—forested mainly with mixed oaks. You can reach the basin via Tarkiln Trail, heading southeast from the intersection of Blankley and Martin Hill Roads (see the Buchanan State Forest public-use map and ask for advice at the district office). In this extensive, rugged area, hikers are advised to have a topographic map (the Beans Cove, Pennsylvania, quadrangle) and a compass.

The Mid-State Trail passes through part of the natural area. Sweet Root Natural Area can be reached via Blankley Road and Wasson and Tarkiln Trails.

12   BOX HUCKLEBERRY

10 ACRES, TUSCARORA STATE FOREST, PERRY COUNTY

I have a mental image of a lean, dark-haired man, tall for the era in which he lived—Spencer Baird was a shade over six feet—striding along on a dirt wagon road near the town of New Bloomfield, Pennsylvania. In the mid-1840s, Baird was a young professor of natural history at Dickinson College in Carlisle. New Bloomfield is twenty miles north of Carlisle, and no doubt Baird had walked the whole way; he was a prodigious hiker who often covered forty miles a day and would wear out several pairs of boot soles in a summer.

Baird had already caught the attention of the famous wildlife artist John James Audubon for describing two species of birds that proved new to science: the yellow-bellied flycatcher, *Empidonax flaviventris,* and the least flycatcher, *Empidonax minimus.* With gun in hand (for collecting bird specimens: Baird's journals record that he shot and stuffed everything from hummingbirds to hooded mergansers), the young naturalist was headed south when he noticed an unfamiliar plant growing along the edge of the roadway.

That the plant was a huckleberry he could tell from the clustered, light blue fruit hanging from short pedicels—fruit that was not particularly sweet, and rather seedy. The plant formed a dense, dark green mat not quite a foot high on the acidic woods soil. The leaves, small, thick, and leathery, lacked the resinous dots found on other huckleberries.

Baird—who ultimately would become secretary of the Smithsonian Institution and a founder of the U.S. Fish Commission—had chanced upon one of the few specimens of box huckleberry, *Gaylussacia brachycera,* located since the pioneering French botanist Andre Michaux first discovered the plant in western Virginia in 1796.

In 1929, a private landowner gave four acres of the Baird-discovered box huckleberry colony to the Pennsylvania Department of Forests and Waters, and since that time the commonwealth has acquired the rest of the site. At ten acres, Box Huckleberry is the state's smallest natural area. A quarter-mile interpretive footpath loops through the site, a west-facing slope forested mainly with white pine and mixed oaks. Hemlock, sassafras, black cherry, Virginia pine, and black locust also grow there. Trailing arbutus shows its clusters of white flowers in early spring, along with northern downy violet and three-lobed violet. In summer, false Solomon's seal, rattlesnake weed, and self-heal come into bloom.

Still, it is the box huckleberry that attracts most visitors to the woodland. Box huckleberry is an evergreen, and a good time to view it is in early spring, before other plants have leafed out. The shiny leaves are oval and one-half to one inch long; the plant's name comes from the leaves' resemblance to those of the boxwood, an ornamental tree from the Mediterranean region. At the natural area, what seem to be patches of box huckleberry actually are connected, and the apparent colony of plants is believed to be a single individual. Box huckleberry grows by sending up suckers from its roots, expanding its overall width by about six inches per year.

Around a hundred widely separated patches have been found in Tennessee, Kentucky, West Virginia, Virginia, Maryland, Delaware, and Pennsylvania. Botanists know of only three box huckleberries in the Keystone State. A huge one covering almost a hundred acres near Losh Run, fifteen miles northeast of the New Bloomfield box huckleberry, was badly damaged by the widening of U.S. Route 322 in the 1970s. In 1989, a botani-

cally minded surveyor found a colony in Bedford County, sixty miles south
of the New Bloomfield plant. Both of these other plants are on private land
and are not accessible to the public.

Botanists believe that the box huckleberry cannot self-pollinate: a grain
of pollen from one flower will not fertilize another flower on the same
plant. Reproduction, as explained by the scientists, goes something like this:
a bee gets nectar from a flower, picking up pollen in the process. The bee
flies to another box huckleberry. (A bee flies fifteen miles?) At the faraway
plant, the bee again takes nectar, leaving behind some pollen. From the pol-
linated flower, a fertile fruit grows. A bird or mammal eats the fruit and
later deposits a dropping, containing a viable seed, in some congenial spot.
"Just try to calculate the probabilities of box huckleberry spreading in the
wild," noted Sam Vander Kloet, a Canadian professor and an authority on
huckleberries quoted in a newspaper article reporting on the discovery of
the Bedford County site.

In 1918, a scientist with the U.S. Department of Agriculture determined that, based on its size and rate of growth, the New Bloomfield box
huckleberry had been flourishing for around twelve hundred years, making
it one of the oldest living things known. The hundred-acre patch near Losh
Run, damaged by the highway widening, was judged to be thirteen *thousand* years old. By comparison, the largest sequoias are around thirty-two
hundred years of age, and the oldest bristlecone pines have seen forty-six
hundred winters.

It was a cloudy day in late April when I strolled through the Box Huckleberry Natural Area. Dogwoods showed their creamy flowers. New leaves
of the mockernut hickory were delicate reddish blades, while those of the
white oak were smaller, with lobed edges, and deep rose in color. Midday,
and not much was moving in the way of wildlife. I heard crows cawing and
a cardinal whistling, a chipmunk scampering past in the leaf litter.

Which allowed me to concentrate on the box huckleberry. The plant
seemed to pour itself over the ground. The leaves were a reflective green,
and the stems bore bell-shaped, hanging flowers, white with a blush of
pink. No bees were busy on this chilly, gloomy day.

The plant did not project the antiquity, the brooding sentience, that
one intuits when looking up at a towering white pine or hemlock—yet, if
we can believe the scientists, the box huckleberry is several times older than
the oldest white pine or hemlock in existence.

Recently I came upon an essay, "The Oldest Living Thing," by the writer Euell Gibbons, famous for his books on foraging, including *Stalking the Wild Asparagus*. Gibbons lived close by in central Pennsylvania, but he was not one to shout the praises of the New Bloomfield box huckleberry. He considered searching for the oldest living thing to be an exercise in futility. He wrote, "while gazing on the box huckleberries . . . I wondered if the little wintergreen plants growing under them might not be older." Gibbons offered, as organisms of great antiquity, the lichens growing on rock faces in arctic regions. He suggested that many plants, such as milkweed and dogbane, might be just as old: they "put up, aboveground, fruiting and seeding plants that last only one season—but life goes on in the underground rhizomes that push on, fork, and sprout new plants endlessly and with apparent immortality."

Gibbons wrote of plants ballyhooed as ancient: "Let us not burden them with superlatives they cannot honestly claim." Although it seemed to me that the New Bloomfield box huckleberry wasn't claiming a thing, as it kept on enlarging, slowly and steadily, on its quiet hillside.

TO GET THERE. From the square in New Bloomfield, go 1 mile southeast on combined PA Routes 34 and 274. Turn right onto Huckleberry Road and proceed 0.5 mile to the natural area, which is on your left (look for a gray wooden sign). Park along the berm.

---

13 FRANK E. MASLAND, JR.

1,270 ACRES, TUSCARORA STATE FOREST, PERRY COUNTY

When forester Bob Beleski wants to enjoy solitude and a serious hike, he heads for Frank E. Masland Natural Area along the North Branch of Laurel Run in western Perry County. One of Beleski's duties is to improve recreational opportunities in the Tuscarora forest district, which offers riding and hiking trails, four state parks, and a system of designated campsites for hunters, hikers, and horseback riders. Beleski guided me through the natural area in early December; we both wore bright orange hats to make ourselves visible to any deer hunters in the vicinity.

Before the gypsy moth swept through south-central Pennsylvania in the 1980s, the Bureau of Forestry characterized the Masland natural area as "the finest oak forest in the state." Today the oaks are thinner on the ground, and many stand as whitening skeletons on the dry ridges that define the wooded valley: Bowers Mountain, elevation 2,030 feet, to the northwest; and Middle Ridge, at 1,673 feet, to the southeast. Yet in the Laurel Run basin—through which red-blazed North Branch Trail extends for about two miles—many impressive trees remain.

Beleski and I passed large black birches, yellow birches, eastern hemlocks, white pines, tuliptrees, black gums, white ashes, mockernut hickories, basswoods, and, of course, oaks: white, red, black, and chestnut oaks, some of them more than three feet in diameter and over a hundred feet tall. According to a Bureau of Forestry publication, the trees are "older than most other second growth stands on State Forest land." The brochure continues: "In reconstructing the past cutting history, it appears as though the upper slopes were heavily cut for extract wood [tannic acid, used to tan leather, was extracted from American chestnuts and chestnut oaks] and the lower slopes and stream bottom were only partially cut. Many old growth trees were left and can be seen today."

As we hiked along, we stopped now and then to identify the leafless trees by their bark patterns. Beleski pointed out where Laurel Run had reshaped its streambed after a 1996 deluge dropped ten inches of rain in twelve hours. Raging through the hollow, the stream dug out new pools where native brook trout fin in the green water. The run shoved boulders around and stranded debris six feet up on the slope above the stream bottom, forty feet from the North Branch itself. The flooding forced Beleski to make a new trail through the valley, completed in 1998. In places, the path follows the stream closely; over other stretches, it climbs up deer trails through mountain laurel and looks down on the sparkling water below.

We found where a bear had swiped its claws across a red maple's smooth bark, but the only wildlife we actually spied were a band of chickadees and a pair of downy woodpeckers. The birds foraged diligently in witch hazel shrubs and on dead oak snags as Beleski and I walked steadily past, all of us trying to stay warm in the twenty-degree weather. A recent study documented sixty-five species of birds using the area: the usual suite of deep-woods species, ranging in size from ruby-throated hummingbirds to wild turkeys. Timber rattlesnakes hunt the mountain slopes for small rodents, including large numbers of chipmunks supported by acorns dropped by the oaks.

In its description of "Pennsylvania Habitats," the *Atlas of Pennsylvania* lists the Masland natural area as a prime example of mixed-oak forest, which it characterizes as "the most common habitat in Pennsylvania, found on rolling hills and slopes throughout the state, and commonly referred to as the oak/hickory forest of eastern North America."

Frank Masland was a carpet manufacturer from Carlisle, about twenty miles east of the area. An active conservationist on the local, state, national, and international levels, Masland once represented the U.S. Department of the Interior on a study of parks and wildlife reserves in Ethiopia and East Africa. In the Bureau of Forestry archives in Harrisburg, I found that the agency had let a contract for logging along the North Branch of Laurel Run in 1945, but canceled it after the contractor failed to begin operations by a specified date. Masland, who owned a camp in the area and was fond of the prime oak forest, had opposed the logging and used his influence to prevent the site from being cut.

TO GET THERE. From Landisburg in western Perry County, head west on PA Route 233 toward Newville. After 3.5 miles, turn right onto Laurel Run Road. Go 10 miles on Laurel Run Road (the road changes from paved to gravel) to a **T** intersection. Turn right (Cowpen Road is on your left) and climb through a gap in the mountain, still on Laurel Run Road. After cresting the ridge and starting to descend, on your right you will pass the trailheads for Turbett Trail and Deer Hollow Trail; 1.1 miles after your turn at the **T**, you reach the North Branch of Laurel Run, in the bottom of the valley. Park there and hike northeastward along the creek. To do a loop hike, return to Laurel Run Road via Deer Hollow Trail or Turbett Trail, turn right, and walk back down the mountain to your vehicle.

A brochure with a trail map is available from the Tuscarora State Forest district office. The natural area is covered by the Blain, Newburg, and Andersonburg topographic quadrangles. Access to the area is by gravel roads that become icy and dangerous in winter: call the district office for road conditions.

14 HEMLOCKS

131 ACRES, TUSCARORA STATE FOREST, PERRY COUNTY

In summer, this grove of old-growth hemlocks offers a shady refuge from heat and glare. In fall, the somber greens of the conifers form a backdrop for the bright yellows, reds, and oranges of the changing deciduous leaves. In winter, snow builds up on the green boughs, the stream is locked away under ice; silence reigns. In spring, migrating birds stop to feed on insects in the diverse, deep-woods habitat. Many of the birds remain, nesting along the pristine stream course or in the dense forest canopy overhead; the males fill the woods with their singing.

The 131-acre Hemlocks Natural Area cradles some thirty acres of old-growth trees (when you are among them, it seems like a much larger stand), most of them hemlocks, in a steep, rocky ravine surrounded by the oak woods typical of south-central Pennsylvania. Back in 1921, the State Forestry Commission gave the site special protection as a forest monument. At that time, you could arrive at the virgin timber only on foot over rough, brushy terrain; today a gravel road leads to a parking lot with a trailhead connected to hiking paths on both sides of northeast-flowing Patterson Run.

The stately hemlocks are three hundred years old. Many of them measure more than two feet in diameter; the largest that has been found is fifty-two inches in diameter and 109 feet tall; and the tallest rises 123 feet into the air and has a diameter of thirty-eight inches.

A tree that large is a habitat unto itself. Mosses and lichens grow on the trunk, thriving in the humidity of the shady grove. Examine a big hemlock's bark, and you will likely find among the deep furrows abundant insects and spiders and the eggs and early growth stages of those invertebrates. Many birds zero in on these foods, including highly efficient bark preeners such as black-capped chickadees, white-breasted nuthatches, and brown creepers—all species that breed and winter at the Hemlocks.

On a recent outing in spring, I lay on my back in the leaves trying to focus my binoculars on a male Blackburnian warbler as he moved among the boughs, perhaps bringing food (moth and butterfly caterpillars are the species' mainstay) to young in a hidden nest. I had a few brief glimpses of the bird's flame orange throat and black-and-orange face as he paused on branches about fifty feet up. The Blackburnian is known as the "hemlock warbler," since it often nests in hemlocks, particularly in the southern part of its range, which follows the spine of the Appalachians south to Tennessee and North Carolina. In the Allegheny National Forest in northwestern Pennsylvania, researchers found that densities of Blackburnian warblers averaged forty-six times higher in old-growth hemlocks than in younger forests that had been logged within the last 170 years.

Giant trees even provide a habitat after they have died and fallen to the ground. At the Hemlocks, look for large hemlocks growing in straight lines along the slopes. The trees probably seeded and began to grow on top of a fallen hemlock, finally sinking their roots into the soil after the old downed tree—known as a "nurse tree"—had moldered away. Black birch and yellow birch, two other trees abundant at the Hemlocks, also may start out as seedlings on a rotting bole.

Unfortunately, there may soon be many rotting trunks in this narrow valley in western Perry County, where Patterson Run tumbles over rocks in a series of small, white waterfalls. The hemlock woolly adelgid, an aphid from Asia, showed up at the Hemlocks in 1999, and its population increased during 2000. Trees hit by the pest show an unthrifty reddish cast to their needles. Damage by the sap-sucking adelgid can combine with drought, invasion by fungi, and native insect attackers to weaken and kill trees, especially old-growth specimens. (For an explanation of the woolly adelgid and its potential impact on Pennsylvania's hemlocks, see the chapter on Sweet Root Natural Area, beginning on page 43.)

In their account of the Blackburnian warbler in *Warblers,* a Peterson Field Guide, Jon Dunn and Kimball Garrett write that "large-scale loss of hemlocks could seriously affect this and other wood-warbler species." Other birds at the Hemlocks include the common raven, broad-winged hawk, chimney swift (probably nesting in tree cavities, another important feature of old-growth stands), belted kingfisher, three species of woodpeckers, four flycatchers, winter wren, wood thrush, red-eyed vireo (the loudest and most persistent singer in spring and summer, its oft-repeated robinlike phrases filling the woods), scarlet tanager, and at least seven wood-warbler species, including the Louisiana waterthrush. Four species of salamanders thrive in the close, damp environment, and brook trout live in the stream.

In 1973, the National Park Service designated the old-growth stand as a national natural landmark. The red-blazed Hemlock Trail leads through the heart of the natural area, starting at the upper parking lot and following

Patterson Run; hikers can bear left on either of two short side trails, climb uphill to Hemlock Road, turn left again, and ascend back to the parking area. The yellow-marked Rim Trail and orange-marked Patterson Run Trail follow higher ground on Rising Mountain to the east of Patterson Run, affording a view down into the big trees' crowns.

TO GET THERE. Drive west from Blain on PA Route 274 for 10 miles. Turn south (left) onto Hemlock Road. After 2.2 miles, you enter the natural area; after a total of 3.8 miles, you come to a parking lot on the left with access to the Hemlock Trail.

From the Pennsylvania Turnpike (I-76), exit at Willow Hill and go north on PA Route 75 for 10.9 miles. Bear right on Route 274 just beyond Doylesburg. After 4.8 miles, turn right on Hemlock Road and follow the directions in the preceding paragraph.

Request a free brochure with trail map from the Tuscarora State Forest district office.

---

15   MT. DAVIS

581 ACRES, FORBES STATE FOREST, SOMERSET COUNTY

In early September, the black gums on the summit of Negro Mountain were already changing color, from summer's slick green to fall's scarlet, orange, and salmon. The last rays of the sun touched the trees' leaves and made them glow. A breeze blew through the aspens, whose tumbling, coin-shaped leaves made a sound somewhere between fluttering wings and trickling water. The wind in the trees, the ratcheting of katydids, and the far-off cawing of crows were all I heard as I climbed the observation tower reaching up into the vast, deep blue sky.

One can make a visit to Mt. Davis Natural Area as demanding or as relaxing as one wishes. That evening I was about done in, having driven many miles and trekked for six hours at another natural area farther north. I was looking for peace and quiet, a place where I could sit and rest, watch and think, and Mt. Davis was the perfect spot.

There were no other cars in the parking lot when I pulled in, and I had the tower—and the view—to myself. And what a view it was. I had read other visitors' accounts of fog and clouds and rain, here on the highest point in Pennsylvania, but this was a beautifully clear evening, and from my perch I looked out over hundreds of square miles.

Meadow Mountain stretched away to the southwest, down into Maryland. Ten miles east, the town of Salisbury sat cradled in rolling farmland. Toward the west and the setting sun, Laurel Ridge was a long, cerulean bar, seemingly without dimension; through the deep notch carved into it by the Youghiogheny River, I could pick out far-off Chestnut Ridge, an even paler blue.

I sat on the cast-bronze relief map of the surrounding terrain and snugged myself down into my jacket. A sharp-shinned hawk sailed swiftly past, following the ridge's northeast-to-southwest orientation, pale feathers on the bird's breast picking up the ruddy light. I heard the mournful wail of a train somewhere far to the west. Under the great round of the sky, I considered how few places in hilly, forested Pennsylvania offer a view so sublime. *I'm the highest thing in Pennsylvania right now,* I said to myself—and grinned at the notion that, pushing fifty, I could still get excited at such a thing.

The natural area is named in honor of John N. Davis, a Civil War veteran and an early settler who owned a tract of twenty-six thousand acres that included the top of Negro Mountain; Davis was also a land surveyor, a teacher, and a minister. In 1912, the U.S. Geological Survey established the fact that the top of Negro Mountain is 3,213 feet above sea level and thus is the highest point in Pennsylvania. In the metal observation tower, I was forty feet higher. I tempered my hubris by remembering that Pennsylvania is the lowest high point in all of the Appalachian Mountain states: the Newfoundland-to-Georgia range subsides to a mere saddle in the Keystone State compared with peaks such as Maine's Mount Katahdin (5,268 feet), New Hampshire's Mount Washington (6,288 feet), and Mount Mitchell in North Carolina (6,684 feet).

Negro Mountain is a thirty-mile-long ridge extending into Maryland, where portions of the mountain are, in fact, higher than the site designated as Mt. Davis. A host of stories explain the mountain's name. The following, as good as any, is from a speech given by Col. Henry Shoemaker, Pennsylvania newspaperman, booster, and demihistorian, in the early twentieth century: "Negro Mountain was one of the first peaks in Pennsylvania to receive a definite name, away back in 1755. . . . Colonel Thomas Cresap, famed as the instigator of the so-called Cresap's war over the border between Pennsylvania and Maryland, was marching to join General Braddock, accompanied by a group of his personal retainers and servants. They bivouacked for the night at the foot of an enormous mountain [where] they were surprised by hostile Indians. . . . The only person killed was the Colonel's favorite Negro body servant, a black of colossal proportions. The Indians were driven off, and the body of the unfortunate Negro dropped down in a deep crevice of the rocks in a shoulder of the mountain, and the party resumed its way." According to Shoemaker, bigotry reared its ugly head soon after Negro Mountain was found to be the highest point in the state, when some people wanted to change its name; but a group called the Pennsylvania Alpine Club stood firmly for the traditional moniker, and it was kept.

The top of Negro Mountain is not a fertile place. Early clear-cut logging, mining, and repeated wildfires destroyed what little topsoil existed here, and cold temperatures (frosts have been reported every month of the year), frequent high winds, and winter ice storms have deformed, gnarled, and stunted the trees. As well as black gum and quaking and bigtooth aspens, various oaks (including scrub oak, a waist-high shrub), pitch pine, black and yellow birches, black cherry, red and striped maples, and sassafras persevere on this tough patch of earth. Around the observation tower, mountain laurel, greenbrier, lowbush blueberry, teaberry, and several species of club moss cloak the ground. In spring, trailing arbutus and painted trillium bloom in the nearby woods.

Looking north from the tower, I spied a stone circle on the ground. Mt. Davis Natural Area is known for these concentric rings of pale gray rocks, so arranged by frost heaving. Each ring surrounds an area where the earth is loose and vaguely humped; over millennia, goaded by freezing and thawing of the soil, the rocks have crept downward and outward to the perimeters of the humps. The rings are about thirty feet across, and they are not easy to discern when leaves are on the trees.

As the sun slid toward Laurel Ridge, flocks of blackbirds came flying over the mountain—long, living snakes made of thousands of birds, the formations twisting and turning in the pellucid light, contracting and expanding, the birds not calling much, an occasional *chack,* the cumulative sound of their wingbeats a quick, airy *whit, whit, whit,* the sound slowly fading as, one by one, the flocks disappeared into the west.

The sun went down at 7:41, behind the Youghiogheny's water gap. In the east, a half moon hung in the darkening sky as I climbed down from my perch.

TO GET THERE. From Meyersdale just west of U.S. Route 219, turn west on Broadway Street, and follow the signs for Mt. Davis through a network of rural roads. Drive to the parking area for the observation tower on the summit, or stop at the picnic area (with restrooms, tables, and drinking water) along SR 2004. From the picnic area, a trail leads southwest approximately 1 mile to the tower on the mountain's gently rolling summit. *50 Hikes in Western Pennsylvania,* by Tom Thwaites, describes a more strenuous 5.8-mile, three-and-a-half-hour walk through the surrounding forest, beginning at the picnic area and following Tub Mill Run, Timberslide, Shelter Rock, and High Point Trails, with a stop-off at the observation tower. A brochure with a trail map is available from the Forbes State Forest district office.

16 ROARING RUN

3,090 ACRES, FORBES STATE FOREST, WESTMORELAND COUNTY

I overshot the parking area and looked for a place to turn around. The driver in the SUV hugging my tail wasn't happy with my decelerating, but maybe he felt less inconvenienced when the bear went running in front of us, left-to-right across the blacktop. I pulled into a driveway and watched as the bruin lumbered on into the woods, in the general direction of a quarry. A nice big bear, probably a mature male and, in the way of bears, totally, startlingly black against the landscape.

While parking at the gravel lot, I was wishing I'd seen the bear (bagged him, so to speak) *before* he vacated Roaring Run Natural Area, a wooded tract on the western slope of Laurel Ridge some twenty miles southeast of Greensburg and forty-five miles from downtown Pittsburgh. Roaring Run is the largest state forest natural area in western Pennsylvania. It protects a complete headwaters stream system in a region where the human population is numerous and steadily growing.

The trail passed through a young forest of mixed oaks, black birch, tuliptree, black cherry, and American beech. Later on my walk, I noticed shagbark hickory, black locust, bigtooth aspen, black gum, sassafras, yellow birch, white ash, basswood, and several other tree species. In this diverse woodland, foresters have counted more than 50 of the 120 trees occurring in Pennsylvania. Beneath the taller trees grow understory species such as striped maple, witch hazel, greenbrier, various tree seedlings, and a host of ground-hugging plants, including jack-in-the-pulpit, violets, trillium,

Dutchman's-breeches, bluebell, toothwort, trout lily, spring beauty, and dwarf ginseng.

Greenbrier tangles the slopes above Roaring Run. I am familiar with this formidable shrub, having snagged myself on it in Florida's swamps, the grouse coverts of central Pennsylvania, and various places in between. Its strong, pliant, vinelike stems, viridian green in color, bear stout, needle-sharp prickles that earn it the name "catclaw" in the South. Deer browse on the tender growing tips, and a variety of birds from songbirds to ruffed grouse eat the thin-skinned purplish fruits and the large, woody seeds they contain.

The trail was marked with blue plastic rectangles tacked to trees. I heard a pileated woodpecker drumming, and the rustlings of a thrush as it foraged next to the path. The way led past big, lichen-covered rocks. Sunlight shafted in through the trees, reflecting from and backlighting the heart-shaped leaves of the greenbrier. Small black cherries lay scattered on the trail; I tasted one, tart enough to pucker my mouth.

It had taken me several hours to drive to Roaring Run, and it felt good to stretch out my limbs and really walk. I followed a route suggested by Tom Thwaites in his book *50 Hikes in Western Pennsylvania:* entering the natural area from the west on Roaring Run Trail, making a big loop, and returning to my starting point via Painter Rock Trail. The seven marked trails at Roaring Run total nearly twenty miles; with the area so close to Pittsburgh, it gets a lot of weekend use by hikers and cross-country skiers, but in the middle of the week, I saw no other visitors.

The intermittent rushing of cars on the highway soon gave way to a different flowing sound: Roaring Run, dividing itself around boulders and cascading over rocks in its gently curving bed. The water sparkled in the sun. Native brook trout, their olive green backs dappled with black and their fins marked with orange and white, flashed as quick as thought when I spooked them in passing; once I spied five fingerlings, all faced upstream and finning slowly in the current, in a spot you could have covered with a hat.

The trail followed a tram road built by loggers in the early 1900s. Additional logging followed those initial operations, with some parts of the natural area cut over three times in less than a century. In the late 1960s, the Western Pennsylvania Conservancy, a private land conservancy organization, bought the drainage and conveyed it to the Bureau of Forestry. The bureau publishes an excellent trail guide showing parking areas, contour lines, and streams; request the map from the Forbes State Forest district office or Bureau of Forestry headquarters in Harrisburg.

Thwaites writes that Roaring Run Trail crosses the stream twenty-eight times as it ascends the rugged valley. I don't doubt it. Low water conditions and my trusty rhododendron hiking staff made for easy crossings. Thwaites advises an upland route along South Loop Trail during high water conditions in springtime.

A splendid fungus shelved out from the trunk of a tuliptree. The fungus had a snowy white bottom and a hard, brown, weathered-looking top. The lower surface area contained thousands of tiny pores, through which the fungus releases millions of microscopic spores, which are like seeds. The white skin makes an excellent canvas on which pictures can be etched and has earned *Ganoderma applanatum* its common name, the artist's conk.

A hawk shot over my head, flying down the valley—I saw its shadow on the ground, then spotted the raptor flashing past just above the treetops. Judging from its size and shape, I thought it must be a Cooper's hawk, an accipiter that preys mainly on birds the size of robins, jays, and flickers, and on mammals as large as squirrels. Later, I got a good look at three sorts of woodpeckers: a crow-sized pileated woodpecker, tapping for grubs on a dead limb; a downy woodpecker no bigger than a sparrow, hanging upside-down on a branch; and a hairy woodpecker, about the size of a robin, a male with a splash of red on the back of his head. I also saw a veery, many robins, wood thrushes, and a band of juncos.

Bob Mulvihill is an ornithologist at nearby Powdermill Nature Reserve, a field station for Pittsburgh's Carnegie Museum of Natural History. Mulvihill has been studying the birds of Roaring Run as part of a larger research project. At least fifty species breed in the natural area, he told me when I phoned him after my visit. Common breeders include the Louisiana waterthrush, Acadian flycatcher, red-eyed vireo, wood thrush, winter wren, Canada warbler, black-throated green warbler, scarlet tanager, veery, American redstart, and dark-eyed junco. The stream valley is alive with their territorial singing in the spring; in late August, when I visited, the birds were almost silent, and no doubt many of them had already left on their southward migration.

Mulvihill's study focused on the Louisiana waterthrush. This small streamside wood-warbler requires clean, clear water flowing through large unfragmented tracts of forest. Louisiana waterthrushes look like thrushes and behave like sandpipers, hopping from rock to rock and striding into the stream to catch nymphs, snails, and other aquatic creatures, and flitting out over the water to snap up flying insects. They build cup-shaped nests out of

A tiger swallowtail rests on a rock next to the rushing waters of Roaring Run, which drains a forested watershed in Westmoreland County.

leaves and grass in cavities along streambanks, hidden among tree roots or other vegetation. According to Mulvihill, breeding densities of Louisiana waterthrushes along Roaring Run are "as high as can be found anywhere in the mountains of southwestern Pennsylvania." His study revealed that Roaring Run has "a very high abundance of many different kinds of aquatic insects, especially mayflies, stoneflies, and caddisflies." In short, it's about as clean and pure as a stream can be.

After three and a half miles, Roaring Run Trail met Painter Rock Trail, and I climbed up out of the drainage. I ate my lunch while sitting on the berm of a woods road, next to a monument marking the spot where D. A. Sheets, C. K. Baker, and Catherine Saylor were killed in a sleigh accident while on their way home from church in January 1896.

Painter Rock Trail led through open woods and past a large red oak with a mass of thick limbs spreading out from its trunk about ten feet up. The red oak was surrounded by much younger trees. I guessed that the oak had once grown in an open area, perhaps along a field boundary. After another mile, I came to Painter Rocks. "Painter" is a corruption of "panther" and probably refers to the puma, or eastern mountain lion, which once inhabited Pennsylvania; perhaps pumas had denned in the cracked, deeply fissured rock formations perched on the lip of the valley.

My feet were tender and my legs weary as I followed the rock-studded trail down toward Roaring Run and the parking area. A scraping sound made me stop.

The bears saw me the moment I saw them. A sow with two cubs nearly full-grown: sleek, and black as they could be against the forest background. The sow's small, thick ears were erect, and her nose twitched back and forth, up and down. I would gladly have given up the trail. But the bears deferred to me and went crashing off through laurel and greenbrier.

TO GET THERE. From Jones Mills in western Westmoreland County, turn south on PA Routes 381 and 711. After 1.2 miles, at a gas station in Champion, turn left (east) on County Line Road, SR 1058. Drive 1.8 miles to a gravel parking area on the left. (Altogether, five parking areas are scattered around the perimeter of Roaring Run Natural Area.) According to Tom Thwaites's *50 Hikes in Western Pennsylvania*, the Roaring Run Trail–Painter Rocks Trail loop covers 8.2 miles and takes five hours; allow another hour if you like to dawdle and nature-snoop as I do.

Be sure to take along the map and guide to Roaring Run Natural Area, available free from the Bureau of Forestry.

17   ALAN SEEGER

390 ACRES, ROTHROCK STATE FOREST, HUNTINGDON COUNTY

The Wampler Road overlook on Gettis Ridge faces knolls, ravines, and mountains: the Rothrock State Forest looks like a green tapestry that has fallen off the wall to lie rumpled on the floor. In the complicated forested terrain, a patch of conifers stands taller than the hardwoods surrounding it. In winter, when the oaks are gray and bare, it is easy to spot the hemlocks' evergreen foliage. In summer, it is not so simple to discern them, but if you know where to look, you will see the conifers of Alan Seeger Natural Area filling a small, flat-bottomed valley. For a long time, I have thought of Alan Seeger as the deep green at the heart of the green.

The place is part of my personal history. My father, Leonard Fergus, was a professor at Penn State. He studied fungi, many of which invade and weaken trees, and break them down once they are dead. For many years, my father taught the school's forest pathology course. Jim Nelson, former chief state forester for Pennsylvania, who helped create the natural area system, was one of my father's pupils; Nelson told me my father's teaching had inspired him to go on to further studies.

Dad often collected mushrooms for the university herbarium. He dug them out of the ground with a pocketknife—never would he pluck them; that might destroy key morphological features—and carried them home in a paper sack. His favorite place to collect was Alan Seeger.

My mother, Ruth Fergus, my younger brother Mike, and I often went along, riding in our green Chevrolet station wagon. It seemed like a major expedition to reach Alan Seeger, although it was only about fifteen miles from home. We would have a picnic beneath the great hemlocks, where the air was always moist and cool, compared with the sunlit parking lot. After lunch, Dad, Mike, and I would go mushroom hunting. Mushrooms are the fruiting bodies of fungi, which are plantlike organisms living in the ground and in wood. Mushrooms are to fungi what apples are to apple trees.

Walking, we concentrated on the ground at our feet, where few green plants grew, because the trees' interlocking crowns shut out the sun almost completely. We found red mushrooms, pink ones, violet, orange, pale turquoise, yellow, green, black, white, and many shades of brown. Mush-

Many different fungi grow beneath virgin
hemlocks at Alan Seeger Natural Area,
including the poisonous Amanita virosa,
known as the destroying angel.

rooms that looked like oysters, hedgehogs, coral, dead fingers, brains, cauliflower, melted butter. Mushrooms that felt as slimy as a slug, or waxy, or rubbery, or silken. Mushrooms that had gills on the undersides of their caps, and others that had tiny pores. Mushrooms that dripped milk when you scored their gills with a fingernail. Mushrooms whose golden flesh turned blue when touched. Mushrooms with hair-thin stems and dainty caps that looked fashioned by elfin craftsmen—next to huge, bulbous, corrupt, rotten-looking specimens. I remember many of the common names: stinkhorn, turkeytail, earth tongue, hen of the woods, old man of the woods, horse mushroom, horn of plenty, beefsteak fungus, dryad's saddle.

I became interested in nature by following my father on his collecting forays. Sometimes I wish I could go back to those days, when my parents were still living, when death was so remote as to have no relevance to life. It is a period that seems bright and serene, suspended in my imagination, and when I leave the real world and venture back in time to visit it, I think about racing lightly down woodland paths, and holding hands with loving adults, and being fully open to the sights, sounds, and smells of a fantastic natural world.

My most recent visit to Alan Seeger was in late May. The natural area surrounds and includes a 118-acre stand of virgin timber, principally eastern hemlocks, with a few large white pines, white and red oaks, cucumbertrees, and tuliptrees mixed in. Oddly enough, the trees appear bigger to me today than they did when I was little (whereas things like buildings and statues and city parks seem smaller to me now than then).

The hemlocks are tall. Some of them top a hundred feet, with burly, shaggy crowns like those of old redwoods. Standing Stone Creek, often referred to simply as Stone Creek, splits and braids among the trees; the air is humid and dense. The largest hemlocks are more than five hundred years old and perhaps as many as a thousand years old. Seventy years ago, a forester described the stand as "the finest example of virgin hemlock on streambed alluvium in Pennsylvania." E. Lucy Braun, in her comprehensive book *Deciduous Forests of the Northeast,* published in 1950, cited Alan Seeger as a classic example of "the hemlock forest type of ravine [where] the hemlock . . . occupies the lower flats [and] hemlock, white oak, and red maple are the most abundant canopy species, together composing about 70 percent of the stand."

Where storms have toppled a hemlock, or where some malady has killed a tree and reduced it to a snag, sunlight comes streaming in, flashing off the large, blade-shaped leaves of the great rhododendron. These massive shrubs stand twenty feet tall beneath the old-growth trees. (An excellent time to visit the natural area is during the first week of July, when the rhododendrons are blanketed with spectacular pink flowers.) The trail at Alan Seeger is a tunnel through the rhododendrons; it would be almost impossible to negotiate the stand were it not for the footpath.

Many birds breed in the old-growth stand: Louisiana waterthrushes, Acadian flycatchers, wood pewees, ovenbirds, Blackburnian warblers, black-throated green warblers, and hooded warblers. Other species can be seen during spring and fall migrations. As I walked on the three-quarter-mile trail through the hemlocks, a warbler chattered at me while flitting surreptitiously among the twisted, arm-thick, interlocking rhododendron trunks. Finally I caught the bird in my binoculars. Its lemon yellow breast was adorned with black radiating streaks like a necklace: a male Canada warbler, a species that breeds in boggy thickets in Canada and at high elevations in the Appalachians.

I thought of my father and his fascination with fungi (not for nothing was he known as Fungus Fergus) when I found *Ganoderma tsugae,* a tough, woody conk shelving out from the mossy side of a fallen hemlock. The mahogany-colored fungus had a sheen to it like fresh shellac. As its species name implies, *Ganoderma tsugae* grows mainly on the eastern hemlock, *Tsuga canadensis.* The fungus was decaying the woody bole, breaking it down into organic matter. Without fungi, trees would rot very slowly indeed. All along the summit of the huge, supine trunk, tiny hemlocks sent up dainty, pale green sprays of needles. Someday perhaps they, too, would become forest giants.

Old-growth pines and hemlocks are remnants of the virgin forest that once covered much of Pennsylvania.

The Pennsylvania State Forest Commission established Alan Seeger Forest Monument in 1921. The name recalls an American poet who died during World War I while serving in the French Foreign Legion. Alan Seeger was killed by machine-gun fire during an attack on a fortified town in France on July 4, 1916. He was a native of New York City, and there is no evidence that he ever visited Pennsylvania.

People have often wondered why more than a hundred acres of old-growth hemlocks were spared the logging that denuded the Seven Mountains, as this rugged region is known. I have heard two explanations.

There was a dispute between two logging companies regarding ownership of the timber. Neither company was sure enough of its claim to turn loose the axmen and sawyers.

A water-powered sawmill stood where Detweiler Run enters larger Standing Stone Creek. A common practice was to hold off on cutting around the mill until the very end, and in this instance the timber company went out of business before leveling the final tract.

TO GET THERE. Just north of the village of McAlevys Fort, turn east off PA Route 26 and proceed 6.4 miles, first on SR 1023 and then on SR 4006, to the natural area parking lot. Across the lot from the picnic area, a wooden sign depicts the trail winding through the old-growth stand. If approaching from the east, drive west 7.3 miles on Stone Creek Road from U.S. Route 322 near Laurel Creek Reservoir, north of Milroy. (Route 322 is divided by a median barrier, and Stone Creek Road is accessible only from the eastbound, or downhill, lanes.)

From just south of the parking area at Alan Seeger, partway up the hill on Seeger Road, the blue-blazed Greenwood Spur–Johnson Trail climbs Broad Mountain through dry uplands very different in character from the hemlock grove.

---

18   BEAR MEADOWS

890 ACRES, ROTHROCK STATE FOREST, CENTRE COUNTY

A foggy morning on one of the shortest days of the year. Two inches of snow lay on the ground, turned to slush by yesterday's rain. A breeze stirred the trees' bare branches, loosing water droplets that drummed on the big, leathery leaves of the great rhododendron, *Rhododendron maximum,* one of the signature plants at Bear Meadows.

Nick Bolgiano had invited me along on an outing, part of the Christmas Bird Count sponsored by a local birding club, in which some twenty parties of dedicated souls were fanning out with their binoculars across Centre County to identify and count as many birds as they could on this mid-December Saturday. Bolgiano, a thin, quiet man in his forties, a statistician by trade, knows Bear Meadows as well as anybody: monitoring the site for the Pennsylvania Society of Ornithology's Special Areas Project, he canvassed the natural area more than forty times between January 1998 and December 2000, when we visited. During that time, Bolgiano recorded 109 different avian species.

He paused on the trail through the quiet woods and pursed his lips. "Pish, pish," he called—urgent sounds like the alarm calls of birds. "Pishing," as birders refer to the technique, can excite and attract feathered creatures within hearing.

A small band of dark-eyed juncos gave a soft, anxious twittering as they cautiously came in. A flash of blue and white, and a jay scolded us loudly while keeping out of sight in a patch of mountain laurel. A golden-crowned kinglet arrived, then seemed to forget all about us as, only ten feet away, it fluttered in place while inspecting the dark green laurel, searching for insect eggs and hibernating spiders and bugs. A brown creeper hitched itself up a nearby tree trunk, sounding a scarcely audible *seeeee* very similar to the kinglet's high-pitched note.

Four species, duly entered by Bolgiano in his notebook.

We moved on. Bolgiano stopped and cupped his hands around his mouth. He let out a string of throaty, measured hoots suggesting the phrase: *Who cooks for you, who cooks for youall?* The mimicry recalled for me a time I had gone winter camping in a conifer-dark stream bottom and been wrenched out of my sleep by a barred owl blaring that same slogan from a hemlock above my tent. I thought Bolgiano's rendition a very good one. However, no barred owl answered—although Bolgiano has seen those secretive predators at Bear Meadows. A raven went *ronk,* perhaps in response to the owl call. Bolgiano dug his notebook out of his jeans pocket. Five species and counting.

The day proceeded, dripping, somber, dim. In the mist, smells seemed intensified: the citrus scent of hemlocks, the tang of tannin-laden bog water, the musk of wet bark. On the ice, we crept past the monument stone at the small parking area, crossed the bridge over Sinking Creek, and took the trail to an observation platform. The now somewhat rickety edifice was built in

1978, and normally it gives a good view of the bog: oval, some 325 acres in extent, a mix of grasses and sedges growing on and around a mat of sphagnum moss furzed with swamp-loving shrubs such as highbush blueberry, leatherleaf, poison sumac, and wild raisin; clusters of standing dead trees along the bog's edge, backed by the deep green of living hemlocks, black spruce, and balsam fir. Today, I couldn't see much of anything, except for nearby winter-bare shrubs and the tea-colored creek flowing sluggishly past. The raven called again, from the murk somewhere above us; maybe he was above the clouds.

A series of springs feed Bear Meadows bog, which specialists classify as a "poor fen," a type of peatland lacking in plant nutrients. Geologists are not sure how the bog, or fen, came into being; most such wetlands developed in low areas overlain by glaciers during the last ice age, but Bear Meadows lies sixty miles south of the southern limit of glaciation. Perhaps a small pocket of ice filled the mountain valley at one time, or a landslide blocked its drainage. The bog, about a mile long and a quarter mile wide, lies on an east-west axis. It is surrounded on three sides by forested mountains rising four hundred to six hundred feet above the valley floor. When the weather is clear, an excellent overview of Bear Meadows can be had from North Meadows Road, which swings above the wetland on the north. In recent years, beavers have built dams on Sinking Creek, causing the bog to expand; Bolgiano told me the water level was the highest he'd seen it since he began going to Bear Meadows back in 1983.

Trees such as black spruce and balsam fir, and many other plants that are more common in areas farther north, find a home at chilly Bear Meadows, whose bowl shape holds the cold air and where frosts may occur well into May. Members of the Pennsylvania Native Plant Society took a field trip there in June 1999 and identified a range of plants, including rare twayblade orchids so tiny they are hard to spot even on the open forest floor. The plant enthusiasts observed common bladderwort floating on the waters of Sinking Creek. (Bladderwort is a carnivorous plant that sucks aquatic insects into bladderlike traps, then digests them.) They found checkered rattlesnake plantain, partridgeberry, butterfly weed, and swamp milkweed. Corn lily, yellow-flowered goldthread, goldenseal, bluebead lily, starflower, and round-leaved and yellow fringed orchids have also been reported. Collectors apparently wiped out the round-leaved sundews and pitcher plants, rare carnivorous species that once grew on top of the sphagnum mat.

My friend Clark Shiffer, an amateur odonatologist, reports that he and other enthusiasts have netted sixty-one species of dragonflies and damselflies at Bear Meadows—more than a third of all the species found in Pennsylvania. Bobcats haunt the bog and the surrounding woodland. Deer, chipmunks, and gray squirrels abound. Black bears feed heavily on the blueberries that ripen in late summer on shrubs whose roots are reliably watered by the sphagnum moss, which holds moisture like a sponge. Bear Meadows probably got its name from bears coming in to feed on the berries; according to local lore, settlers built pens out of logs to trap the bears.

Bears also relish the autumn fruit of black gum trees, many large and ancient specimens of which grow in the band of damp woods around the bog. Many of the trees have thick, twisted trunks and plated, deeply furrowed bark that looks like alligator skin. Migrating songbirds snap up the black gum berries by the thousands. The leaves of black gums turn a brilliant orange-red before most other deciduous trees show their fall colors. Biologists term this early vivid display "foliar flagging" and suggest that it is an invitation to birds to come and gorge on the fruit, which offers a high fat content. The birds then scatter the trees' seeds in their droppings.

Bolgiano and I tramped along on the trail encircling the bog. The breeze had swung around to the north, and it began pushing the fog out of the valley. By now Bolgiano's list had swelled: black-capped chickadee, hairy and downy woodpeckers, white-breasted and red-breasted nuthatches. In other winters, he has spotted redpolls, pine siskins, and red and white-winged crossbills, seedeaters driven south from their normal wintering range by food shortages among the conifers in their boreal home. At Bear Meadows, the birds find many of the same trees and seeds that sustain them during normal winters in the north.

Since we still hadn't gotten a good view over the bog, we left the trail and went downhill. And hit a wall of rhododendron. We squirmed, ducked, and sidestepped our way through the shrubs with their springy, twisted trunks, some of which were thicker than my forearm. I made a mental note to return in July, when the rhododendrons, taller than my head in places, would put forth their showy pink blooms. In spring and summer, Bolgiano finds Canada, black-throated blue, and hooded warblers nesting among the dense foliage of the rhododendrons.

In 1842, Spencer Fullerton Baird, a professor of natural history at Dickinson College in Carlisle (he later became secretary of the Smithsonian

Institution), set off on a long walk through central Pennsylvania. In a letter to his brother, he wrote of a June sojourn to "the Bear Meadows," describing "a Meadow on top of a Mountain so Boggy that you can thrust a stick through the roots & moss 15 feet. The place is filled in most places with a dense growth of Rhododendron, Hemlock, Black Spruce, Tamarack &c. It contains many very curious and beautiful flowers; I saw 4 ravens."

A half century after Baird toured Bear Meadows, a logging company bought five thousand acres surrounding the bog. Pines and oaks were cut for lumber, and other tree species were processed into paper pulp. Joseph Rothrock, a professor at nearby Pennsylvania State College and the first chief

On the edge of Bear Meadows bog, birder Nick Bolgiano tries to elicit the response of a barred owl by mimicking the species' call.

forester for Pennsylvania, noted that the largest white pines cut in and near Bear Meadows were four and a half feet in diameter at the base, although the typical diameter was about two feet.

Bolgiano and I paused beneath thick, towering hemlocks that the loggers for some reason had spared. Some of the black spruce were also quite large, and since spruces grow slowly in the nutrient-poor bog, many of them must have been very old. According to Bolgiano, colorful Blackburnian and yellow-rumped warblers nest high in the conifers during spring and summer. Small stands of balsam firs stood scattered in the swampy woods, where the crowns of the trees linked together and shut out the light. Upslope from the bog, red spruces were dark green pyramids among the linear gray-brown trunks of the hardwood trees. The overlapping boughs of the spruces flexed in the risen wind.

As the day waned, the wind grew chill. It sang in the tops of the conifers and whistled through the bare branches of oaks, gums, and birches.

Bolgiano had seen or heard fifteen species of birds. "About what you'd expect for a winter outing," he said. "If it had been May or June, we probably would have hit fifty."

TO GET THERE. From the traffic light in the village of Boalsburg, just east of State College, travel east on U.S. Route 322 for 1.9 miles to Bear Meadows Road (SR 2001). Turn right on Bear Meadows Road, passing Tussey Mountain Ski Area on the left. Stay on Bear Meadows Road a total of 5 miles to the bog; a small parking lot is on the right side, along with a stone monument, on which a plaque put up by the National Park Service designates Bear Meadows as a national natural landmark.

South of the parking area, a trail leads westward to an observation platform with a view over the bog. To circumambulate Bear Meadows, leave the observation platform and, keeping the bog on your right, follow a well-used footpath in a clockwise direction. Altogether, this loop covers 3.5 miles; for part of the way, the trail is blue blazed. The path is level, rocky, and often wet. The black and red spruces and balsam firs grow along the northern edge of the bog.

In winter, access roads to Bear Meadows are not maintained, and they get dangerously icy. To conduct his midwinter bird surveys, Bolgiano leaves his car at the ski lodge and hikes to the natural area on foot.

Bear Meadows is on the McAlevys Fort, Pennsylvania, topographic quadrangle.

---

19   BIG FLAT LAUREL

184 ACRES, ROTHROCK STATE FOREST, HUNTINGDON AND CENTRE COUNTIES

Serious birders rise early in the day. Greg Grove had asked me to meet him on Bear Gap Road at 6 A.M. A few minutes after six, we were hiking on the Mid-State Trail into Big Flat Laurel Natural Area, at the juncture of Greenlee Ridge and Thickhead Mountain, elevation twenty-four hundred feet. It was May 26, a clear, chill morning, and at first the birds were silent.

The trail wound among chestnut oaks, some of them killed by gypsy moth defoliation fifteen years ago but still standing, bereft of bark and pale in the first light. The orange-blazed footpath led us past pitch pines and black gums and black birches and shadbush and, fortunately, because it is not pleasant trying to fight your way into and out of such places, through

Mountain laurel swells its buds in late May and blooms profusely in early June at Big Flat Natural Area.

thickets of mountain laurel, *Kalmia latifolia,* blanketing much of the natural area. The glossy green shrubs were covered with flower buds, tight and a livid shade of pink, about a week shy of opening; I sometimes think I like the bright buds of the laurel even more than the blossoms that follow.

I listened hard. When the trees are full of leaves, you can know that a bird is present by hearing it—you may have little chance of ever seeing it, particularly in such a thick place. What I heard was the squeaking of our leather boots, our footfalls on the beaten path, and the traffic of trucks and early commuters on U.S. Route 322, three miles to the west, twelve hundred feet lower down, and a world apart from this high, rocky flat in the Rothrock State Forest.

Grove stopped and lifted a finger. "Hear that squeaking? That's a cowbird. They're here in the morning, dumping eggs. Then they go back to the farms down below." The brown-headed cowbird is a nest parasite: the female seeks out the temporarily vacated nests of other birds, surreptitiously lays an egg, and departs. The host birds raise the demanding, fast-growing cowbird hatchling, which sometimes cheats their own offspring out of the food they need to survive. I was surprised that cowbirds would venture into such a large, unbroken chunk of woods. However, birds have wings, and a three-mile flight is a pretty short hop: from farm to forest in five minutes, then back again.

A dark-eyed junco fed on the ground ahead on the trail. "At least we'll see one bird today," Grove joked. Actually, I had seen some other birds already: a hen turkey and a gobbler, his naked head a startling pale blue, while I was driving up Bear Gap Road en route to our meeting.

Grove, in his late forties, is a professor of molecular biology at Penn State University. Birding is his avocation. He lives on the edge of Rothrock State Forest and visits it regularly, binoculars in hand, ear cocked for birds calling. He monitors three areas in Rothrock—Detweiler Run, Alan Seeger, and Big Flat Laurel Natural Areas—for the Pennsylvania Important Bird Area program, sponsored by the Pennsylvania Audubon Society.

"I just heard a hermit thrush go," he said.

The call was a single introductory note followed by trembling, liquid phrases. A Mohawk legend holds that the hermit thrush once outflew all the other birds, arrived in heaven, and there learned its sublime song. The hermit thrush is a bird of the mountains in Pennsylvania, breeding at higher elevations and more often in coniferous forests than the closely related and much more abundant wood thrush.

Now the towhees had begun: one to the left of the trail, a couple others to the right. Grove opined that the eastern towhee (also called the rufous-sided towhee) and the ovenbird are the two most common breeders at Big Flat. *Drink your tea,* the towhees sang.

Towhees and thrushes I can make out, but birds with subtler songs sometimes frustrate me. I have damaged my hearing over the years—first by shooting rifles in an indoor range, later by pounding nails and running a power saw—and now I sometimes watch a bird lift its head and open its bill and (apparently) belt out a song that I never hear above the buzzing, ringing, and whining sounds that fill my head.

Grove pointed to where an ovenbird was singing. It took me a while—I had to advance along the trail, get closer to where the bird was hidden—before I made out the emphatic *tea-cher, tea-cher, tea-cher.*

Grove told me that he, too, had damaged his hearing through shooting. Now, when listening for birds, he wears a hearing aid in one ear. He heard (I didn't) the bouncy, high-pitched song of an indigo bunting. He whispered, "There's a black-and-white warbler very near us right now."

Straining, I finally caught the thin, repetitive *weesee weesee.* A chestnut-sided warbler: *please please please ta meetcha.* A myrtle warbler: Roger Tory Peterson, in *A Field Guide to the Birds,* simply calls this song "weak, colorless, and irregular."

The trail curved out into an open area, then went across an expanse of pale rocks. In the boulder field grew mountain ash; the trees, straggling and spindle-trunked, bore white flowers that later would become scarlet, berry-like fruits. We were at a spot known as Indian Wells Overlook. Grove tapped his boot toe on the edge of a low, dry area about five feet wide. "For what it's worth, these depressions are the Indian wells, although who knows whether Indians really made them."

We sat on rocks as the sun rose in the clear sky. In the wooded bowl below us lay Bear Meadows Bog. Beyond the bog were green ridges, some long and straight, some truncated or bending back on themselves. The ridges carried on toward the northeast, where knobbed hills disappeared into the haze; through my binoculars, I could see tan and green fields and tiny houses and barns catching the light. On the southern horizon were Grass Mountain, backed by Spruce Mountain, with Stone Mountain and Jacks Mountain and possibly Blacklog and Shade Mountains, all wooded, receding in ever paler shades of blue.

A yellow-billed cuckoo sounded its *gowk gowk gowk,* and a moment later it flew past, giving us a good look at a normally very shy forest bird. A goldfinch winged overhead, and Grove said he could hear the bird's flight call, which he described as a faint *potato-chip, potato-chip.* A blue jay landed in a snag and gave its squeaky-hinge call. We saw some unusual birds for a deep-woods setting: a mourning dove perched on a bare branch, eyeing us nervously before flying off on whistling wings. A chimney swift flitted up and down on sickle-shaped wings. Two great blue herons labored past, their necks tucked back against their angular bodies, gray silhouettes against the blue sky.

A flock of cedar waxwings came past on whooshing wings. Periodically the flock would break up into smaller groups, one of which landed in a fire cherry poking out of the rocks about thirty feet away. Cedar waxwings are highly social birds that feed in flocks during most of the year. They eat mainly fruit, and they also take insects, readily available at Bear Meadows Bog down in the valley. Cedar waxwings wait until summer to nest, when shrubs and trees have produced enough fruit to nurture their young.

Grove and I focused our binoculars on the waxwings, perched in the morning sun. The birds had brownish backs, pale lemon bellies, black face masks, crested heads, brilliant yellow tail tips, and small tufts of crimson feathers on their wings like dabs of bright sealing wax.

"You can hardly believe that such an exquisite thing exists," Grove said.

TO GET THERE. From U.S. Route 322, 1.9 miles east of the traffic light in Boalsburg, turn right on Bear Meadows Road, SR 2001, at a sign for Tussey Mountain Ski Resort. After 1.4 miles, keep left on paved Bear Meadows Road. Stay on Bear Meadows Road another 3.5 miles, turn right on North Meadows Road, and go 2.5 miles to Gettis Ridge Road. Park in the vicinity and follow the Mid-State Trail north into the natural area. Big Flat Laurel Natural Area borders larger Bear Meadows Natural Area on the west. To catch the peak of the mountain laurel blooming, schedule your visit for the first week in June.

The natural area is on the McAlevys Fort, Pennsylvania, topographic quadrangle.

---

20   DETWEILER RUN

463 ACRES, ROTHROCK STATE FOREST, HUNTINGDON COUNTY

Winter's snow had mostly melted. The mountains were gray, with a touch of lavender from the swelling buds of the red maples. Wood frogs called from a vernal pond, and a raven's shadow fled across the leaf-strewn ground. It was a promising April day along Detweiler Run, which flowed noisily in its rocky bed, calling out in a high rushing sound with lower crumping and gurgling tones.

Butterflies seemed to be everywhere. The apparently fragile creatures had spent the winter hibernating, tucked away beneath tree bark or in cracks among rocks, while the snow lay deep and the wind howled and the run was silenced beneath ice. Now, from the muddy edges of puddles, two dark brown butterflies came starting up on red-banded, white-spotted wings; the red admirals fluttered off swiftly and erratically through the woods. A tortoiseshell wafted past me and landed on a tree. It folded shut its orange-and-dark-brown wings, whose margins looked like intricately torn paper. The undersides of the wings showed a pattern of mottled grays and browns, blending the butterfly in perfectly with the bark of the white oak on which it had landed.

Tiny blue butterflies known as spring azures seemed to be chips of sky brought down to earth. On a maple, a much larger butterfly lapped up sap at one of a row of holes drilled in the bark by yellow-bellied sapsuckers. A mourning cloak butterfly, it slowly opened and closed its wings, revealing their upper surfaces in a series of slow flashes: a deep, rich maroon edged with gold. Female mourning cloaks lay their eggs on trees' twigs. After hatching, the caterpillars feed on the foliage. As they grow, the caterpillars shed their skin several times; then they pupate, entering into a resting state inside a chrysalis, a thin-skinned, semirigid enclosure resembling a mummy's case, from which they later emerge as adult butterflies. In all, two generations arise each summer, the second of which enters hibernation in adult form, to awaken again the following spring.

In her book *More Outbound Journeys in Pennsylvania,* nature writer Marcia Bonta notes that summer butterflies at Detweiler Run include tiger swallowtails, red-spotted purples, white admirals, and great-spangled fritillaries, a range of species whose "numbers, size, and beauty rival those you can see in tropical rainforests."

The blue-blazed Greenwood Spur of the Mid-State Trail followed Detweiler Run closely. According to a 1928 edition of the *Pennsylvania Department of Forests and Waters Bulletin,* "The Detweiler Run State Forest Monument comprises a tangle of giant original forest trees, mostly white pine and hemlock, with an understory of almost impenetrable rhododendron." Passing by the rhododendrons guarding the stream (the locals call it "buck laurel"), I was grateful for the well-used trail giving easy access to one of the most beautiful stands of old-growth timber in Pennsylvania.

The rocky path led past black and yellow birches, red oaks, ashes, and cucumber magnolias of ordinary second-growth size. Soon the blue paint blazes gave way to orange, where the Greenwood Spur met the Mid-State Trail. The Mid-State went northeast on an old logging railroad grade into the old-growth timber: huge tuliptrees, their straight trunks ringed with sapsucker feeding wells; hulking, twisted white oaks; and hemlocks that were not simply tall, but massive, with thick trunks and deeply furrowed bark. There were gnarled, moss-covered roots for resting upon, the stream making its cheerful music, and springs along the trail for replenishing the canteen. The hemlocks grew close by the stream, while lofty white pines stood on the south-facing slope above the watercourse. Although leaf-out had not yet begun, many shades of green enlivened the forest: the dark hemlocks and paler pines, the glossy leaves of the rhododendrons, bluish lichens splotching the tree trunks, moss dappling boulders and cloaking smaller rocks, and ferns, which had survived through winter, their fronds now lying prostrate on the ground.

I've heard it said that the big trees along Detweiler Run were left uncut because a boiler blew up on a log-hauling steam engine, causing timbering operations to be suspended, and the state bought the land before the logging could be resumed. Another bit of folklore holds that parts of the locomotive lie rusting along the run, hidden in the rhododendron.

From the 1928 *Pennsylvania Department of Forests and Waters Bulletin:* "Conditions in this monument picture very truly the primeval forest of the State. . . . Former State Forest Ranger Ross, a local authority on the wild life of Pennsylvania, says that the wolves made one of their last stands in central Pennsylvania in the dark, gloomy depths of Detweiler Hollow, sallying forth at night in search of game, howling dismally from the mountain tops, or with dark, furtive eyes watching the shingle shavers from the edge of the forest." Shingle shavers were men who snuck in to illegally fell the best of the remaining pines, shaved out shingles from their knot-free wood, and carried the shingles on their backs to distant settlements where they were sold.

"In the dark recesses of this great forest tangle live some of the rare warblers and other forest-loving birds," the description continued. "The late Dr. J. T. Rothrock stated that the duck hawk, one of the rarest varieties of hawks in the State, nested in these big trees."

Greg Grove, a veteran birder living near the Rothrock State Forest, has spent many hours in Detweiler Run Natural Area. He has not spotted the duck hawk, which we know today as the peregrine falcon, although perhaps some day it will return as a nesting species. Grove finds the following birds to be common breeders, however: downy and pileated woodpeckers, wood pewee, Acadian flycatcher, solitary and red-eyed vireos, black-capped chickadee, white-breasted nuthatch, brown creeper, veery, wood thrush, and scarlet tanager, along with eight warblers: black-throated blue, black-throated green, Blackburnian, black-and-white, hooded, and Canada warblers, as well as ovenbird and Louisiana waterthrush. Winter wrens, golden-crowned kinglets, and hermit thrushes also may nest in the natural area.

The Rothrock State Forest, and particularly Detweiler Run Natural Area, has been identified as a Pennsylvania Important Bird Area by the

Audubon Society, as described in the publication *A Guide to Critical Bird Habitat in Pennsylvania.*

It's a great place for butterflies, too.

TO GET THERE. From U.S. Route 322, 1.9 miles east of the traffic light in Boalsburg, turn right (south) on Bear Meadows Road, SR 2001. Follow Bear Meadows Road for 5 miles to Bear Meadows Natural Area; from there, go up and over Thickhead Mountain, making a hard left but staying on Bear Meadows Road at its intersection with Wampler Road. Continue 0.6 mile to where Bear Meadows Road makes a sharp right, and park on the left near gated Detweiler Road. In winter, and in some years well into spring, sections of the roads can be icy and extremely treacherous.

For a circuit of the natural area, descend on the orange-marked Mid-State Trail to Detweiler Run. Follow the trail to the left on a northeast heading. This section of the Mid-State is rocky and requires sturdy hiking shoes. You can walk as far as the blue-blazed Ax Handle Trail, which climbs the slope back up to Detweiler Road (the road parallels both the Mid-State Trail and Detweiler Run), or you can continue on to a pipeline right-of-way, which also allows an ascent to Detweiler Road. On grassy Detweiler Road, turn left and walk back to your vehicle.

The natural area is included by the McAlevys Fort and Barrville topographic quadrangles.

---

21   LITTLE JUNIATA WATER GAP

624 ACRES, ROTHROCK STATE FOREST, HUNTINGDON COUNTY

For me, it is a place of passage. Hiking into the gap carved through Tussey Mountain by the Little Juniata River, I enter a hidden world of vegetation subtle and soaring; a refuge for reptiles, amphibians, birds, and mammals; a portal into the recent and the geological past.

The Little Juniata Water Gap is a deep declivity cut through a wooded mountain ridge in central Pennsylvania; it looks like an ax notch on the horizon. The Little Juniata River snakes its way through the 1.6-mile-long gap it has created. In some places the river is narrow and swift, in others wide and placid.

Water gaps can be found throughout the Ridge and Valley Region of the Appalachian Mountains, which extends from Pennsylvania south to Alabama. The long ridges, stone-capped and covered with trees, lie on a northeast-to-southwest orientation, the result of continental shifting nearly three hundred million years ago. Tributaries flow along in the agricultural valleys, then turn at right angles and cut through weak zones or fractures in the ridges to reach larger waters. "Like a thief through a gap in a fence" is the way the writer John McPhee describes the river flowing through Delaware Water Gap, 150 miles to the east. Geologists believe the ancient rivers kept to their courses while the Appalachians were gradually uplifted from a level plain. For fifteen million years, the rivers maintained their elevation and gradient, sawing down through thousands of feet of slowly rising sandstone and shale.

The gaps eventually became footpaths for Native Americans, including the Susquehannocks, who lived in the vicinity. Then came European settlers with their wagon roads and canals. Later, engineers routed railroads and, ultimately, highways through the gaps: it's easier to follow the ready-made corridors than to climb and descend the steep, stony slopes. At Little Juniata Water Gap, the river lies at around 710 feet; Tussey Mountain crests more than 1,300 feet higher up.

The top of Tussey bears evidence of past human activity: old quarries, abandoned in the 1950s, now overgrown with black birch and striped maple. Miners labored here after Tuscarora quartzite, hard rock capping the mountains, unyielding rock that allowed the ridges to endure while softer rocks eroded away to form the valleys. The quartzite went for ganister bricks, used to line steel and copper furnaces. You can still see funicular routes cut into the slope, down which the rock was lowered.

Of more than forty major water gaps in Pennsylvania, the Little Juniata is one of very few without a highway running through it. True, a rail line angles partway in, with freight trains frequently clattering past; but the railroad tunnels away through the mountain, leaving the gap behind, and the trains are but temporary intruders in what is otherwise a quiet, natural place.

On a day in late September, I visited the water gap, north of the town of Alexandria. The small parking lot was empty, and it looked as though I would have the place to myself on this Indian summer day, with hazy blue skies and the temperature in the eighties. I often seek out the gap in summer, when it is the coolest place around, the chill breath of the river held in the gorge between Tussey Mountain on the east and Short Mountain to the west.

Sycamores stood thick-trunked along the river, dropping yellow-brown leaves onto the slow, green glide of the Little Juniata. Red oaks jutted up

The Little Juniata River cut a 1.6-mile-long water gap through Tussey Mountain.

taller than the sycamores. The rich bottomland forest included white ash, tuliptree, basswood, white oak, cucumber-tree, sugar maple, and other species. A red-bellied woodpecker scolded from among the trunks, and the raucous rattle of a belted kingfisher sounded from the river. At the water's edge, a great blue heron jumped into the air, tucked up its stilt legs, and fled upstream.

Along the path, autumn's flowers had just about faded away. I found blue-stemmed goldenrod, white snakeroot, and tall bellflower with its five-lobed blue blossoms. In other seasons, violets, jack-in-the-pulpit, cone-flowers, and columbine bloom amid the brush. Poison ivy and stinging nettle fence the footpath.

Near a stone railroad bridge that arches across the river, the trail climbed above the Little Juniata. The train tracks were on my side for several hundred yards, and then they crossed the river again on another bridge. Not far beyond the second bridge, the railroad disappeared into the tunnel through Short Mountain.

The path descended into the heart of the water gap. A view of the stream opened before me: big, rounded tan rocks, tree-covered islands, stones along the bank plastered with dun-colored mud. In a stretch of slow water, trout rose languidly to take aquatic insects; ripples and rings spread

In some places in Little Juniata Water Gap, the river is narrow and swift; in others it is wide and placid.

across the surface. From the woods, a ruffed grouse drummed, the sound of its wing thuds speeding up and then dying away suddenly. Although it was late in the year, I kept a sharp eye out for copperheads and timber rattlesnakes. Red-bellied, water, and milk snakes and several types of salamanders also inhabit the natural area.

On my right rose sandstone cliffs whose shelves and cracks supported ferns and saplings. The cliffs revealed strata laid down when eastern North America lay beneath a shallow sea, before the Appalachians buckled upward: I hiked through the eons. The breeze sifted through the hemlock trees. When I emerged from the hemlocks' gloom, I sat on a rock at river's edge. Taking off my boots, I dipped my feet in the flow. The current cooled my feet while nudging them gently downstream. Pleasantly I remembered a day when my then-six-year-old son and I sought relief from the July heat with a dip in the Little Juniata. Holding hands, we rode the roller-coaster current around a big rock, then floated slowly through a deep pool.

A bird with a wide wingspan came gliding up the river and lit in a snag. It was an osprey. Soon the fish hawk flapped off its perch and flew back the way it had come.

The osprey reminded me of another aspect of Little Juniata Water Gap: a level of avian passage high above the river. From the parking lot, a second trail climbs Tussey Mountain to a series of overlooks and rock slides from which one can see the surrounding ridges and valleys. Each fall, raptors migrate along the ridges in their southward journeying: hawks, ospreys, vultures, and, particularly in November and December, golden eagles. When the wind

From rock slides and talus slopes high above the Little Juniata, hikers can watch for migrating birds, including raptors.

blows from the north, it is deflected upward by the ridgetops. The aerial travelers get a free ride, borne on a standing wave of air.

Sitting on my boulder, I watched as leaves ghosted past underwater, pale golden shapes that slowly twisted and turned. A monarch butterfly, on its own migration south, fluttered along a few feet above the Little Juniata. The river smell, green and piquant, hung in the air.

I resumed the path and was almost to the north end of the gap when the heron I'd scared earlier came flapping back downstream. A scraping and a muted banging sound followed the bird. One voice, then another. A canoe approached, the paddlers picking their way between rocks. They did not see me as they passed.

TO GET THERE. From the village of Water Street, where U.S. Route 22 and PA Route 453 intersect, go east on Route 22 for 0.5 mile. Turn left toward Alexandria. At 1.2 miles, turn left (north) at the Mead Paper Products factory and follow SR 4004 through the village of Barree. Make a sharp left and take the bridge across the Little Juniata River. At a **T** intersection just beyond the bridge, turn left again and drive 0.6 mile to the Bureau of Forestry parking area. The trail into the water gap is on the east bank of the Little Juniata. The path up the mountain begins on the side of the parking lot opposite the river.

The natural area is covered by the Alexandria, Pennsylvania, topographic quadrangle.

22 ROCKY RIDGE

150 ACRES, ROTHROCK STATE FOREST, HUNTINGDON COUNTY

Mr. Gruver was not interested in birds. I had paused on the trail leading up Rocky Ridge while trying to focus my binoculars on some warblers feeding on gnats in the trees; he was still looking for plants.

"Striped pipsissewa," I heard him say, as I found a bird and focused on it—only to have it flit into the next tree, where the new leaves obscured it.

"Over here's perfoliate bellwort."

The bird, which finally moved into my field of vision, proved to be a male Blackburnian warbler, one of the loveliest of the North American wood-warblers, with an orange throat and face set off by black head stripes, and a black-and-white body. Near it was a myrtle warbler, also a male, with bright patches like dabs of yellow paint adorning its head, sides, and tail.

The mixed flock moved off among the treetops, and I returned my attention to Gruver, a spare, agile seventy-nine-year-old, a retired ceramics scientist who is an avid botanist. I realized then that he didn't even have binoculars with him. "I'm not a naturalist," he said with a shrug. "Birds don't stay put long enough to let you get a good look at them. Not like plants."

It was the first week in May. The dogwoods were at the peak of their flowering, and one could still see far distances through the woods in which the fresh new leaves of the trees seemed to float like a golden-green haze. May: when many plants were flowering at Rocky Ridge Natural Area, 150 acres of fertile forest near Martin Gap in Huntingdon County.

Already we had seen wild geraniums and blue, yellow, and white violets. The five-petaled yellow flowers of cinquefoil shone like sunbursts. Gruver introduced me to the perfoliate bellwort at his feet: its single lemon yellow flower hung down like an unopened miniature beach umbrella. *Perfoliate,* he said, because the plant's upright stem seemed to pierce each of the long oval, pointed-tip leaves. "Take a sniff," he said. "The flower is quite fragrant."

Unfortunately, all I could smell was my sunscreen.

It was a hot day, and the sun lit up the dogwood blossoms that spread like snowbanks through the woods. A tiger swallowtail floated past. The

From spring until autumn, violets and many other wildflowers bloom at Rocky Ridge Natural Area.

The Link Trail leads past sandstone boulders studding the top of Rocky Ridge in northern Huntingdon County.

male catkins, or flowers, of oak trees lay fallen on the ground; they looked like fuzzy yellow-green caterpillars. Already I had noted five kinds of oaks: white, chestnut, red, scarlet, and black.

Gruver and I continued climbing up the Link Trail, which conveniently passes through the natural area. (The Link Trail is so named because it links the Mid-State Trail, in central Pennsylvania, with the Tuscarora Trail in the south-central part of the state.)

I was already familiar with some of the plants Gruver pointed out. Round-lobed hepatica, which had already flowered. Yellow lady's slipper, a large, spectacular orchid with lush green leaves whose flower buds looked a few days shy of opening. Pink lady's slipper, or moccasin flower, also not yet in bloom. Field pussytoes, whose woolly, white flowers really do resemble a cat's toes. Mayapple, also known as mandrake; because its fleshy, branching root system bears an uncanny resemblance to the human body, mandrake was once assumed to possess magical powers. Almost everywhere I looked, I saw fringed polygala, better known as gaywings, a small, ground-hugging evergreen plant that I rarely notice, except in spring, when it puts out beautiful paired, violet-pink flowers.

Many more plants were new to me, probably on account of my bad habit of walking about with my eyes directed upward, searching for uncooperative, irrelevant birds. Early meadow rue, with dangling, greenish white flowers. Miterwort, sometimes called bishop's cap, whose small, intricately fringed white flowers climbed up opposite sides of a vertical stalk. Wild ginger ("The flower smells like carrion; it attracts flies, which pollinate the plant," Gruver said), wild yamroot, wild comfrey, wild indigo, wild lupine.

At Rocky Ridge, the forest is well stocked with tall, straight timber prospering in the rich limestone soil. In addition to the spectrum of oaks, the hardwood species include tuliptree, shagbark and mockernut hickories, red and sugar maples, and black gum, with basswood, butternut, American beech, black cherry, and hop-hornbeam mixed in. In the moist bottom where Martin Gap interrupts Rocky Ridge, hemlocks and white pines shade a small stream. The ridge is scattered with Table Mountain pine, a conifer of the southern Appalachians that ranges north into southern Pennsylvania. Table Mountain pine is a slow-growing tree that ekes out a living on dry, rocky sites. Its large cones, armored with sharp spines, may take up to twenty years to ripen.

Gruver led the way along the ridge, calling out plants as he went. Partridgeberry. Sessile bellwort. Wild sarsaparilla. American comfrey.

Chunks of sharp-edged, frost-cleft limestone lay among the botany. We came to a different sort of stone: massive, contorted, greenish gray boulders that squatted like ogres on the ridgetop. Rocks the size of panel trucks, scabbed with the lichen known as rock tripe. The rocks were sandstone of the Oriskany formation. Wedged precariously into fissures between the boulders were broken-off chunks the size of basketballs and hay bales. At the base of the stones, sand weathered off the slabs was stippled with dozens of small, cone-shaped excavations. The pits had been dug by ant lions, also called "doodlebugs," and any ants or other small insects that slid down the craters' slopes would become meals for the predatory larva lying buried at the bottom of each pit.

From the boulders, a fine view opened to the northwest onto farmland in Standing Stone Valley; across the valley, Tussey Mountain hovered, pale through the haze of oak pollen in the air. The water gap at Barree interrupted the ridge, and the upturned prow of Canoe Mountain showed beyond the gap. Behind us to the east, Stone Mountain lifted its forested bulk to almost twenty-two hundred feet of elevation, a thousand feet higher than Rocky Ridge and fifteen hundred feet above the Standing Stone Valley floor.

Where a powerline right-of-way crossed Rocky Ridge, Gruver revealed himself to be more of a naturalist than he'd let on. "I was here just yesterday," he said, "and saw a northern fence lizard sunning himself on that boulder." We snuck up on the boulder, but no fence lizard was visible. Above us, turkey vultures soared on rising currents of air heated by the exposed rocks.

Gruver left the trail and led us down through open woods. Sweet cicely: "Note the hairy stem and the fernlike leaves." He crushed a bit of the plant, whose sharp licorice smell overcame my sunscreen. Gill-over-the-ground; bluet; Solomon's seal; tall rattlesnake root; gall-of-the-earth. I let myself be distracted once again by a thrush singing from a branch. Its ascending, flutelike phrases and the pale rings encircling its eyes convinced me that it was a Swainson's thrush, a common spring migrant in Pennsylvania forests and a rare breeding resident in the state's northern tier.

In the bottomland woods, Gruver found seven different ferns: Christmas, hay-scented, rattlesnake, maidenhair, rock cap, sensitive, and interrupted. He confided to me that he never carried food or water while walking. Indeed, he was an ascetic-looking man, I observed while munching on my sandwich and taking a tug on my water bottle. He failed to notice a blue-gray gnatcatcher acrobatically flitting about catching insects. He seemed not at all tempted by the stream, whose pools of cool, clear water looked like perfect places for soaking hot and tired feet.

He speculated on what might happen to the great diversity of plants as the years passed and the trees reached maturity and cast more shade on the forest floor. Probably their numbers would lessen. "But see how these tuliptrees have blown down," he said. We picked our way among the fallen trunks; the trees' root systems must have failed to anchor them during a storm. In sunlit openings created in the forest canopy, flowering plants grew abundantly.

I asked Gruver to name the absolute best time of year for a visit to Rocky Ridge. "You should come here every two weeks from the middle of April right through to the middle of September," he said.

TO GET THERE. From PA Route 26 north of Huntingdon, turn south on Martin Gap Road, SR 1017. After about a mile, cross a bridge and continue on to Rothrock State Forest land. Where the road forks, go right on Frew Road, which is rough but passable by automobile. After 0.5 mile, park at a pull-off on the left by a gated forest road. The Link Trail crosses Frew Road and, on a westward heading, climbs Rocky Ridge. Follow the Link Trail, marked with orange paint blazes, until you reach a powerline right-of-way. Descend on the right-of-way to Frew Road, turn left, and walk back to your car.

23   CHARLES F. LEWIS

384 ACRES, GALLITZIN STATE FOREST, INDIANA COUNTY

The hawk left the ground on pale, fast-beating wings. Climbing at a steep angle, it rose above the trees. The raptor flew burdened by the weight of the prey clutched in its talons: a gray squirrel, whose bushy tail plumed beneath the hawk's belly. The bird finally topped out above the forest, set its broad wings—their span approached four feet—and glided down the hollow.

It was a cool morning in late October, and the red-tailed hawk was on its autumnal migration, which might take it as far south as Florida. The bird had found a meal at the Charles F. Lewis Natural Area, a steep wooded valley in the side of Laurel Ridge, whose stream, Clark Run, flows into the Conemaugh River. The run, fed by rains that had fallen earlier in the week, raced down its bed fifty feet below the trail. The stream sheeted over long, slanting slabs, then tumbled between boulders.

All around me, leaves swirled down like giant snowflakes. The tall tuliptrees were shedding their yellow foliage; so were the sugar maples. The basswoods and birches had mostly dropped their leaves, which gave off a yellowish glow from the ground. Adding to the color flooding the hollow were the bright yellow leaves and crinkly yellow flowers of witch hazel shrubs, and the pale yellow leaves of striped maples. The American beeches had turned bronze. Red maples showed a dazzling orange-red. Against all of this temporary brilliance reposed the steadfast greens of streamside rhododendrons and hemlocks.

Fog cloaked the top of the mountain as I climbed the trail along Clark Run. My staff and boots helped me keep balanced on the rocky, slippery path. Fallen leaves lay like golden snow on and beneath green ferns cloaking the bank. The sun broke through the fog, turning the crowns of the tuliptrees a blazing yellow and lighting up the smooth blackish bark of black birches growing on the rocky south-facing slope across from where I hiked. Prickly brown husks of beechnuts lay on the trail: a source of food for the squirrels whose hollow, knocking calls filled the valley.

I flushed out another redtail; it was perched in a tree, no doubt listening and looking for squirrels. A pileated woodpecker called from deep in the woods. A white-breasted nuthatch froze against a tree trunk, its straight black beak held out at an acute angle. By now, most of the perching birds had departed for wintering grounds farther south. Birders report indigo buntings, Acadian flycatchers, blue-gray gnatcatchers, Louisiana waterthrushes, and numerous warbler species breeding in the natural area.

Charles F. Lewis lived from 1890 to 1971. A newspaperman and conservationist, he served as the first president of the Western Pennsylvania Conservancy, a citizens' organization that, since its inception in 1932, has bought thousands of acres to be set aside as public parks and natural areas. Part of the conservancy's mission is to conduct conservation education programs for children and adults, and the Charles F. Lewis Natural Area, less than two miles from the city limits of Johnstown, is an excellent outdoor classroom where visitors can observe different forest types and natural forest regeneration.

Starting in the mid-1800s, the Clark Run drainage was timbered off several times—first for lumber, later for mine props and charcoal. The railroad hugging the bank of the Conemaugh River has sent fires racing up the steep slope on the southern edge of the natural area; there, thickets of mixed oaks are gradually becoming forest again. Along Clark Run, which roughly parallels the Conemaugh before turning south and draining into the river, are several habitats and forest types. At the mouth of the ravine, deep, sandy soils support a northern hardwood cove community, with yellow birch, tuliptree, basswood, and sugar maple. Farther up the drainage are additional northern hardwoods, including black cherry, black birch, red maple, and American beech. Gradually, as the elevation increases and the soils become drier and thinner, a mixed-oak forest takes over.

Clark Run Trail makes a 1.8-mile loop through the natural area. It is blazed with yellow paint markings on trees—difficult to discern on the day I visited, when yellow leaves came spinning down with each breath of wind. Three-quarters of a mile up the run, where Clark Run Trail intersects with a level, gradually ascending woods road, I turned right for ten or so paces and then made a left onto the orange-blazed Rager Mountain Trail. This three-mile extension climbs to the natural area's eastern boundary, a powerline right-of-way with a view into the Conemaugh Gorge. The trail extends beyond the natural area boundary into state forest land, then loops back to reconnect with Clark Run Trail near the natural area's west end. The highest point on Rager Mountain Trail is twenty-four hundred feet above sea

On its way to the Conemaugh River, Clark Run cuts through the Charles F. Lewis Natural Area.

Autumn is a beautiful time of year to visit.

level, and the trailhead for Clark Run Trail starts off at around thirteen hundred feet.

On Rager Mountain Trail, I spotted the crown of a striped maple thrashing back and forth; lowering my gaze, I spied a four-point buck punishing the tree with his antlers. I watched until the wind shifted and carried my scent to the buck. He stared at me for a minute, then dropped his head and slunk off through the woods.

Rager Mountain Trail passes rock ledges reputed to be rattlesnake and copperhead dens. "Get into your rattlesnake mode," I was told by a forester in the district. Despite my awareness, I didn't see any of the retiring reptiles, which may already have gone into their winter dens.

I had almost finished the trail when I rested for a while on another powerline right-of-way, this one on the natural area's western edge. I looked down on green-tinted Conemaugh River, where it cut through Laurel Ridge, swirling around low, brushy islands. Overhead, pale motes circled slowly against the blue: hawks, climbing in rising columns of air, gliding their way steadily southward.

TO GET THERE. The natural area is adjacent to and east of PA Route 403 in the Conemaugh River Gorge. From Johnstown, drive 5.9 miles north on Route 403 from where it branches off PA Route 56. If coming from U.S. Route 22, proceed 3.5 miles south on Route 403. Look for a gravel parking area and a prominent wooden sign at the mouth of Clark Run.

A box at the parking lot may contain brochures describing the natural area, its flora and fauna, and its trails; request the publication in advance by contacting the Gallitzin State Forest district office. Also see *50 Hikes in Western Pennsylvania*, by Tom Thwaites, which gives a detailed description of the five-mile Rager Mountain Trail–Clark Run Trail loop.

24 BEAR RUN

15 ACRES, BALD EAGLE STATE FOREST, CENTRE COUNTY

This small fragment of old-growth forest stands along Bear Run in eastern Centre County near the Union County line. The magnificent hemlocks and tuliptrees are surrounded by second-growth oak and maple woodland typical of the mountains of central Pennsylvania.

Les Johnson, assistant forest manager in the district, recalls one huge hemlock falling during a winter storm in 1972. At thirty-five feet above the butt, the tree was more than thirty-two inches in diameter; he estimates its age at more than four hundred years. Johnson suggests that the grove of mature trees was left by timber cutters as a shady rest area, for themselves and for draft animals used during logging operations, or perhaps in a spot where steam locomotives stopped to take on water: several logging grades converge in the area, and the mill itself was a quarter mile upstream on Bear Run.

Bear Run includes only a handful of virgin trees, hemmed in on three sides by gravel roads. However, it's a nice place to linger for a time in the shade, as loggers may have done a century in the past. Nearby Snyder-Middleswarth Natural Area (page 109) is larger, quieter, and gives a better impression of what Pennsylvania's forests must have been like before European settlement.

TO GET THERE. From the village of Woodward on PA Route 45, turn south on Woodward Gap Road. The road climbs Thick Mountain and then descends to Bear Run; you arrive at the natural area after 2.5 miles. The tall trees stand immediately to the southeast of where Bear Run Road intersects Woodward Gap Road.

25   HALFWAY RUN

407 ACRES, BALD EAGLE STATE FOREST, UNION COUNTY

I tried to picture it when it was tundra: the ground bare or lightly cloaked with mosses, lichens, and low shrubs. Glaciers had not covered the valley; the farthest the ice had come was fifteen miles north. But it would have been cold, so cold that trees wouldn't grow. Almost thirteen thousand years in the past: What animals had lived along Halfway Run then? Snowy owls, lemmings, musk oxen? Maybe mammoths roamed the area, or stag moose, or long-haired bison, harried by giant short-faced bears—these last creatures were long-limbed and fleet, with foreshortened faces and broad muzzles, more like cats than the bears we know today, and believed to be the most powerful predators of the Pleistocene Epoch in North America.

Exactly where those animals ranged is not well known. Many Pleistocene species, particularly the large mammals, have gone extinct. Others, such as snowy owls, lemmings, and musk oxen, withdrew to the north as the ice age ended, as glaciers retreated and the tundra followed the shrinking ice fields toward the pole. Here in the Northeast, the environment changed radically as the climate warmed, with forests of broadleaf trees overspreading the land. Yet there are marks on the landscape recalling for us that strange and not-so-distant past. Some of the marks, known as pingo scars, can be seen at Halfway Run Natural Area.

We visited Halfway Run on a day in March, before vegetation had crowded up to obscure the scars, which are visible remnants of icy outcroppings that marked the land during the Pleistocene. I went with my twelve-year-old son, Will, a friend of his named Tommy, and Tommy's father Rick, a professional geologist who wanted to see some pingos. At first we walked through a mature woods next to Halfway Run, a clear brook about ten feet wide. A breeze whispered in the tops of tall white pines and large hemlocks whose thick evergreen crowns blocked out the spring sun. Away from the run, the conifers were replaced by yellow birch, American beech, sugar maple, and white and red oaks. Mountain laurel grew in clusters beneath the trees.

We came to a water-filled basin about twenty feet wide and fifty feet long. The basin lay about a hundred feet uphill from the stream; it was

Halfway Run features water-filled pingo scars, remnants of ice-cored hills formed during the last ice age.

shaped like a teardrop and oriented perpendicular to Halfway Run. A pingo scar? We scratched our heads. Kind of small and nondescript. Wood frog egg masses bobbed in the water like soggy balls of cotton. A band of juncos flew through the woods, their white outer tailfeathers flashing.

We arrived at another pond that appeared much like the first. It was starting to look like we were on to something. Soon we were skirting one watery depression after another. Some of the scars were large—seventy-five feet wide and two hundred feet long, boggy and partly filled in with sphagnum moss and clumps of sedge. All were roughly parallel, like beads on a string. Sometimes they appeared distinctly separate; in other places, one scar connected with the next. We crossed Halfway Run and found a similar series of formations on the other side.

Before our outing, I had read in the journal *Geography* (October 1987) an article, "Pleistocene Pingo Scars in Pennsylvania," by Ben Marsh. Marsh is a professor at nearby Bucknell University. He wrote of finding fifty-five "well-preserved pingo scars" along the upper mile and a half of Halfway Run. He defined pingos as "ice-cored hills that grow at the sites of springs and seeps in regions of discontinuous permafrost." His article explained how rising groundwater built up pressure beneath the permafrost layer; the overlying soil was pushed upward by the water flowing out of the ground and then freezing. Pingos require average soil temperatures a few degrees below freezing, "cold enough to freeze water below the surface in some places," wrote Marsh, "but warm enough to permit recharge of the aquifer through gaps in the permafrost."

Pingos can swell from ten to almost two hundred feet high. I found a picture of one in the encyclopedia: a dome-shaped, barren hill, like a big pimple, on the Mackenzie River delta in Canada's Northwest Territories. *Pingo* comes from an Inuit word, *pinguq*. Pingos don't grow forever: at some point the covering soil is stretched too thin, and it splits, exposing the ice. Gradually, the ice core melts. "Long-term warming and an end to permafrost conditions would also cause pingos to melt," Marsh wrote. What's left is a low earthen rampart surrounding a depression that is "the cast of the ice body." Many pingo scars are elongated downslope; they're usually wet and may hold a bog fed by the spring that created the pingo in the first place. Until Marsh identified the formations along Halfway Run, the only pingo scars known in the United States were on a plain in Illinois.

At Halfway Run, muck in the larger pingos lies fifteen feet deep. When Marsh dug up sediment samples, he found well-preserved plant parts, including pieces of wood. Subjected to radiocarbon dating, the wood proved to be 12,800 years old.

As we stood looking at a pingo, I described how it had formed to my geologist friend. Rick listened to my layman's explanation, then supplied the witticism "Ergo, the pingo." The boys were happy to echo the phrase until we told them to pipe down. Then they threw sticks into the water and played around on the depression's edge, looking as if they might fall in. (Tommy eventually did.)

Some of the Halfway Run pingo scars were dry enough to support hemlock seedlings and larch trees. Sphagnum and low blueberry covered the ground. It was complicated terrain: boggy patches interwoven with tree-grown hummocks, tangles of mountain laurel, and big humps left by the roots of windthrown trees. At the headwaters of Halfway Run, the scars seemed to blend together; the effect was not unlike that of a Florida cypress swamp, with crazily leaning trees, moss, and pools of dark, slow-moving water.

It was the breeding season for wood frogs, and in the distance a male sounded his quacking call. A barred owl barked out its crackpot *Who cooks for you, who cooks for youall?*—barred owls not being at all shy about vocalizing during midday. We passed an old pine stump, lichen-flecked, fire-blackened, slowly breaking down into rust-colored humus. Logged nearly a century ago, the stump was a remnant of Pennsylvania's original forest—although, in the context of pingos, tundra, and permafrost, the meaning of "original" had suddenly become blurred.

TO GET THERE. Halfway Run is near R. B. Winter State Park. From PA Route 192 just east of the park, go north 0.7 mile to Sand Mountain Road. Turn right, continue for 0.5 mile, and park at a turnout on a powerline right-of-way. The pingo scars lie to the left (east) of the right-of-way on both sides of Halfway Run. Wear rubber boots to fully explore this wet, spring-fed terrain. When you have finished your tour, walk north back to Sand Mountain Road, turn left, and hike back to your vehicle.

Take along a compass and, at a minimum, the Bald Eagle State Forest public-use map. The Hartleton, Pennsylvania, topographic quadrangle covers the natural area.

---

26   THE HOOK

5,119 ACRES, BALD EAGLE STATE FOREST, UNION COUNTY

A big black bird swept across the strip of sky above Buffalo Creek. The bird was a raven, and there is no other avian species that so perfectly symbolizes the Hook Natural Area, a five-thousand-acre wooded wilderness in the mountains of central Pennsylvania.

The raven had a long, wedge-shaped tail and a four-foot wingspan. Sunlight flashed off its ebony feathers and off the bird's great, sharp-tipped beak, useful for tearing flesh from the carcasses of winter-killed deer or stealing eggs or young out of other birds' nests. Eighty years ago, when Pennsylvania's forests lay in ruins, the brushy, logged-over mountains charred repeatedly by fires, many people were lamenting the loss of the wilderness-loving raven, which they assumed would go extinct. But ravens are adaptable birds. Although their population dwindled, the shy, secretive, intelligent omnivores held on. Today ravens are becoming common again in Pennsylvania, especially in remote areas such as the Hook.

The ravens—and there were at least two of them—croaked and cackled and made whimsical sounds like hammers pinging against pipes as they soared and banked and tumbled, playing in the sky. I felt sure they had seen my hiking partner and me, and that we human intruders constituted a mildly interesting diversion in the ravens' home range. It was also possible that the birds were part of a family group that had recently disbanded, vacating their home territory to go wandering about—sticking, of course, to the wild and rugged terrain that ravens prefer.

It was a cool, comfortable day for the middle of August. Since it was late in the summer, my friend Dean and I had not heard or seen many birds: broods had fledged, and some species had already begun to head south on their fall migration. Had we visited the Hook in spring, we might have found breeding pairs of hooded, black-and-white, black-throated green, black-throated blue, and pine warblers; Louisiana waterthrushes; Acadian flycatchers; winter wrens; and other deep-woods species. The Hook is listed as an Important Bird Area by the Pennsylvania Audubon Society, and birders have reported more than 175 species (both breeding birds and migrants) from the natural area.

We had climbed down into the Hook on the steep Molasses Gap Trail, following a crease in the side of Little Mountain. As it descended, the trail crossed and recrossed a small stream. Along the freshet grew hobblebush, with large, red berries and deep green leaves, and dense stands of rhododendron. Boulders covered the slope to the west of the trail, where black birches thrust up from among the pale rocks, and green ferns filled the intervals between the slabs.

Molasses Gap Trail intersected with a blue-blazed footpath next to the North Branch of Buffalo Creek. We turned left onto the trail and soon crossed the creek on a large, wooden bridge. In 1995, the Bureau of Forestry arranged with the Pennsylvania Air National Guard for a military heavy-lift helicopter to airlift the bridge to the site, where it was lowered onto the original stone abutments of a railroad trestle that had once crossed the creek.

"The Hook" probably comes from the logging era, when timber cutters had to hook their rail line around the prows of Jones Mountain and Buck Ridge, which come nose-to-nose in this high mountain valley. Today the hiking trail is located on the old railroad bed.

Northern hardwoods cloaked the stream bottom: black and yellow birches, red and sugar maples, white ash. Hemlocks lined the stream. Several tall white pines seemed to predate the loggers, who probably passed on the trees because they were split or had other flaws, making them less valuable as lumber. After about half a mile, Dean and I came to an area where

With more than five thousand acres, the Hook Natural Area is larger than several wild areas in the state forest system.

the forest changed dramatically from northern hardwoods to mixed oaks: the birches and maples occupied the damp ground along the stream, while from the drier south-facing slope just across the brook rose the pale trunks of white oaks.

We were alone in the valley, but the place was not silent. As Dean and I ate our lunches, we listened to the ravens conversing far overhead. We lifted our heads at a loud, tearing sound, then three or four shorter ripping sounds, then a loud thud: a limb falling through leafy branches to the ground not far from where we sat.

We decided to hike up Mule Shanty Trail, which climbed gradually toward the northwest along narrow Panther Run. Dense rhododendrons stood on the shady side of the stream. On the opposite slope were boulders and rock formations with overhangs, crevices, and shallow caves. The Hook is known for a healthy timber rattlesnake population, and the rocks looked like prime denning sites.

Mule Shanty Trail led to a small clearing. After snooping around for a while, we located the remains of the shanty where the loggers had stabled mules used during timber-hauling operations. I found one rusty link of a heavy chain lying on the ground amid the rotten boards.

Hobblebush, a woodland shrub, grows along the Molasses Gap Trail, one of several routes leading into the Hook.

The Hook is an excellent place for solitude and scenery. Because the North Branch of Buffalo Creek is in the municipal watershed for the town of Mifflinburg, camping is prohibited in the natural area.

I recommended the Hook to another friend not long ago, and when she and her family hiked down Molasses Gap Trail late one afternoon, a flying squirrel skimmed suddenly past her head. It landed on a tree next to her shoulder, flattened itself momentarily against the bark, scurried up the trunk, and launched itself into the air again. With all four legs spread wide, forming the sail that held it aloft, the small squirrel went gliding down the hill.

TO GET THERE. From PA Route 45, 0.7 mile east of Hairy John Picnic Area, turn left on Sheesly Run Road. Go 2.1 miles to an intersection with Stoney Run Road. Continue straight ahead through the intersection on Buffalo Flat Road. After 2.3 miles, turn right at the **T** near an old stone hunting camp and drive another 2 miles east on Old Shingle Road. Park at the sign for Molasses Gap Trail.

Molasses Gap Trail descends northward into the natural area. When you reach the bottom of the valley, set a stick against a tree, or heap up several stones, so that on your return you will notice the rather obscure turnoff for Molasses Gap Trail. Bear left, following the well-used footpath along the North Branch of Buffalo Creek. The trail soon crosses the helicoptered-in bridge. You are now in the heart of the natural area.

The simplest, safest route is to continue on to a sign for Mule Shanty Trail and then turn around and retrace your steps. As an alternative, turn left on Mule Shanty Trail and hike up the hollow to Jones Mountain Road. Turn right on the graded forest road and walk approximately 1 mile to a sign for Molasses Gap Trail. Turn right on Molasses Gap Trail and hike back through the Hook, find your turnoff, and climb up to Old Shingle Road, where you parked your car. Carry a compass and a copy of the Hartleton, Pennsylvania, topographic quadrangle.

50 Hikes in Central Pennsylvania, by Tom Thwaites, presents a longer eight-mile walk through the Hook.

Forest roads in the area are not maintained during winter.

---

27   JOYCE KILMER

77 ACRES, BALD EAGLE STATE FOREST, UNION COUNTY

"I think that I shall never see / A poem lovely as a tree . . ." Most Americans know those lines, which open Joyce Kilmer's poem "Trees," long popular for its sentiment and its simple philosophy.

Joyce Kilmer Natural Area is one of thirteen original forest monuments designated by the Pennsylvania State Forest Commission in 1921. The site honors the New Jersey native, who died at the age of thirty-one while fighting in France during World War I. Another poet killed in the war, Alan Seeger, had a forest monument—later reclassified as a natural area—named after him as well (see page 63). Kilmer also is eulogized with the Joyce Kilmer Memorial Forest, thirty-eight hundred acres of old-growth timber in the Nantahala National Forest in North Carolina.

From the small parking area, my son Will and I hiked across the flat summit of Paddy Mountain. The trail led through mountain laurel, low-bush blueberry, and chestnut oak. Gypsy moth caterpillars had attacked the trees' leaves on the mountaintop, denuding most of the oaks. We spotted a scarlet tanager in a black gum that the caterpillars hadn't ravaged and heard a wood thrush give its solemn, shapely song. We saw a cuckoo. I wasn't fast enough with the binoculars to identify the cuckoo as to species: both yellow-billed and black-billed cuckoos home in on gypsy moth infestations to gorge on the superabundant pests and feed the caterpillars to their young.

We felt our way down the steep trail. Civilian Conservation Corps workers built the path in the 1930s (a CCC camp once stood in the gap between Bear Mountain and Stitzer Mountain, near the lower, northern end of the trail), and recently someone had marked the way with blue paint dots sprayed on the trunks of trees.

We found ourselves in a dim, cool world where shade was restored. The hemlocks—part of the original forest that had covered the mountains before logging commenced—were shorter, smaller, and more densely limbed than old-growth hemlocks growing in fertile, better-watered places. They were stocky, upright trees, some of them dead, one a limbless snag so riddled and excavated and hammered at by woodpeckers that it resembled a bizarre, impressionistic totem pole.

Beneath the conifers spread a roomy, open understory. Fallen needles and hemlock cones, dry hardwood leaves, small branches and twigs, and chips of bark made a scanty covering over the rubble of sandstone. Thick tree roots sprawled across the ground, then plunged between the slabs: pale roots of yellow birch, rusty brown roots of hemlock. Red maple, black birch, chestnut oak, and red oak also persevered on the hardscrabble site.

The density of the stand did not allow for sweeping views. The trees seemed more like creatures than plants in their solid, dignified presence. They were silent and real and powerful in the angled light of a June evening.

TO GET THERE. In Woodward, in eastern Centre County, turn south off of PA Route 45 onto Woodward Gap Road. Drive 3.4 miles, and turn left on Paddy Mountain Road. Paddy Mountain Road is rocky and rutted; I crept along it, dodging the exposed rocks and wishing I'd brought the pickup instead of the station wagon. After 2.9 miles, park on the left at a wooden sign for the natural area. The trail crosses the top of the mountain and descends into the virgin hemlock stand. Hiking to the downslope limit of the stand and returning takes less than an hour. The natural area can also be reached by walking upslope from Bear Run Road, just southwest of where it intersects Route 45. The Bald Eagle State Forest public-use map shows the natural area and the access trail.

28   MT. LOGAN

512 ACRES, BALD EAGLE STATE FOREST, CLINTON COUNTY

The hemlocks' branches reached all the way to the ground. Gradually the space between individual trees increased, and on the trees' trunks the lower branches were dead or missing. As my son Will and I worked our way into the stand, the evergreen canopy merged overhead. The shade deepened. The air felt fifteen degrees cooler than it had just a hundred yards away on the sun-baked rocks capping Mt. Logan.

A hermit thrush sang sweetly in the gloom, and a blue jay gave its *wheedelee* call. Most of the hemlocks' trunks looked no more than eighteen to twenty inches in diameter. The largest one we could find had a seventy-five-inch circumference, which meant that its diameter was not quite two feet. The trees were about forty feet tall, the same height as the second-growth oaks that surrounded the fifty-acre conifer stand. The hemlocks were old-growth trees, although they appeared vastly different from the tall, graceful, columnar specimens that characterize virgin hemlocks growing on more favorable sites. Before visiting Mt. Logan, I had spoken with Les Johnson, assistant forest manager for the Bald Eagle State Forest; Johnson thought he remembered hearing that corings done in the 1950s on the Mt. Logan hemlocks had revealed ages of over two hundred years. "They're pretty small for being that old," he said, then added with a laugh: "Those trees had to bring their own dirt with them."

The eastern hemlock was not a particularly valuable lumber species at the turn of the twentieth century, when the forests on Bald Eagle Ridge, of which Mt. Logan is a part, fell to the notching ax and crosscut saw. Often the loggers would cut a hemlock, spud its bark off for use in tanning leather, and leave the bole to rot. It's likely the trees on Mt. Logan were spared because they grew near the top of a steep, stony slope, and because they were small. The expense of getting them to the mill or the tannery was judged to be too high.

The Mt. Logan hemlocks reminded me of how Chris Bolgiano, in her book *The Appalachian Forest,* characterized a patch of stunted old-growth white oaks on a rocky North Carolina mountain: "They were living sculptures, the most perfect biological expression of which that ridge was capable."

On Mt. Logan the hemlocks grew out of piles of rocks. Their roots pushed the stones apart. The soil was sparse and thin, composed mainly of rotting hemlock needles and cone scales. The lacy, green fronds of spinulose woodferns arced out from isolated clumps. Here and there, where light penetrated to the ground, a shrubby striped maple or witch hazel grew. Very few hemlock seedlings were present beneath the old trees. Scattered piles of dark, oblong droppings suggested that white-tailed deer were browsing off the new growth that normally would sit in wait beneath the tall trees, ready to push upward when a gap opened in the canopy.

Will and I climbed back to the summit of Mt. Logan. The mountain's top is a sharp hogback of Tuscarora quartzite. This sandstone variant was at one time sunk deep in the earth, where high temperatures and pressures metamorphosed the rock, melting its quartz component, which then solidified again. Hard and weather-resistant, the quartzite caps many of the mountains in Pennsylvania's Ridge and Valley Region. The rock is a pale tan, almost white, and on top of Mt. Logan it stands in low cliffs ten to twenty feet in height. Below the cliffs lie boulder fields, also known as talus slopes: jumbled, tilted, clack-together slabs ranging in size from dictionaries to pool tables. Geologists identify the talus slopes on central Pennsylvania ridges as periglacial features that developed during the last ice age, around fifteen thousand years ago. In the tundra landscape of that era, the slabs broke off from the ridgetops and slowly crept downslope, their movement abetted by repeated freezing and thawing.

Atop Mt. Logan, white pines have taken root, some of them twisted and deformed. Will and I ate lunch in the pine-scented shade and watched as small, metallic purple wasps landed on the rocks, then went running

The summit of Mt. Logan is a sharp ridge of Tuscarora quartzite.

swiftly about, their antennae and wings flicking as they hunted for insects or spiders. Such a wasp immobilizes its prey with a sting and then carries it off to a nest chamber; it stashes the prey in the nest, lays an egg on it, and seals the chamber. As it develops, the wasp larva consumes its paralyzed cell-mate alive.

Black-capped chickadees scolded us from the branches just above our heads. A pair of cedar waxwings sallied forth from a snag to catch flying insects. Red-eyed vireos called repeatedly from the treetops below us. Turkey vultures sailed past, riding on currents of heated air rising from the rocks. The rocks were decorated with colorful lichens: pale gray-green blotches, deeper green rosettes, orangey sunbursts, olive-colored blisters.

The north end of the exposed summit offers a limited view to the southwest down Nittany Valley. Thick woods to the north and west block what would otherwise be a breathtaking vista: Mt. Logan, elevation 2,108 feet, rises 1,500 feet above the West Branch of the Susquehanna River just east of Lock Haven.

A man named Henry Shoemaker apparently gave Mt. Logan its name. A newspaperman during the early twentieth century, Shoemaker had a

Jumbled slabs of Tuscarora quartzite at the top of Mt. Logan provide a habitat for invertebrates, small mammals, and reptiles.

large log summerhouse at the village of McElhattan, below the peak. Logan was an Indian, the son of the Oneida chief Shikellemy, who was a representative of the Iroquois confederation and an ally of the first white settlers in the region. According to Shoemaker, in a speech he delivered in 1923, Logan often camped "in the gap at the foot of the mighty mountain which bears his name. It was there that he fell in love with a white girl, Jura McAvoy, who followed him to the wilderness, and tradition states that her white lover tracked the eloping pair, and, surprising Logan while drinking at the Zeller Spring, in Sugar Valley, Clinton County, shot him in the hip, making the proud chieftain a cripple for the rest of his life." It's not known whether this tale has a basis in fact; Shoemaker was a noted raconteur who never let the truth stand in the way of a good story.

Will and I left the ridge and retraced our steps on Winchester Trail, which wound among the boulders on the south-facing slope of Mt. Logan. We kept our eyes peeled for timber rattlesnakes; the reptiles often den in crevices and beneath rocks on talus slopes such as this one. Tom Thwaites, author of *50 Hikes in Central Pennsylvania,* told me he hiked up Mt. Logan and heard rattlesnakes buzzing under the rocks. "I didn't include that hike in my book," he said, "at first because I was afraid of the rattlesnakes' effects on people, and then later because I worried about people's effects on the endangered snakes."

Today Mt. Logan is classified as an amphibian and reptile protection area, where it is illegal to disturb, collect, or kill any snakes.

TO GET THERE. I recommend using the Bald Eagle State Forest public-use map and the *Pennsylvania Atlas and Gazetteer* to arrive at this hard-to-access natural area. To explore Mt. Logan and the surrounding forest, use a compass along with the Loganton, Mill Hall, and Jersey Shore topographic quadrangles. (The natural area lies where the three maps come together.)

Attempt the following approach only in a vehicle with ample road clearance, such as a sport utility or a pickup truck, and do not chance it during bad weather or in winter.

From the Mill Hall exit on I-80, take U.S. Route 220 north. Go about 0.75 mile to the first major intersection, and there turn right on Auction Road, SR 2008. Go 3.7 miles (through an intersection with Long Run Road, after which Auction Road changes its name to Beagle Road) to a **T**; turn left and go 0.2 mile, then turn right. You are now on East End Mountain Road. Go past a shale pit on the left and continue up the road, which steepens and reverts to a gravel surface. After 2 miles, you come to the intersection of East Mountain Road, Dug Road (a gated Bureau of Forestry roadway), and Nittany Ridge Road. Turn left on Nittany Ridge Road, which is rocky and may be badly rutted, depending on the season. Continue 2.4 miles on Nittany Ridge Road to its intersection with Kammerdiner Road.

Park and hike east (right) on Kammerdiner Road, going about a quarter mile to a sign announcing Mt. Logan Natural Area and the Winchester Trail, part of the natural area's western boundary. Follow the blue-blazed Winchester Trail uphill to the summit. Hike east along the exposed ridge for about two hundred yards, then go due north (downhill on the north-facing slope) about 100 yards to the old-growth hemlocks.

29   ROSECRANS BOG

152 ACRES, BALD EAGLE STATE FOREST, CLINTON COUNTY

In late August, purple-blue fruit still spangled the highbush blueberries. The shrubs' leaves were green, except for the zones surrounding their veins, where a red fire had been kindled. The first of the fall colors had come to the red maples as well, which here and there held up a scarlet branch. A bumblebee worked industriously, collecting nectar from the small, pink flowers of the marsh Saint-John's-wort that grew thickly among the sedges and grasses on the edge of the wetland.

When I stepped out of the woods, a big, brown raptor dropped from a dead tree, caught the air under its wings, and flapped straight away; I raised my binoculars quickly but could not identify the bird by species, although I figured it was probably a red-tailed hawk on account of its large size. Cedar waxwings fluttered above the pond, fifty or more of them trying to

Deer, ducks, hawks, and herons are a few of the creatures inhabiting small but productive Rosecrans Bog.

catch insects, their thin, high, sibilant notes reaching my ear. Weaving among the cedar waxwings, flying with strong, direct wingstrokes and with many graceful twists and turns, tree swallows caught their own insect prey.

Dead trees stood in the water on the edge of the pond. The dead trees, and a low partial dam at the pond's downstream end, showed that a beaver colony had once lived there. The dam had backed up the water and killed the trees by flooding and suffocating their roots. Judging from the dam's disrepair, the beavers had long since moved on.

Scanning the standing dead timber with my binoculars, I spotted several masses of sticks wedged into forks between branches: the nests of great blue herons. A moment later, as if in confirmation, a heron lifted from the far edge of the marsh and flew slowly away. Great blue herons nest in wetlands such as Rosecrans Bog, and also in remote woods that can be quite far—ten to fifteen miles—from the water where they find their fish and frog prey.

Rosecrans Bog was once a small nonglacial bog with an open mat of sphagnum moss. In the 1960s, beavers dammed the drainage basin, flooding the bog mat and the surrounding timber. Today the sphagnum mat has been replaced by aquatic vegetation, mainly spatterdock cowlilies, leafy, green plants with big, rounded, bright yellow flowers.

Wild cranberry, mountain holly, northeastern bulrush, pod-grass, and water sedge are some of the other plants reported from Rosecrans Bog in the past. Cavity-nesting birds that breed in the area include the eastern bluebird, common flicker, wood duck, barred owl, black-capped chickadee, great crested flycatcher, and downy, hairy, and pileated woodpeckers.

I heard numerous rustlings among the spatterdock and the *kohee, kohee* call of a wood duck hen followed by a splash as she set down on the water. It was late in the day, and I couldn't stay longer at what I judged to be a beautiful place fairly throbbing with life. The sun was on its way down when I reluctantly left Rosecrans Bog.

TO GET THERE. From the Loganton exit on I-80, take PA Route 477 north toward Salona. After 0.4 mile, turn right on Pine-Loganton Road. After another 0.8 mile, watch closely for Cranberry Road to the right, posted with a wooden Bureau of Forestry sign stating, "DEAD END ROAD, ROAD NOT MAINTAINED, TRAVEL AT OWN RISK." A four-wheel-drive vehicle with good clearance can possibly negotiate the muddy, deeply pitted track, but a more sensible plan is to park and walk. Park on the berm of Pine-Loganton Road, or a few hundred yards farther on the left, near the entrance to the public water supply area for the city of Lock Haven.

On Cranberry Road, walk 1 mile to an access path leading to the left, which follows the border between private land and the natural area; when you reach Jamison Run, turn right (northeast) and hike to the open bog. Or stay on Cranberry Road until you see the bog through the trees to your left. The wetland appears on the Loganton, Pennsylvania, topographic quadrangle under the name "Cranberry Bog." There are no trails, marked or otherwise, in the natural area, although foresters at the district office are planning a path to provide access across state lands from Pine-Loganton Road.

---

30   SNYDER-MIDDLESWARTH

500 ACRES, BALD EAGLE STATE FOREST, SNYDER COUNTY

At first I thought it was a weasel. The slender predator bounded along on the bank of Swift Run less than thirty feet away. Our attention immediately leapt from the towering, thick-trunked hemlocks that filled the mountain valley to the lithe, dark creature as it snaked its long body between downed logs, and over and around mossy rocks.

It was a mink, a member of the family Mustelidae, related to the river otter, the fisher, and the smaller weasels. Its body was a uniform chocolate brown. Its coat glistened in the diffused light that reached ground level in the old-growth forest. The mink had short legs, a short muzzle, and a pointed nose. It was about ten inches long from nose to tail—which meant it was probably a young animal, born in the spring and possibly on its own for the first time in its life. A life that might be brief, should a hawk or fox be watching, because the mink seemed oblivious to any danger as it ran unconcernedly and, I now saw, somewhat clumsily along the stream's edge.

My twelve-year-old son, Will, had already scrambled his own binoculars out of his daypack. He and I followed quietly along on the footpath, keeping up with the mink. I placed the back of my hand against my lips and made a squeaky kissing sound—in the past, I have called up weasels by imitating the distress cry of a small animal such as a vole or a mouse.

The mink stopped and stood on its hind legs. It hurried toward us, through the ferns and moss and low plants and tree seedlings and woody detritus that make an old-growth forest such a teeming, diverse place. The youngster popped its head up ten feet away and stared at us with bright black eyes. We must have looked at one another for fifteen seconds. Then the mink turned, jumped over a fallen branch, dived into the creek, and swam to the far side—where it was joined by a second mink.

I had formed the opinion that the young mink was dispersing, leaving its natal territory. The second mink was larger, a paler shade of brown, obviously the youngster's mother. She ran straight to the pup. We heard faint, high-pitched chipping sounds. The mother licked the young mink on its head and neck. The youngster broke away and resumed loping down the valley. The mother also paid little attention to us; she set off hunting, pausing to stick her nose into nooks and crannies, checking between rocks. She darted beneath a green mat of sphagnum moss, struck with her muzzle once, twice, and emerged with a dark brown creature struggling in her jaws. Even with the binoculars, I couldn't tell if she'd caught a rodent, a shrew, a salamander, or a frog. With the prey in her mouth, she swam back across the stream, climbed the bank, and sprinted off, following her pup.

Obeying a natural imperative to leave its home, the youngster was declaring its independence, setting out to find a territory of its own. The mother mink was equally driven to continue nurturing and helping her own flesh and blood. As I lowered my binoculars, I heard Will whisper "Awesome"—just about the first time my son, the indoor dweller, the computer devotee, dragged from one natural experience to the next from the time he was an infant, had openly acknowledged the wonder of what he saw.

Snyder-Middleswarth Natural Area contains some of the finest old-growth forest in Pennsylvania.

Snyder-Middleswarth Natural Area includes more than 250 acres of pristine old-growth forest, one of the largest such stands in the Pennsylvania state forest system. I was amazed by the tremendous amount of downed material, mainly tree branches and trunks, slowly decomposing and offering shelter and feeding niches to a host of creatures ranging from millipedes to minks to black bears.

The natural area is named for two figures in Snyder County history: Simon Snyder, born in 1759 and the third governor of Pennsylvania; and Ner Middleswarth, an officer in the War of 1812 and a distinguished statesman.

Will and I visited in late June. The trail climbed past yellow birches and hemlocks. The yellow birches, with their peeling bark, looked like whiskered giants. The hemlocks were taller: several at Snyder-Middleswarth have been measured at over 140 feet. One hemlock had fallen across the trail; about 25 feet above its base, someone had chainsawed an opening for walkers. I started counting the annual growth rings. Ones near the center were wide, indicating that the tree had expanded its girth quickly, perhaps catching the sun in a clearing created when a giant predecessor had itself come crashing down. As I neared the edge, the rings became tightly compressed—228, 229, 230—showing the slow growth of a mature specimen. Two hundred and thirty rings. It may have taken the tree 20 years to become 25 feet tall, making it 250 years old. The hemlock had been a seedling before Simon Snyder was born, at about the time of the last and decisive of the bloody French and Indian Wars, around 1750, when this part of central Pennsylvania stood on the colonial frontier.

Will picked a *Boletus* mushroom—one of several species in this genus whose yellowish tan flesh bruises purple, a chemical change that occurs as soon as the soft tissues are injured. On another fallen hemlock grew tiny, dark brown fungi; through a hand lens, they looked like undersea coral, and when touched by a finger, the fronds released clouds of spores. From the trunk of a standing hemlock protruded a large, cream-colored blob of a fungus, like risen dough dotted with beads of honey. Almost everywhere we saw the broad, woody, glossy-surfaced half circles of *Ganoderma tsugae,* found frequently on hemlocks.

Big trees are, of course, the defining element in an old-growth forest. But such a woods is more than a collection of sylvan giants. It is an entire ecosystem, a habitat with many zones, from ground level upward. Fallen trees, their trunks up to five feet thick, break down over the decades through the agency of fungi and microorganisms. Over centuries, debris builds up deeply on the forest floor; the duff holds more moisture than soils in newer forests and retains moisture longer during drought. Shade-tolerant seedlings of black birch, yellow birch, and hemlock are more apt to root on a rotting "nurse tree" than in the surrounding soil. Trees of small and medium height stand waiting for their share of the light, which will come streaming in after a nearby dominant tree falls. The mix of tall, older trees and shorter, younger specimens gives an old-growth forest a characteristic ragged-looking aspect.

Many other plants thrive, including hobblebush, striped maple, and witch hazel, shrubs that Will and I spotted along Swift Run. Ferns, mosses, and lichens grow abundantly in the humid setting. We sat on a moss-covered log and watched the comings and goings of spiders, moths, ants, wasps, and a tiny elongated insect that looked exactly like a hemlock needle: it took a huge, galvanic leap when Will went to touch it. Studies of food chains in old-growth forests have found five times the mass of invertebrates that exists in younger groves. Millipedes and centipedes abound. You need to be careful around some species: a friend took his son to Snyder-Middleswarth, and the boy, scrutinizing a millipede too closely, was temporarily and agonizingly blinded when the creature squirted a chemical defense compound in his eyes.

The invertebrates are preyed on by a variety of birds and small mammals. Woodpeckers, warblers, thrushes, sparrows, juncos, and flycatchers live in great numbers in old-growth stands. When Jerry Hassinger, a biologist for the Pennsylvania Game Commission, ran small-mammal traplines in Snyder-Middleswarth, he was astonished at the population densities of masked shrews *(Sorex cinereus)* and short-tailed shrews *(Blarina brevicauda)* that he found. Studies done in old-growth forests in the southern Appalachians revealed many more salamanders, and a much greater number of species, than in younger managed forests.

As Will and I hiked farther into Snyder-Middleswarth, the sky clouded over. Thunderclaps echoed up and down the valley. The wind lifted the boughs of the hemlocks and made the birch leaves rattle against each other. Drops of rain fell, bright beads plummeting from the sky. We stood beneath a giant hemlock, where the great boughs kept us dry. High in the crown of a nearby tree, a tiny warbler flitted among the raindrops, chasing insects.

TO GET THERE. From Troxelville on PA Route 235, turn west onto Timber Road at a sign for Snyder-Middleswarth and Tall Timbers Natural Areas. Timber Road becomes Swift Run Road at the state forest boundary. Keep following the signs for Tall Timbers. Pass Rock Springs Picnic Area. After 4.8 miles, you arrive at Snyder-Middleswarth Picnic Area. Park in the gravel lot and, at a stone monument announcing the area's status as a registered national natural landmark, follow the trail into the natural area.

The well-trodden footpath leads through old-growth forest along the north bank of Swift Run. Walk as far as a wooden bridge, then cross the run on the bridge and hike along the south side of Swift Run back to the picnic area; on this return route, the trail climbs above the run, giving you an elevated view of the old-growth forest. Or you can continue along Swift Run Trail past the bridge, turning back whenever you wish.

In *50 Hikes in Central Pennsylvania*, Tom Thwaites describes a trip that covers 3.4 miles and takes two hours. Hikers follow Swift Run Trail west through the natural area, ascend Tower Trail on the natural area's western boundary (look for a line of blue paint blazes leading down to the run and then up the opposite slope on a south heading) to the top of Thick Mountain, turn east on Thick Mountain Trail, and descend to Swift Run Road and back to the parking area. Carry a compass along with the Thwaites book or the Weikert, Pennsylvania, topographic quadrangle.

31   TALL TIMBERS

660 ACRES, BALD EAGLE STATE FOREST, SNYDER COUNTY

It reminded me of a passage in *Woodcraft,* a classic of camping and outdoor skills penned in 1920 by Nessmuk, otherwise known as George Washington Sears, of Wellsboro, Pennsylvania: "It ended as nearly all trails do; it branched off to right and left, grew dimmer and slimmer, degenerated to a deer path, petered out to a squirrel track, ran up a tree, and ended in a knot hole."

In fact, the trail into Tall Timbers Natural Area vanished in a mountain laurel thicket. As near as I could tell, I had reached the area where Swift Run went from being a legitimate watercourse to an intermittent stream, one of those broken blue lines on the topographic map. The stems of mountain laurel had been gouging my shins for the last hour. I'd worn shorts on this hot day, a stupid thing to do, since I fully understand that trails neatly marked on topographic maps may not exist on the ground. I slapped at a mosquito on the back of my neck. Nessmuk had this preparation, three parts pine tar, two parts castor oil, and one part pennyroyal oil, which he slathered onto his skin until it built up into a good glaze, deterring mosquitoes and black flies, pernicious North Woods pests.

I was on the lookout for timber rattlesnakes. The reptiles like to hang out in mountain laurel thickets, especially in high mountain valleys forested with acorn-bearing oak trees, where chipmunks abound. Chipmunks sounded their alarm whistles all around me as I threaded my way through the thicket. Buck Mountain rose to the north and Thick Mountain to the south, both covered with jumbled rocks, perfect for rattlesnakes to hibernate in. Although, of course, the rattlesnakes wouldn't be hibernating now. They would be lying in wait in the laurel thickets, their chins resting on logs, ready to detect vibrations made by chipmunks scampering along.

I wasn't scared of snakes, just respectful. Tall Timbers is among the twenty-eight out of sixty-one natural areas designated by the Bureau of Forestry and the Pennsylvania Fish and Boat Commission as special regulation areas for the complete protection of all amphibians and reptiles. Which meant it was more than likely that large numbers of rattlesnakes live here.

I had planned to hike the whole way up the valley to Red Ridge Road, but I wasn't seeing enough wildlife to warrant shredding my shins on the laurel. (I wouldn't have minded seeing a rattlesnake—at a safe distance, of course.) Continuing up the run, I encountered, rather bloodily, a strong greenbrier vine that my right foot pinned down and my left shin rammed into, sending me sprawling in the mountain laurel.

A good time to stop and eat a sandwich. I sat with my back against a pine and tallied up what I'd seen. Huge old-growth hemlocks along Swift Run: they had towered above me all the way through the adjacent Snyder-Middleswarth Natural Area, en route to Tall Timbers. The names are misleading, because the trees at Tall Timbers are not as tall as the trees at Snyder-Middleswarth.

Shafts of sunlight on glossy, upturned rhododendron leaves and on the shrubs' pink and white blooms. Peaceful groves where tiger swallowtails wafted past on their yellow-and-black wings. Where it entered Tall Timbers, the trail had been obvious enough, a string of light blue paint dabs on tree trunks. The hemlocks had given way to pines, gray and black birches, red maples, and chestnut oaks as I gained elevation and the valley flattened out. The trail had given way to laurel and nothing but laurel.

A blue jay voiced its raucous call. A great crested flycatcher sounded its *wheep wheep,* and a red-eyed vireo serenaded the world monotonously and invisibly from a perch in the forest canopy.

Birds began feeding past me: a mixed flock, perhaps brought together by chance in a good feeding area. In the winter, birds of several species will often join into a flock, a strategy that boosts their chances of finding food and detecting predators. However, I was surprised to see such a band in mid-July, when most birds remain spread out through the woods defending individual territories. An American redstart butterflied up on orange-and-black wings, hovered in midair, and suddenly dipped to catch a fly. A black-and-white warbler crept up a tree trunk, hunting for insects in bark crevices. A brown creeper and a hairy woodpecker searched for food among the bark ridges of nearby oaks. I spotted a black-throated blue warbler (he should have been down by the stream, in the hemlock shade) and a yellow-rumped warbler (like the black-throated blue, the yellow-rumped usually nests in conifers; the species nears the southern limit of its breeding range in the mountains of central Pennsylvania). Rounding out the mix were black-capped chickadees and a white-breasted nuthatch.

The birds brightened my day considerably, even if they didn't take the sting out of my shins. It is a nice feature of Ridge and Valley Pennsylvania that the landforms lie in a northeast-to-southwest direction, so that the hiker generally knows his position; and I understood that if I climbed to the ridge on my left, turned left, and walked east (finding, I hoped, Thick Mountain Trail, which the topo map promised was up there), sooner or later I'd be back at my car at Snyder-Middleswarth Picnic Area.

Two steps, and I had crossed Swift Run. A white tail flagging through the laurel directed me to a deer path. The deer path led to a logging skid, a century-old track that conveniently angled up to the ridge. Thick Mountain Trail was a highway compared to what I'd left behind.

TO GET THERE. Follow the directions to Snyder-Middleswarth Natural Area given at the end of the preceding chapter. Swift Run Trail leads west through Snyder-Middleswarth, providing access to Tall Timbers. A compass and the Weikert, Pennsylvania, topographic quadrangle or the Bald Eagle State Forest public-use map will help get you into and out of Tall Timbers Natural Area.

32   MARION BROOKS

917 ACRES, MOSHANNON STATE FOREST, ELK COUNTY

A foot of snow covered the ground when my friend Gary and I ventured into Marion Brooks Natural Area. We had cross-country skis and snowshoes in the truck and opted for the latter, since we'd be bushwhacking—forsaking marked trails and striking off through the February woods.

We parked where Losey Road intersects with the Quehanna Highway. Losey Road hadn't been plowed, but enough four-wheel-drive vehicles had traveled it that the walking was easy. We hiked north on Losey Road, headed for the Paige Run drainage. The natural area, formerly known as Paige Run Natural Area, was renamed in the 1970s to honor Marion Brooks, a conservation-minded resident of nearby Medix Run, Pennsylvania, who worked to improve the water quality in north-central Pennsylvania and helped establish strip mine reclamation laws.

Our boots crunched in the snow. White clouds with spumelike tops outlined long, narrow hallways of blue sky. The low, weak sun now and then peeked out from between the clouds. A gusty west wind made the treetops sway and blew clouds of snow across Losey Road. Where the road met Paige Run, we donned snowshoes, turned left, and followed the narrow stream toward the northwest.

We passed rust-colored stems of cinnamon ferns; the ferns would sprout luxuriantly and stand three feet tall by next summer. We circled patches of lowbush blueberry and islands of mountain laurel. We trudged among sassafras, red maple, and black gum. It was mostly open country, lightly wooded, with scattered white and pitch pines. In places, deer had pawed down through the snow to feed on grasses and the roots of the ferns.

A porcupine's track was a trough that wandered through the snow and led us to a grove of hemlocks. Ralph Seeley, a friend of mine who has built many hiking and skiing trails in the region, had pronounced Marion Brooks Natural Area "porcupine city." (The rodents eat his trail signs.) This porcupine, however, had chewed on the green tips of the hemlocks. In so doing, it had clipped off many twigs, which in turn had been fed on by deer; their heart-shaped tracks marked the snow beneath the conifers.

Breaking trail was hard work, and Gary and I switched the lead frequently. The valley was broad and flat, studded with huge old stumps weathered gray, some of them fire-blackened. The white pine stumps were more than a century old.

The pines spoke of a bygone era, when most of the region, known as the Quehanna Plateau, was covered with virgin white pine, hemlock, and various hardwoods. Loggers set up lumber camps crewed with men known as "wood hicks." The Quehanna lay too far from the West Branch of the Susquehanna for the white pine, the most valuable of the timber, to be lashed into rafts and floated downriver to market, something that was done in other parts of northern Pennsylvania. Instead, the loggers built "splash dams" out of earth and wood, spanning the small headwater streams. From September to March, the wood hicks felled the pines, bucked them into logs, and used horses to skid the logs to splash dams. There the logs were marked with their owner's insignia and stockpiled. As the snow melted in late winter, the gates of the dam were shut. Opening the gates caused thousands of logs, now floating in an artificial lake, to race out in a torrent of water. A series of splash dams propelled the logs to the West Branch, where they floated downstream; eventually they were captured and sorted at the booms—huge chains strung across the river—at Lock Haven and Williamsport.

From the 1860s to the late 1880s, timber barons took almost all of the white pine from lands that are now the Moshannon State Forest. Then they built logging railroads and proceeded to cut the rest of the trees. By around 1912, the Quehanna Plateau consisted of eroded hills, scoured stream basins, and vast expanses of brush, created when the root systems of cut-off trees sprouted up through the discarded tops and limbs of the logged forest. Fires periodically raged through the debris, blackening the sky for days on end and bringing the region to an even greater desolation.

You can still see the remains of the splash dams and the abandoned logging grades (Ralph Seeley has located many of his trails on the old grades) and the long-lasting pine stumps, which look like grave markers on the blueberry-and-sedge barrens.

Gary and I snowshoed up Paige Run. The barrens gave way to a meager forest of chestnut and white oaks, red maple, and sassafras. The Quehanna has poorly drained, acidic soil and a short growing season. We got ourselves semi-lost in a great thicket of mountain laurel, whose springy stems grabbed at our snowshoes and attempted, sometimes successfully, to pitch us headlong into the snow. "Mountain laurel and snowshoes don't mix too well," I muttered. Gary grinned and replied: "Mountain laurel doesn't mix too well with much of anything."

After working our way around the big tangle, we took a south compass heading to get back to the truck. A band of crows flapped overhead. We cut a line of coyote tracks and a half dozen deer trails. Large boulders stood among the trees, melted free of snow. Soon we came to one of the prime features of Marion Brooks Natural Area: a nearly pure stand of birch.

These were not the tall, straight paper birch of the Minnesota canoe country—graceful trees that can reach eighty feet, trees from which the Indians harvested the strong, light, flexible bark and used it to sheath their canoes. The trees at Marion

At Marion Brooks, a nearly pure stand of paper birch sprang up on soils depleted by repeated wildfires following logging.

Brooks were thirty to forty feet tall, growing in weedy clumps in the impoverished soil. Foresters believe that the repeated wildfires after the logging era scorched the soil in much of the Quehanna, burning away the organic matter. On a few sites, such as Marion Brooks, all that would grow back was the pioneering birch. Some of the trees are said to be paper birch, *Betula papyrifera,* and some of them are the similar-appearing gray birch, *Betula populifolia.* Donald Culross Peattie, in his classic *A Natural History of Trees,* pronounced the gray birch "a stunted sister" to the paper birch, which is also known as canoe birch.

The trees release a toxin that may make it tougher for other species to root and grow, a competition-reducing strategy that botanists call allelopathy. Today, however, the birches are dying. They have reached the ends of their eighty- to ninety-year life spans. As they fall, wrapped in their moisture-trapping bark, they rot quickly, returning precious organic matter to the soil in this much-abused part of Pennsylvania.

TO GET THERE. From Karthaus in northeastern Clearfield County, drive west on PA Route 879 1.6 miles to a stop sign. Turn right onto SR 1011, the Quehanna Highway. Go past a state correctional facility at Piper and past the Wykoff Run Natural Area. After 13.9 miles, turn right into the parking lot for Marion Brooks Natural Area. The white birches begin just beyond a stone monument with a plaque dedicated to Mrs. Brooks. Losey Road angles off to the right from the parking area.

You can also reach the natural area by exiting I-80 east of DuBois and driving northeast on PA Routes 255 and then 555. At the village of Medix Run, turn right on the Quehanna Highway. Marion Brooks is 8.8 miles east, on the left side of the road.

Request a Moshannon State Forest public-use map and a Quehanna Trail map from the Moshannon district office or the Bureau of Forestry in Harrisburg. The Quehanna Trail map is based on USGS topographic data. Use it and a compass whenever you leave the highway on this confusing, relatively flat upland plateau.

People have contracted Lyme disease from tick bites gotten in the Quehanna. When hiking during spring, summer, and fall, tuck your pants into your socks and further seal the seams with rubber bands. Consider using clothing sprays containing the chemical repellent permethrin. Remove and wash your clothes immediately after a hike. Take a shower, and thoroughly inspect yourself for ticks.

---

33   SPRUCE SWAMP

87 ACRES, LACKAWANNA STATE FOREST, LACKAWANNA COUNTY

Spruce Swamp offers access to intriguing wetland plants and uncommon trees. Hikers can walk around the fringes of the "swamp," peering in. In fact, the wetlands is a glacial kettlehole bog, a depression formed by a melting chunk of ice left behind when glaciers withdrew from the Pocono Mountains at the end of the last ice age, around ten thousand years ago. If visitors come shod in rubber boots, they can venture onto the bog to study the hardy, highly adapted plants.

The swamp's namesake tree is the black spruce, *Picea mariana,* found in New England and Canada as far north as the subarctic limit of tree growth. Black spruce also shows up in the cold, high-mountain bogs, such as Spruce Swamp, that pock the Appalachians as far south as Tennessee. Black spruce has short, sharp needles that are squarish in cross section, and small, rounded seed cones. Its trunk is generally straight, usually studded with many dead branch stubs, and the evergreen crown, high up at the top of the tree, often has a scraggly, tufted appearance. Beard lichens may cloak the branches. In a wet habitat such as Spruce Swamp, a black spruce usually sends out a flat, shallow root system. The roots spread over the quaking bog surface, which is formed from a layer of sphagnum moss: plants, both alive and dead and decomposing, that slowly fill in the kettlehole depression.

Tamarack, also called eastern larch, is another northern tree found at Spruce Swamp. It is Pennsylvania's only deciduous conifer, which means it sheds its foliage—needles, rather than the broad leaves of deciduous hardwood trees—in autumn, then grows a new set the following spring. In summer, larch needles are a pale blue-green. In late September, when I visited Spruce Swamp, the tamaracks were turning a warm golden yellow. To identify the tree, look for its feathery foliage (each branch looks like a crooked pipe cleaner covered with tufts of short needles) and small, oval seed cones less than an inch in length. Tamarack doesn't like the shade; it favors open parts of the bog. Black spruce, by contrast, grows well in dim light, and it clusters in thickets, with young trees growing beneath old ones.

Rhodora azalea, leatherleaf, Labrador tea, bog rosemary, and highbush blueberry mingle in the sunlit glades at Spruce Swamp. These shrubs are known as heaths. Heaths have adapted to grow in places that are damp, chilly, acidic, and poor in plant nutrients. Most bogs get their water not from moving groundwater, but from accumulating rain and snow, so few nutrients—such as calcium, potassium, and phosphorus, which come mainly from the breakdown of minerals in rocks—enter the system.

Bog plants grow slowly. They resist winter's cold winds, and conserve water and the few nutrients they manage to glean, by having tough, leathery leaves. Some species have evergreen leaves. Leatherleaf—widespread and common at Spruce Swamp—tends to keep its olive green leaves for more than one growing season, although never more than two. The leaves of leatherleaf and many other bog plants produce toxins that repel most vegetation-eating animals, although deer, rabbits, hares, and birds will occasionally take a nibble, and some insects have evolved to feed on them. At times, bog plants reproduce by dropping seeds, but mostly they colonize an area by spreading, sending up sprouts and pushing down roots from buds located low on their stems. This growth habit usually makes a bog a crowded, hard-to-penetrate place, at least for human visitors.

When I hiked into Spruce Swamp, the aspen leaves were turning gold and twinkling like thousands of coins. The red maples wore their autumnal cloaks of exclamatory red. I followed a deer trail through the wetland. The narrow path wandered between tussocks of leatherleaf, through the contorted, interwoven stems of highbush blueberry, and in among the black spruces. In the hardwood forest ringing the swamp, American beeches shone a rich, brassy gold in the slanting light. The whistling of a broad-winged hawk on high and the wind ruffling the aspens' leaves were the only sounds I heard.

TO GET THERE. From the Blakeslee exit on I-80, go north 5.5 miles on PA Route 115. Turn right on Buck River Road (SR 2040) toward Thornhurst. (At the village of Thornhurst, note the historical marker concerning the millionaire railroad manipulator Jay Gould, who, in the mid-1800s, was part owner of a tannery near the town.) After 4.8 miles on Buck River Road, turn left on Bear Lake Road (SR 2016) in the direction of Dupont and Wilkes-Barre. Go 1.9 miles and turn left onto gravel Tannery Road.

Pass Renfer Road and Fire Line Road, both on the right. After 1.2 miles, look for a sign for the natural area, where Tannery Road intersects with Phelps Road on the left, and a grassy lane leads to the right (north) beyond a gate. The small parking lot is on the left. The grassy lane runs north-south and forms the western boundary of the natural area, while Sunday Trail (part of the Pinchot Trail system) skirts the area on the north and east. Tannery Road forms the south boundary. A sign notes that there is no winter maintenance of Tannery Road.

Request a free map of the Pinchot Trail from the Lackawanna State Forest district office or the Bureau of Forestry headquarters in Harrisburg.

---

34   BRUCE LAKE

2,845 ACRES, DELAWARE STATE FOREST, PIKE COUNTY

A cold north wind blew my canoe down the lake. A belted kingfisher fled ahead of me, sounding a metallic chattering call; the blue-backed bird lit in a snag and watched as I floated past. The clear September sky reflected off ripples that went wind-driven across the water, a ceaseless train of wavelets lapping against the canoe's hull.

The wind pinned the canoe against the mat of sphagnum moss at the lake's south shore. A large dragonfly with a striped abdomen and sun-glittering wings made a soft clattering sound as it flew all along the canoe, then hung hovering in the breeze above one gunwale.

In the bog, tamaracks held up their feathery, yellow-green boughs above the ruddy leaves of highbush blueberry shrubs. Black spruces stood dark on the bog mat. In the zone where wetland met dry land, red maples were turning a brilliant red. White pines stood head and shoulders above the hardwoods in the forest surrounding the bog and the lake; the undersides of the pines' boughs were shaded a dark green, and their pliant, upright needles showed a bright pale green. Not a house or a cabin fronted the forty-eight-acre lake; it could have been a scene from Canada or Maine. And the wind was chill enough to remind me of northern places—as if the ice sheet that had left its mark on the Poconos had not really gone for good but only withdrawn temporarily.

Twenty thousand years ago, the Pocono Plateau—on which Bruce Lake Natural Area is situated—lay hundreds of feet beneath a continent-spanning belt of ice. Grinding slowly across the land, the glaciers picked up boulders, carried them along, and dropped them: the big slabs that today can be seen scattered through the woods in northeastern Pennsylvania. As global temperatures rose, the ice sheet began to melt and the glaciers withdrew northward. Huge chunks broke off the glaciers. As the stranded ice chunks melted, they deposited small rocks and silt around their edges. Water collected in the depressions made by the bergs' great weight, surrounded by the banks of sediment. Thus were born Bruce Lake and many of the other lakes, bogs, and swamps that dot the rolling, low-relief landscape.

I paddled past a beaver lodge and maneuvered the canoe down a narrow channel fringed with yellowing grasses. A wren foraged in a patch of sedge, but before I could get a good look, the bird flitted off into a blueberry thicket. Was it a marsh wren—a species rare in Pennsylvania, but one that could potentially breed in a large, isolated wetland such as this one? More likely it was a house wren, either a local breeder or a bird on its southward migration that had dropped in to feed on insects among the diverse plants of the bog.

The canoe ground to a halt where the channel narrowed. I picked a few blueberries from an overhanging branch. Most of their sweetness was gone, but the distinctive taste remained, and I reckoned this was the last such snack I'd have this year—although if I'd had the time to search, I might have found cranberries. Cranberry plants thrive in the acidity of the bog, and their pea-size fruit ripens to a bright reddish pink in early autumn.

Bruce Lake Natural Area lies north of Promised Land State Park. As well as Bruce Lake, the natural area includes the sixty-acre Egypt Meadow Lake, backed up behind a small dam built by Civilian Conservation Corps workers in 1935. There are several splendid swamps and an extensive trail network. The only flaw in the system is Interstate 84, which forms the natural area's northern boundary and broadcasts an appalling amount of engine drone into what is otherwise a pristine, restorative place. Since it is near several cities and in a region where the human population is steadily increasing, Bruce Lake Natural Area gets a lot of recreational use. On the Monday when I visited, I met three other hikers. (In most natural areas, it was rare for me to encounter another human on a weekday.)

Bruce Lake is about twenty feet deep. Low rock ledges line its north and east sides. At its southern end lies a large floating bog composed of built-up layers of sphagnum moss. In the bog grow pitcher plants and sundews (for an explanation of those plants' carnivorous feeding habits, see the account for Reynolds Spring Natural Area, page 194). Rare orchids, cattails, cinnamon and sensitive ferns, leatherleaf, spirea, and viburnum also sprout in the bog. Trees in the wetland include balsam fir and alder. Rhododendrons form impassable thickets.

After turning the canoe around, I worked my way back up the stream channel and paddled along on the lake's east shore, where the steep bank took the bite out of the wind. I beached the canoe near a patch of exposed bedrock with glacial striations on its surface: pale scars clawed into the stone by rocks frozen in the bottom of the glacier that had advanced and then receded so many years ago.

A rocky trail around Bruce Lake led past clumps of sheep laurel, a small shrub whose leathery evergreen leaves are smaller than those of the closely related mountain laurel. Sheep laurel is the more northerly of the two species and is found commonly in northern New England. Many of the oaks—white, chestnut, scarlet, and red—were dropping their acorns and I heard the little thuds all through the woods. The trail passed black gums, pitch pines, and a smattering of red spruces. The red spruce is also a northern species, with deep green aromatic needles and a classic Christmas tree shape.

Alerted by spiny, tan-colored husks on the trail, I found one of the largest chestnut trees I've ever seen in Pennsylvania. The American chestnut was the most common tree in much of the state's forests until a fungal blight nearly wiped it out in the early 1900s. The tree was almost a foot in diameter at breast height. The blight had infected the trunk—shown by the fungus's fruiting bodies, orange dots patching the bark near a branch stub—and I hoped that this particular chestnut was one of the few individuals that seem to have some resistance to the disease.

A side trail gave a view over Bruce Lake, where a great blue heron flew off across the water, so low that its wingtips almost touched the surface at every measured beat. Bald eagles and ospreys hunt for fish in Bruce and Egypt Meadow Lakes and in the many active beaver ponds in the area. Bobcats take prey ranging from voles to snowshoe hares and even an occasional deer in the extensive shrubby swamps, including three-hundred-acre Balsam Swamp and the somewhat smaller Panther Swamp. Black bears abound. Gray foxes, gray and red squirrels, chipmunks, and a wide range of songbirds also inhabit the natural area. A forester spoke of going fishing with some friends at Egypt Meadow Lake; they spotted a family of four river otters, which, he told me, "swam up close and really checked us out."

Around Bruce Lake, the land is rolling, and the same type of habitat—mountain laurel and mixed oaks—stretches for long distances. As close as it is to the interstate, this remains a wild place. That fact was driven home in a tragic way in January 1994, when a middle-aged couple from Canada went cross-country skiing in the natural area. Although the man had taught winter survival skills, he and his wife entered the area without adequate food or warm clothing. They left the marked trail and became lost. Floundering about in deep snow, they froze to death.

TO GET THERE. From the Promised Land exit of I-84, travel south on PA Route 390 1.5 miles to a parking area on your left. (You will pass another parking area for the natural area only a few hundred yards south of the interstate.) Walk around the locked steel gate, and proceed on a well-groomed woods road to Egypt Meadow Lake and Bruce Lake.

A map of the Promised Land Trail System is available from the Bureau of Forestry and also at Promised Land State Park, about a mile south of Bruce Lake Natural Area. In addition, the park brochure has a map of the natural area and interlinking trails in the park, many of which are used for cross-country skiing.

35 BUCKHORN

535 ACRES, DELAWARE STATE FOREST, PIKE COUNTY

The view into the Delaware River gorge would have been spectacular had it not been pouring down rain. As it was, I could just make out the green wooded mountain that reared up on the far side of the curving watercourse; then the clouds closed in again, rain sluiced off my hat brim, and the vista disappeared.

I was with Tim Ladner, assistant district forester in the Delaware State Forest. Ladner was new to the Poconos, having transferred there from south-central Pennsylvania only two months earlier. This was his first time at Buckhorn Natural Area, just as it was my first visit there.

We left the rain-obscured view and walked around Stairway Lake, held behind a low dam. We followed a grassy woods road uphill through scrubby mixed oaks, red maples, and black birches shedding yellow leaves in the rain, the leaves falling onto the slick evergreen foliage of acre upon acre of mountain laurel. The rain beat down on the laurel. It beat down on our shoulders and backs and hats.

When I had telephoned James Connor, chief forester of the Delaware district, and asked him what made the Buckhorn special, he had spoken of its remoteness, its wilderness quality. The natural area protects a watershed draining north into the Delaware. It is situated on a peninsular upland that juts eastward like a big elbow ending at Matamoras, Pennsylvania, near the three-way border between the Keystone State, New York, and New Jersey. The state forest land within the elbow—which is defined by the river's ninety-degree bend at Matamoras, opposite Port Jervis, New York—has been proposed for wild area status. Ultimately, Buckhorn will become a natural area within a wild area. "It's probably the wildest place left in the Poconos," Connor told me.

I saw no reason to doubt him. Ladner and I had hiked more than a mile to reach Stairway Lake. We hadn't seen another soul, other than a white-breasted nuthatch and a few bedraggled chickadees and seven dis-trustful ducks on the lake, and we were uncertain how much farther we needed to go to actually reach the natural area.

The road wound through a strangely pitted and hummocked landscape. This part of Pike County has great quantities of bluestone, a hard, fine-

grained sandstone used for everything from building blocks to
cemetery monuments. The most
profitable application for bluestone
was in curbs and sidewalks in bur-
geoning nineteenth-century cities,
including Scranton, Wilkes-Barre,
Trenton, Passaic, Philadelphia,
New York—even such far-flung
metropolises as Minneapolis and
Havana. Workers quarried the
stone by hand, using pry bars,
chisels, and sledgehammers. Slabs
were hauled down the mountain
in wagons, then loaded onto railcars and canal barges.

After a while, the road that
Ladner and I were following disappeared underwater. Not rain water,
although the rain was still coming
down hard, but water backed up
behind a beaver dam. The dam

Beavers dammed this small stream, creating a wetland near the edge of Buckhorn Natural Area.

was a lattice of small and large sticks and branches plastered with leaves and
mud. We circled the pond to the east. A series of dams had flooded many
trees over several acres. The beavers had cut down trees ranging from ones
as thick as my arm to oaks that were bigger around than my waist. Other
trees stood along the water's edge with hourglass-shaped cuttings on their
trunks, ready to be chewed through and felled. The beavers' smell was very
strong: the aquatic rodents secrete a pungent oil, castoreum, from glands at
the base of the tail and mark the boundaries of their colony with it.

A black duck flew up from the water and disappeared into the rain and
gloom. Brilliant red maples stood out like beacons among the dark hemlocks and the still-green oaks. Lowbush blueberry was going red along the
edge of the pond, where backed-up water had reached the shrubs' roots. In
the forest were more quarry pits, along with unraveling stone foundations
and rotting boards.

In time, we circumambulated the beaver pond. We looked at maps that
were rapidly becoming soaked and threatening to fall apart in the rain. We
checked our compasses. Although we believed we were in the natural area,

we were not completely sure of it. The high plateau was faintly rolling, uniform in its mix of oaks, blueberry, mountain laurel.

We found deer droppings and coyote scat on the trail. Timber rattlesnakes are known to den in the many sandstone ledges in the vicinity. Buckhorn Natural Area has a vernal pond where amphibians breed in springtime. Black bears, bobcats, otters, minks, foxes, porcupines, bald eagles, ospreys, hawks, owls, ravens, and songbirds share the woods.

After a certain pitch of misery had been attained, Ladner and I took a vote on whether to head back to the truck. The results were unanimous. We began retracing our steps. Gray clouds brushed the tops of the mountains. In the rain, the slumped-in quarries lay filled with gloom.

On the old road, Ladner stopped, bent, and straightened, holding something in his hand. An old horseshoe, lost by some long-ago draft animal, two bent, rusted nails still dangling.

TO GET THERE. In Milford, from the center of town, go north on Broad Street (combined U.S. Routes 6 and 209). After 2.7 miles, turn left on Cummings Hill Road. Drive uphill and continue past a gas pipeline right-of-way at 3.3 miles and a gated forest road at 4.0 miles. Cummings Hill Road starts heading downhill, curving to the right and then to the left. Look for a parking area at 4.6 miles.

The trail starts off from the parking lot, where a marker announces that Stairway Lake is 1.5 miles away. The trail follows the state forest boundary, marked with white paint blazes on trees, crossing Bush Kill (a small creek) and several wet areas. After about 0.75 mile, it intersects with a woods road. Turn left on the road, noting the spot so that you can recognize it on your return. Go around Stairway Lake on the north, still following the road. Pass the beaver dam. When the road bends to head southwest, the natural area is on your right.

Alternatively, Buckhorn Natural Area can be reached by driving west from Milford on Route 6; turning north on Schocopee Road; turning right on Fire Tower Road; and parking at the boundary between state forest land and State Game Lands 209, administered by the Pennsylvania Game Commission. Walk in a northeast direction for about 0.75 mile, following the marked boundary between the two public land holdings. According to state foresters, a wildfire recently burned several hundred acres in the vicinity, and many of the boundary trees have died and fallen down.

Before visiting Buckhorn Natural Area, ask for advice from Delaware State Forest personnel. Buckhorn is a rugged, wild area subject to rapid weather changes. If you wish to explore it, take along the Pond Eddy, New York, topographic quadrangle, plus a compass. Allow a full day in case you become lost.

36 LITTLE MUD POND SWAMP

182 ACRES, DELAWARE STATE FOREST, PIKE COUNTY

I got as far as the edge of Little Mud Pond Swamp, and contented myself with standing on a rock ledge (bobcats den in the rocks, according to the foresters) and looking out over the dense vegetation barricading this small wetland. Little Mud Pond Swamp is basically impenetrable to upright bipeds, although hunters' trails—allowing access for pursuit of deer, bears, and showshoe hares—testify that at least some hardy souls venture into it.

Little Mud Pond is a boreal conifer swamp dominated by black spruce of uneven ages, in some places so dense that little light penetrates and few plants exist below the canopy. A five-acre bog at the core of the wetlands has an unstable quaking bog mat covered by leatherleaf shrubs and mudflats. Three to four acres of open water form one large pond and several smaller pools. Along with the black spruce are tamarack, red maple, and white pine trees. During a brief site visit, a botanist found forty-five trees, shrubs, and plants, including highbush blueberry, tall huckleberry, rhododendron, sheep laurel, mountain holly, cinnamon fern, Virginia chain fern, bog rosemary, spatulate-leaved sundew, pitcher plant, pogonia, and several species of sphagnum moss.

The surrounding upland forest is typical of the Poconos: chestnut and white oaks sprinkled with pitch pine and red spruce, undergrown with mountain laurel and low blueberry. On a short hike, I saw ample signs of white-tailed deer, a blue jay, and a yellow-shafted flicker. A hunter I spoke with said the swamp is negotiated most easily in winter, when the vegetation is less dense; the visitor may find tracks of bobcats and snowshoe hares in the snow.

TO GET THERE. Little Mud Pond Swamp lies south of U.S. Route 6 in Blooming Grove Township. You have to be good with a compass and topographic map to get there. The following directions put you in the general vicinity:

From the Lords Valley exit of I-84, go north on PA Route 739 4.4 miles to Germantown. Turn right (east) on Route 6. Pass a sign for the Pennsylvania Fish and Boat Commission's Greeley Lake Access Area on the left. After 2.6 miles, at mile marker 210, turn right onto a woods road at a small, white hunting camp (camp number 19C618). Park in the vicinity and continue on foot, using the Rowland, Pennsylvania, topographic quadrangle. An old woods road, Weaver Trail, bounds the northern edge of the natural area.

37 PENNEL RUN

936 ACRES, DELAWARE STATE FOREST, PIKE COUNTY

The Thunder Swamp Trail System, a twenty-eight-mile network built by Youth Conservation Corps workers in the 1970s, provides excellent access to two state forest natural areas; one of them is Pennel Run.

I was glad I'd worn sturdy hiking boots, because the way leads over a great many rocks that jut up through the thin soil of the Poconos. Assistant district forester Tim Ladner and I had parked at a lot along Snow Hill Road and hiked north from there. Soon after starting off on our September tramp, we came to two huge white pines standing side by side along the trail. Staring up at the tall, straight giants, Ladner wondered aloud why two such impressive sticks of lumber had been left by the loggers who cleared off the region around the turn of the twentieth century. Maybe the trees were on a boundary line and it wasn't known who owned them. In any case, the pines will probably never be cut: it is Bureau of Forestry policy to leave trees standing in a two-hundred-foot corridor around any state-designated hiking trail, should a logging job be let in the vicinity.

Thunder Swamp Trail followed Spruce Run, a shallow, meandering stream of tannin-dark water and a tributary of Bushkill Creek. It crossed the run on a wooden bridge supported by stone-filled wire baskets called gabions. On either side of Spruce Run stood a beautifully diverse forest of white ash, tuliptree, white oak, sugar maple, and shagbark hickory, with yellow birch and hemlock crowding the waterway.

After 1.6 miles, a spur trail branched off to the west toward the natural area; we began hiking uphill among shelves of rock in an open forest of spindly chestnut oak, red maple, and black birch trees. A flock of Canada geese flew over, honking above the clouds, and a band of chickadees bounced through the forest understory of serviceberry, witch hazel, and mountain laurel, feeding as they went.

The spur trail came to a T at Hay Road on the eastern boundary of the natural area. Tom Thwaites described an outing to Pennel Run in his *50 Hikes in Eastern Pennsylvania* and reported finding wild azaleas and pink lady's slippers blooming along Hay Road during May.

The loop through the natural area covers three miles. As Ladner and I walked steadily through an upland forest composed largely of the same nondescript, even-age chestnut oak, red maple, and black birch, I found myself wondering why the more diverse forest along Spruce Run hadn't been chosen for the natural area, or at least included in it.

The trail crossed Pennel Run on stepping-stones. It grazed the edge of Utts Swamp, where winterberry holly held brilliant red berries and cinnamon ferns were turning bronze and yellow with the coming fall. Red spruce, speckled alder, and green ash trees brought some welcome variation to the woods.

TO GET THERE. Take the exit off I-84 for PA Route 402. Drive approximately 14 miles south on Route 402, and turn right on Snow Hill Road. Proceed 2.3 miles to a gravel parking area on the right.

From just west of the parking lot, Thunder Swamp Trail heads north along Spruce Run. After 1.6 miles, a spur trail turns off to the left (west), and after 0.5 mile, it reaches Hay Road and the edge of the natural area. The hiker can then make a 3-mile loop by following the red-blazed footpath either clockwise or counterclockwise, returning via the spur trail and Thunder Swamp Trail to the parking area. The route covers 7.2 miles and takes about four and a half hours. Equip yourself with the Thunder Swamp Trail System map, available free from the Bureau of Forestry's Harrisburg headquarters and the Delaware State Forest district office.

---

38   PINE LAKE

67 ACRES, DELAWARE STATE FOREST, PIKE COUNTY

On a clear, windless evening in late September, the bog showed off the first colorful signs of autumn: scarlet and orange leaves on the red maples, sphagnum moss turning a deep church-carpet red, and burnt orange, head-high fronds of cinnamon ferns. The huge ferns looked prehistoric in the way they jutted up like fountains from the morass of tangled, interlocking plants that grew on the mat of sphagnum ringing Pine Lake.

I worked my way south along the shore. The lake appeared to be about 150 yards wide by 350 yards long. My rubber boots sank ankle-deep in black mud. It felt like I was walking on a thick mattress; the bog mat, made up of a layer of living and dead sphagnum moss, shook and quaked as I set my feet and advanced my weight, while trying to keep my balance by leaning on my hiking staff. Lichens scabbed the trunks of tamaracks and black spruce trees. Winterberry holly shrubs raised their toothed yellow leaves

An exceptional diversity of bog plants grow on the sphagnum moss mat surrounding Pine Lake.

and bright red berries. A catbird squalled from the depths of a blueberry thicket, and three robins landed in a skeletal dead spruce. A spiderweb held beads of dew that caught the late silvery light.

The rumble of truck engines and the whining and drumming of automobile tires made it impossible to forget that Pine Lake Natural Area lies less than a mile from Interstate 84. But the site remains a plant lover's paradise. After botanists from the University of Pennsylvania surveyed the area in 1983, they wrote: "The plant life there shows little sign of disturbance and is high in species richness. It is certainly one of the most outstanding bogs we've seen on our rare plant search in eastern Pennsylvania."

In addition to the tamarack and black spruce trees, the botanists found shadbush, bog rosemary, leatherleaf, water-willow, mountain holly, rosebay rhododendron, and hardhack. Among the thirty-eight herbs that the scientists identified were large and small cranberries, dwarf mistletoe, nine species of sedges (including *Carex cephalantha,* listed in Pennsylvania as a plant of special concern), swamp candles, buckbean, royal fern, white fringed orchid, pitcher plant, round-leaved sundew, and marsh fern—all species adapted to the acidic, chilly growing conditions of boreal bogs.

I stood on the edge of the lake, whose calm waters reflected the first stars twinkling in the sky. My nearest companion was a red maple whose crown just rose above the highbush blueberries and whose trunk was about four inches thick. I wondered how old the tree might be, how many growing seasons were recorded, unseen, in the density of annual rings in its wood. Like the tamaracks and spruces, the maple wore greenish and pale gray lichens on its bark and draped from its lower branches, and I felt distinctly the antiquity of this stalwart plant that had thriven in such an austere, demanding place. It made me consider myself—and the road that my kind had laid down for our machines—as the truly ephemeral things on the land.

TO GET THERE. Unless you can negotiate access through private property to the south of the natural area, you must follow a difficult and circuitous route to reach Pine Lake.

From the Promised Land exit on I-84, head south on PA Route 390 for 0.2 mile and turn right on Old Greentown Road (TR 351). After 4.8 miles, turn right on Beaver Dam Road. After 0.5 mile, park at a sign for a state forest timber sale, being sure not to block the gate.

On a wooden stile, climb over an electrified six-strand deer fence. (The Bureau of Forestry will remove the fence when the trees grow beyond the reach of deer.) Hike north through the logged area on a dirt haul road, and when you reach a powerline right-of-way, turn right (east). Let yourself out of the timber sale by unhooking and then reclosing the springy wires of another electric fence. Continue east along the powerline to a small stream that drains out of Pine Lake—at which point you'll need to turn right (south) and head upstream.

A potential explorer needs to be better than I am at reading a topographic map (the Greentown, Pennsylvania, quadrangle, which unfortunately does not include the powerline right-of-way) to discern which drainage it is that leads south to the lake. A forester told me that an old logging road goes back to the swamp on the eastern side of the stream—although you have to know where it departs from the powerline. Best to have a forester at the district office show you on the map.

---

39 STILLWATER

1,931 ACRES, DELAWARE STATE FOREST, PIKE COUNTY

Settled into a steady hiking gait, I stepped along on Thunder Swamp Trail. And came to a halt as a dark shape rose from behind a stump twenty yards from the path. The big bear glanced at me for a brief moment, then dropped to all fours, turned, and raced off, all power and grace as he

The lazy, meandering character of Little Bushkill Creek gives Stillwater Natural Area its name.

dodged past a fallen tree trunk, his silken coat rippling and catching shafts of the sunlight that penetrated the forest canopy. It was appropriate that the bear disappeared into the fastness of Big Bear Swamp, which takes up some four hundred acres, a fifth of the land in the Stillwater Natural Area.

I checked on what bruin had been doing there behind the stump. He must simply have been dozing, for I found no evidence of feeding, no claw marks, shattered wood, or shreds of moss or rotten bark on the ground.

Two hundred yards farther on, the sudden waving tail of a doe, as she rocketed out of a bed in the laurel next to the trail, put my heart in my throat once again. I took a few more steps, and deer were boiling out all over the place, including a buck with a nice set of polished white antlers.

A Bureau of Forestry report describes Stillwater Natural Area, in southern Pike County, as "a representative portion of the poorly drained, heavily glaciated low plateaus of the Poconos." In this area, during the ice ages, glaciers scoured the bedrock of shales and sandstones and heaped the rocks and sediments into low ridges and outcroppings interspersed with shallow valleys clogged with glacial debris. Stillwater Natural Area consists of two large parcels connected by a narrow corridor of public land. The eastern parcel surrounds Big Bear Swamp, and the western one includes Little Bushkill Creek, whose lazy meandering character gives the natural area its name.

The well-maintained Thunder Swamp Trail—created by Youth Conservation Corps workers in the 1970s—provides access to both parcels. Look as hard on a map as you want, and you won't find any "Thunder

Swamp" in the area; it's rumored that the YCC members simply liked the name. The trail is rocky and has many wet spots, requiring sturdy, water-resistant footwear.

The rolling, jumbled, low-relief terrain makes a denizen of Pennsylvania's Ridge and Valley Region, like myself, somewhat ill at ease and capable of being thoroughly turned around and disoriented in this region, where there are few well-defined mountain ridges to help a hiker fix his or her location. Add in the uniform second-growth oak forest, and acre upon acre of sweet fern, bracken fern, huckleberry, and (especially) mountain laurel, and you have an environment that, were it not for trails like Thunder Swamp and its various side loops, would be difficult indeed to find your way around in.

Black spruce, white pine, hemlock, red maple, and yellow birch grow in Big Bear Swamp. Shrubby portions of the wetland are thick with alder, highbush blueberry, winterberry holly, and viburnum: a first-rate place for bears to feed, breed, and hide. I would expect minks, bobcats, and snowshoe hares to use the habitat, as well as a variety of wetland-loving herons and songbirds during the spring and summer breeding season. Thunder Swamp Trail skirts the swamp and mounts to a modest overlook near its northwest corner.

In September, when I visited Stillwater Natural Area, I saw and heard literally hundreds of chipmunks—chipmunks rustling in the leaves, scurrying along with acorns puffing out their cheek pouches, sitting on stumps and scolding. Gray squirrels worked at harvesting hickory nuts, which came plumping to the forest floor. I flushed a pair of ruffed grouse that were feeding on huckleberries near the path. A band of foraging wood thrushes chacked querulously at me, and a sharp-shinned hawk lifted from the ground and flashed off through the woods, showing its slate blue back and its white-and-black-banded tail. A blue jay half glimpsed among hemlock boughs gave its "squeaky hinge" call, usually employed during early courtship flocking in the spring and perhaps used in this instance to keep a family group or a feeding band together. Fresh coyote droppings on the trail reminded me of the pack I'd heard yipping and yodeling as I stood on the porch of my rental cabin at nearby Promised Land State Park the evening before.

TO GET THERE. From I-84, take the exit for PA Route 402 and drive south for about 10.1 miles. Turn left on Old Bushkill Road (SR 2003) and drive 1.5 miles, then turn left on Flat Ridge Road. Go past Broadhead Road to the right and a parking area for the Thunder Swamp Trail and Painter Swamp; after 2.5 miles, turn right on unmarked Coon Swamp Road. After less than a hundred yards, park at a yellow gate.

Walk along Coon Swamp Road for 0.7 mile to a junction with Thunder Swamp Trail. Turn left (east) on the trail. After approximately half a mile, the trail crosses Little Bushkill Creek on a wooden bridge. The path then swings to the left (east) and intersects with the loop encircling Big Bear Swamp; when I hiked this route in September 2000, there was a small cairn of rocks at the intersection. You can walk around the swamp clockwise (turn to the left) or counter-clockwise (turn right). Be sure to carry a compass and the Thunder Swamp Trail System map, available free from the Bureau of Forestry. Tom Thwaites's *50 Hikes in Eastern Pennsylvania* details an 8.8-mile trek that visits both Big Bear Swamp and nearby Painter Swamp.

Headed back to the car, I took a red-blazed side trail through the western portion of Still-water Natural Area. For part of its distance, the trail followed the edge of Little Bushkill Creek, passing a nice campsite in a grove of hemlocks. (Camping is allowed on the Thunder Swamp Trail System; request a free permit from the Delaware State Forest district office.) Altogether, my hike covered 8.5 miles and took five hours.

40   JAKEY HOLLOW

58 ACRES, WYOMING STATE FOREST, COLUMBIA COUNTY

It might have become just another logged-out, eroded gully, full of slash and brush, its old-growth pine and hemlock skidded away and milled into prosaic products like barn siding and wall studs. Instead, thanks to the fore-sight and generosity of two octogenarian brothers, Jakey Hollow is a wooded refuge, an oasis of old-growth trees tucked away in the otherwise agricultural countryside of Columbia County.

On the August day when my son Will and I hiked down the broad, gentle trail into Jakey Hollow, we scared out a band of crows, which launched themselves from the treetops and flew off on loudly flapping wings, cursing us roundly. In the wake of their departure, we heard (in addition to near-constant grinding and clashing from a quarry less than a mile away) the *wer-wer* call of a white-breasted nuthatch, the whistle of a cardinal, and the screechy scream of an unseen hawk. We paused to watch several young wood thrushes foraging, and Will picked up a blue jay's feather like a splinter of sky fallen on the ground. The trail led to the floor of the hollow, where the thick-trunked pines and hemlocks stood.

In 1990, Ward and Henry Crawford sold to the state of Pennsylvania the fifty-eight acres of Jakey Hollow that they owned. The brothers wanted to ensure that the big trees—at which they had marveled for many decades, since taking boyhood shortcuts through the hollow on their way to school—would never fall to the saw. Between five and ten acres are believed to be virgin timber, and the remaining woodland has not been cut since 1913. Although Jakey Hollow lies twenty-five miles south of the rest of the Wyoming State Forest, the Bureau of Forestry was glad for the chance to own the site and immediately designated it a natural area. Today Jakey Hollow is surrounded by fields farmed for corn, soybeans, and alfalfa, in a landscape that is becoming increasingly dotted with houses.

In the moist, shady hollow, down which a small, unnamed stream runs, eastern hemlocks are the dominant trees. Will and I wandered about stretching a tape measure around the enormous trunks. One venerable giant had a girth of ten feet, four inches. A nearby white pine taped out at nine feet, ten inches. A hundred feet up, their tops merged with the crowns of other hemlocks and pines, forming a complicated canopy that included also the leafy uppermost branches of sugar maples, black birches, black cherries, red oaks, and American beeches, whose leaves, in slightly varying shades of green, shimmered in the gentle wind.

Along the stream stood thick beds of jewelweed in spectacular orange-and-red flower. Evergreen wood, lady, Christmas, and sensitive ferns grew in small clumps or sent their green fronds arching above the ground. Partridgeberry crept across the forest floor. There are no formal trails in Jakey Hollow, but visitors can move about following paths that others have worn down. As Will and I strolled up the hollow, we heard the calling of pileated woodpeckers, robins, and blue jays. Colorful mushrooms sprouted from the leaf duff. We found several specimens of the hoary-looking *Strobilomyces floccopus,* better known as the old man of the woods. This mushroom has a coal gray cap tufted with blackish spiky scales that look like nubbly upholstery. Unlike many of the larger, fleshy fungi, the "old man" resists decay and lasts for a long time; I've often found it standing desiccated and wizened, covered with greenish mold, in the fall.

We reached a line of posters announcing the end of the state land. Beyond, the logged-over woods contrasted with the old-growth forest. We turned uphill. After a short climb, we headed back down the hollow, staying on the slope and passing through a mix of skyscraping pines and large hardwoods, including many chestnut oaks. A storm had brought down a big oak, whose trunk was smothered beneath blackberry canes. Good numbers of the tart berries necessitated a quietly industrious fifteen-minute pause in our walk. Purple, seed-filled fox droppings left on top of the tree's barkless trunk showed that at least one other visitor had enjoyed the fruit.

Downstream of where the access trail bottoms out in the hollow, the forest is mostly hemlock with some nice tuliptrees, white ashes, and white and red oaks. One of the red oaks had snapped off about thirty feet up; on the ground, along with the tree's broken crown, were dark brown, sweet-smelling combs of a honeybee colony that had lived in the hollow trunk.

That summer I had already seen many stands of beautiful virgin trees in quiet, near-wilderness settings. I found myself distracted during our walk, when sounds intruded, of cows mooing, roosters crowing, tractors mowing hay, trucks beeping mechanically as they backed up, stone being quarried and crushed. But Jakey Hollow is a special place. It is a refuge where migrating birds can rest on their journeys, where resident birds can breed, and where mammals can hunt and rear their young; where people can see a sliver of presettlement forest and think about the land as it once was.

TO GET THERE. From the Bloomsburg exit of I-80, go north on PA Route 42 toward Millville. After 1.0 mile, turn left at a stop sign. Still on Route 42, continue 2.3 miles and then turn right on Melick Hollow Road, opposite signs for the HRI Bloomsburg Asphalt Plant and the Hanson Bloomsburg Quarry. Cross Little Fishing Creek on a bridge. After Melick Hollow Road turns sharply to the right, take the first left, on dirt-surfaced Crawford Road. Drive uphill 0.4 mile and look for a sign on the left (in the woods' fringe and not easily spotted from the road) marking the trail down into the natural area.

---

41 TAMARACK RUN

234 ACRES, WYOMING STATE FOREST, SULLIVAN COUNTY

Natural areas aren't necessarily hiker-friendly. Natural days are not always congenial. My brother Brian was visiting from California in early June, and it was a cold and rainy afternoon when we looked in on Tamarack Run Natural Area.

The boggy tract is thick with thigh-high leatherleaf and chest-high blueberry, surrounded by a forest of eastern hemlock and white pine plus northern hardwoods: American beech, birch, sugar and red maples, and black cherry, a mix of species typical for northern Pennsylvania. It's possible that tamaracks, or larches, grew there at one time, but none seem to inhabit the site today. The bog occupies a mountain basin at around eighteen hundred feet of elevation. It gives its waters to Rock Run, draining northward into Little Loyalsock Creek, and to Tamarack Run, trickling south to join the main branch of the Loyalsock. Trails border the bog on the northwest and northeast, and the gravel-surfaced Loyalsock Road, with a nearly ninety-degree bend, forms the southwestern and southeastern sides of the approximately square natural area. The two trails—Rock Run Trail and Sones Trail—are poorly marked and confusing, intersected in many places by logging roads.

The bog looks like a bit of Maine or Quebec plunked down in northeastern Pennsylvania. Along with the sphagnum moss, which forms a thick mat throughout the wetland, grow several unusual plants. One is creeping snowberry, *Gaultheria hispidula.* Brian and I looked for this low-growing member of the heath family, which we thought might be in flower—the small, white, bell-shaped blossoms appear in May and June—but were unable to find it; with the rain pelting down, maybe we didn't make a sufficient effort. Creeping snowberry has tiny, oval leaves alternating on each side of the plant's several stems, which straggle across the ground. The white berry has a wintergreen taste.

Two endangered plants are reported from the bog (and also from the soggy northern end of Sones Pond, half a mile east and outside the bounds of the natural area): small floating manna grass *(Glyceria borealis)* and Tuckerman's pondweed *(Potamogeton confervoides).*

Brian and I wore rubber boots and rainsuits; we stepped carefully so we wouldn't sink to our knees in the soupy places. Wild azaleas bloomed among the leatherleaf, showing off their hot pink flowers; their perfume lay in pockets among the vegetation, mingling strangely with the methane gas that bubbled to the surface when we trod on the yielding floor of the bog.

At one point—I think it was after I'd let go of a branch and it whipped back to smack him wetly in the face—Brian smiled faintly and said, "What percentage of people would actually enjoy what we're doing right now?" The only reply I could think of was that it was better than bog-hopping on a hot, muggy day, when your shirt is plastered to your back, when deerflies zero in on every immobile surface and mosquitoes attend in clouds.

In fact, the fragrance of the azaleas—and the hammering of a pileated woodpecker (the bird had found an especially resonant snag, and its territorial drumming echoed through the swamp)—and a black-throated blue warbler flitting hyperactively after insects during a break in the rain, white patches on his sides glinting in the dim light—and the verses of hermit thrushes drifting through the somber woods—more than justified the outing.

TO GET THERE. From U.S. Route 220 north of Laporte, turn northwest on PA Route 154. Go 1.8 miles and turn right on Rock Run Road. Continue for 2.0 miles, crossing Loyalsock Creek and a portion of the Loyalsock Trail, until you come to Loyalsock Road. Turn left (west) onto Loyalsock Road, passing Sones Pond on the right, and after another half mile, look for the bog and Tamarock Run Natural Area on your right.

The area is covered by the Eagles Mere, Pennsylvania, topographic quadrangle.

---

42   KETTLE CREEK GORGE

774 ACRES, WYOMING STATE FOREST, SULLIVAN COUNTY

I like the woods in the rain: the saturated colors and the sharp odors, but primarily the sound—a constant dripping, small noises in different pitches, at times steady, at times fitful, gusts blowing in the treetops and drops falling on the forest floor, on logs and ferns and leaves. I believe that rain in the northern hardwood forest—a woods composed mainly of beech, birch, black cherry, white ash, and sugar maple—sounds different than rain in the oak woods, such as that surrounding my home. Perhaps it is the shapes of the leaves, which may affect the sound of the raindrops hitting them. The tone is somehow higher and brighter among the northern hardwoods.

On our way to Kettle Creek Gorge, my brother Brian and I hiked through such a woods. The smooth trunks of the American beeches had a sheen like wet cement; those of the yellow birches, with their feathery, curling bark, looked like new copper. The trees' boughs were heavy with water, and they bent low, dipping their rain-glazed viridian leaves toward Loyalsock Trail.

The yellow-green fronds of New York ferns arced up in open places. Shining club moss carpeted the ground in other areas, its foliage a brilliant, light-reflecting green even in the dim light. Witch hazel, striped maple, and black birch saplings grew thick where sugar maples, killed by the fungus-induced disease anthracnose, stood dead or had toppled to the ground.

Loyalsock Trail climbs almost seven hundred feet in a northerly direction from Brunnerdale Run to the mountain above Kettle Creek Gorge Natural Area; from there it plunges into the canyon. On our way up, my brother Brian and I scared a new fawn out of its hiding place. It went skittering off

Loyalsock Trail provides access to the large, wild Kettle Creek Gorge Natural Area.

on its spindly legs, weaving uncertainly among the hazel withes until it finally disappeared among the greenery. We spotted false morels growing out of a rotting log, pink coral fungi, and clumps of edible oyster mushrooms (unfortunately, just out of reach) bracketing the trunk of a tree.

A short side trail led to Angel Falls. There are two falls, one above the other, and on this rainy day, during a rainy June, both of the waterfalls ran full. The upper falls was one of the prettiest cataracts I have seen in Pennsylvania. The water came down in white cascades over the nearly vertical rock walls, splashed onto a flat ledge, shattered, coalesced, and ran in braided foaming rivulets over and through a stony rubble. Fog and spray hung in the air. The rushing sound was constant.

We stopped at a sweeping vista over Kettle Creek Gorge. The clouds parted just long enough for us to see down into the valley's intensely green depths. A yellow-bellied sapsucker, its red, black, and white head brilliant in the gloom, circled around the trunk of a maple; a redstart fed in a nearby tree's crown. Above the pattering of the raindrops, we heard the oft-repeated *teacher teacher teacher* of ground-dwelling ovenbirds. The calls of hermit thrushes and wood thrushes, similarly sweet but slightly different in tone and pattern, came drifting through the woods. We frightened one thrush out of a nest in the crown of a fallen tree; four tiny young raised opened, begging mouths. I thought about waiting for a positive identification when the adult bird came back, but it was so cold and damp that I was afraid the nestlings would become dangerously chilled if our presence postponed their parent's return.

The trail angled down into Kettle Creek Gorge. The canyon is almost nine hundred feet deep at its mouth, near the village of Ogdonia, where Kettle Creek briefly joins Ogdonia Run before flowing into larger Loyalsock Creek. Kettle Creek holds wild brook and brown trout; today it ran fast and clear, white riffles lying between deep, jade-colored pools. We both would have liked to hike downstream all the way through the gorge, the heart of the natural area. But it was already past noon, and we needed to be back home in Centre County by evening. The rain picked up again, drumming on the leaves and dimpling the stream.

It wasn't a hard decision to turn and head out, retracing our steps back to the car. Neither was it difficult putting Kettle Creek Gorge on my mental list of natural areas to come back to.

TO GET THERE. Follow PA Route 87 north from Montoursville for 20.4 miles. Look for a sign for the Camp Lycogis parking area, at the intersection of Route 87 and Ogdonia Road. Take the gravel-surfaced Ogdonia Road 2.9 miles to the southeast, and turn left at the fork onto Brunnerdale Road. Continue on Brunnerdale Road 0.3 mile to a parking area on the left. The Loyalsock Trail, marked with 2-by-6 yellow rectangles with a 1-inch horizontal red stripe, leads you to the natural area. A side trail branches off to Angel Falls.

Hikers should carry a compass and walk in and out keeping to the Loyalsock Trail. At a minimum, take along the Wyoming State Forest public-use map. Because the Loyalsock Trail has been relocated in certain places since the map was printed, you may also want to have along the Hillsgrove, Pennsylvania, topographic quadrangle. For information on the 59-mile Loyalsock Trail, including how to obtain a guidebook and a set of maps, contact the Alpine Hiking Club, P.O. Box 501, Williamsport PA 17703, or visit the website www.hutchey.com/kta/loyal.htm.

43 ALGERINE SWAMP

84 ACRES, TIADAGHTON STATE FOREST, LYCOMING AND TIOGA COUNTIES

Two trees unusual for Pennsylvania grow at Algerine Swamp: black spruce and balsam fir, denizens of the North whose range dips southward in the chilly upland bogs of the Appalachians.

To find them, I headed west off Gamble Run Road through shady, hummocky woodland. Although it was late July, the air was cool enough for a long-sleeved shirt. Tall clumps of cinnamon fern, numerous mosses, and a cornucopia of fungi covered the damp forest floor. A thunderstorm had swept through the evening before, and this morning the colors were brilliant: varied sparkling greens of mosses and other low plants, dotted by mushrooms that were tan, cream, rose, orange, yellow. I spotted enough specimens of the edible bolete, or cèpe (this meaty mushroom is found in Europe as well as in North America), that I could have filled a bushel basket.

Hidden among the oaks and maples, a pair of hermit thrushes countered one another in a melodious, competitive duet that changed to scolding *tuk-tuk-tuk* calls as I trespassed on the birds' territories. I stopped to admire dwarf cornel, or bunchberry, its six leaves in a lush green whorl, from whose center rose an upright stalk holding a ball-shaped clutch of brilliant red berries. Creeping snowberry spread its tiny, dark green leaves across the ground. The five-petaled, delicate white flowers of dewdrop scattered the forest floor. A ruffed grouse flushed in a sudden wing-stutter: wet-feathered and loath to fly, the bird had allowed me within ten yards. Had it been feeding on the abundant lowbush blueberries, sweet fruit that had also been claiming a good share of my attention?

I caught a fresh piney scent and realized I'd been smelling it for some time. One of the trees I was seeking was standing inconspicuously all around me: knee- and waist-high seedlings of balsam fir, small, pyramidal spires whose dark, gleaming needles looked so perfectly formed that, had I seen the trees at Christmas in someone's living room, I'd have suspected: *artificial.* But these were real trees, thriving in the shade of taller hemlocks, pines, and hardwoods.

Balsam fir is common in the vast forests of northern Canada. I have often seen the trees, and smelled their clean fragrance, in the canoe country

Black spruce and balsam fir are northern trees found in chilly upland bogs such as the one at Algerine Swamp Natural Area.

of northern Minnesota. The balsam fir is the only fir native to
Pennsylvania, and its range extends
south in the mountains as far as
Virginia. Wrote Donald Culross
Peattie in *A Natural History of Trees,*
"the delicious spicy fragrance of
Balsam needles is the dearest odor
in all of Nature." The short needles
grow in opposing rows on the
twigs and look a bit like fletching
on an arrow. The wood is light—
only twenty-six pounds to the
cubic foot, dry weight (white oak,
by comparison, is forty-eight
pounds)—and is weak and quick
to decay once it lies on the
ground. Its main commercial use
is as pulp for paper. Balsam fir
releases many tiny, purplish seeds
from its cones, which are held

upright (distinctive among the
conifers) on the tree's upper
branches. Chickadees and crossbills
relish the seeds, and deer browse
the soft needles and branch tips in
winter.

*The pitcher plant traps insects in its vaselike,
water-filled leaves. These rare plants are
protected within the Algerine Swamp Natural
Area.*

Spotting an area of light to the north, I headed in that direction. Soon
my rubber boots were poised on the quaking, saturated sphagnum mat of
Algerine Swamp. On the edge of the peatland, I found several older balsam
firs. Tiny blisters of resin studded the trees' smooth, grayish bark. The firs
were shaped like tall pyramids, each branch angling slightly upward.

Another tree—its foliage scrubbier and sparser than that of the balsam
fir—pushed up from the bog. Black spruce is slightly less shade-tolerant
than balsam fir. It frequents cold, poorly drained swamps; it is the dominant
tree in the muskeg bogs of Canada, although up north it also colonizes dry
sites away from the water.

"Steeple-shaped" is the way many authors describe the black spruce. The trees at Algerine Swamp had plumes of dark bluish green foliage near the tops of their trunks. The trees were not tall: thirty feet, maximum, with many of them only head-high. Growth is slow when a tree's roots have no contact with mineral soil.

In a quaking bog, the roots of a black spruce may spread out as a mesh, like a snowshoe, to stabilize the tree on the uncertain surface. As it grows taller and becomes heavier, the tree may sink down into the bog. From its trunk, it pushes out side roots, which send up their own shoots. The shoots take root and become trees, so that the taller parent—perhaps wind-toppled or with a broken-off trunk—is surrounded by a ring of younger, shorter versions of itself.

Lichens clung to the trunks and dead branch stubs of the black spruces at Algerine Swamp: blue-green scabby lichens and pale green fuzzy ones. Out on the bog mat grew white pine, pitch pine, and eastern hemlock, as well as the black spruce and balsam fir. The breeze coaxed separate sounds from the evergreen foliage of each. The scudding clouds, the mingled scents of the conifers, and the deep and raspy voice of a raven gave the morning a decidedly northern air.

TO GET THERE. From the general store in Slate Run, drive north on PA Route 414 for 3.9 miles to Gamble Run Road. Turn left. Ascend Gamble Run Road past Algerine Lane (at 2.1 miles) and Buskirk Trail (at 2.3 miles), until the road begins to descend; the sign for Algerine Swamp Natural Area is on the left, 3.0 miles from where Gamble Run Road left Route 414. Park on the left just beyond the sign and head west, using a compass and the Cedar Run, Pennsylvania, topographic quadrangle (on which Algerine Swamp, bisected by the Tioga-Lycoming County line, is labeled "Tamarack Swamp"). Red Run drains from the bog's west end.

About half of Algerine Swamp is privately owned. A wire fence and a series of signs mark the border between private and Bureau of Forestry holdings.

An excellent outing can be spent shared between Algerine Swamp Natural Area and Reynolds Spring Natural Area (page 194), about a mile to the north.

44   BARK CABIN

73 ACRES, TIADAGHTON STATE FOREST, LYCOMING COUNTY

It was the strangest sort of rain: nuts and fragments of nuts, pattering down through the leaves and landing on the ground at my feet. I stared up into the crown of a hickory towering over my head. The tree was either a pignut or a bitternut hickory, judging from its tight, shallow-fissured, pale gray bark, and by the size of the nut—about an inch and a half in length—that smacked the ground beside me.

I took a few steps forward on the trail, not wishing to be beaned by one of those hard, green missiles, and spotted a shape high in the canopy: the gray squirrel leaped to a new branch and resumed cutting nuts.

I had not been prepared for the diversity of tree species I was finding at Bark Cabin Natural Area, which the Bureau of Forestry booklet characterized simply as "a remote grove of old growth eastern hemlock in 73 acres along a tributary of Bark Cabin Run."

Northern red oak, straight and thick, showed bristle-tipped leaves against the milky August sky. A black cherry: its bark like flat, gray wood chips pasted onto a thick cylinder. An American beech, whose pale green leaves showed a hint of yellow, predicting the color it would assume come fall. White ash, white oak, and white pine: all of them impressively big trees, their different-textured crowns meshing high overhead. I spotted one of the tallest, thickest, straightest paper birches I have seen in

In the understory beneath old-growth trees at Bark Cabin Natural Area, a witch hazel spreads its leaves to capture sunlight.

Pennsylvania, almost as robust as the birches I've canoed past on wild rivers and lakes in Minnesota. And an improbably tall bigtooth aspen, its crown right up there with the red oaks and hemlocks. The stand also included large chestnut oaks, red maples, yellow birches, black gums, and tuliptrees. Immense white pine stumps had ferns growing out of their jagged sawdust tops and roots as thick as my waist, relics of the logging era. They made me think: now *those* were really big trees.

I sat with my back against the largest hemlock I could find. On the other side of the giant trunk lay a heap of sawdust, which meant the tree was at least partly hollow. The hemlock probably would not live many years longer, and indeed, some other hemlocks at Bark Cabin Natural Area lay broken and rotting on the ground, or stood bare of bark, absent their branches, their trunks pocked and riddled by woodpecker holes.

A gray squirrel gave its catlike squalling call, punctuated by bouts of chattering. A band of blue jays sent their agitated *jay-jay* calls echoing through the woods. Soon a red-tailed hawk went flying between the trees, and I understood what had roused the jays' ire.

TO GET THERE. Drive north from Waterville on SR 4001 toward Little Pine State Park. After 3.2 miles, turn left on Boone Road. Soon after the turn, go straight past a log house (avoiding a road for a commercial campground that bears sharply to the left), and soon you will see a sign for state forest land. After 2.2 miles, turn right on Okome Road. Drive another 2.9 miles, and turn right on Schoolhouse Road. After 0.2 mile, turn left on Hackett Road; this road is rough and rutted, and unless you have a four-wheel-drive with good clearance, you should park and walk.

The Mid-State Trail crosses Hackett Road 0.8 mile from the Hackett Road–Schoolhouse Road junction. Turn left (northwest) on the trail, which starts off as a forest road through a grove of white pines. Take care not to miss the turnoff, signaled by a double orange paint blaze, where the Mid-State Trail leaves the forest road to the right. Stay on the Mid-State until it crosses the Ott Fork of Bark Cabin Run. Turn left off the footpath and, with the run on your left, walk through the open understory of the hemlock grove until you come to a logged area. The largest trees in the natural area are near the boundary with the logged-over private land; you will see them if you turn right at the border and explore the woods, keeping the boundary line on your left. When you arrive at a powerline right-of-way on the left, turn right and keep walking among the trees until you join the Mid-State Trail again. Make another right turn, and retrace your steps to Hackett Road.

The Cammal, Pennsylvania, topographic quadrangle includes the Ott Fork of Bark Cabin Run. The natural area is on the northwest bank of the stream.

45   DEVIL'S ELBOW

404 ACRES, TIADAGHTON STATE FOREST, LYCOMING COUNTY

It was late August, and the last of the highbush blueberries hung ripe and overripe, head high on the shrubs' arching stems. As summer faded into fall, the leaves of the bog plants were beginning to brighten, showing flecks and tints of maroon, orange, and red.

The pitcher plants were reddening, the deep, rich color of their veins now spreading to cover the entire pitcher-shaped, water-containing leaves of the carnivorous plants: so many pitcher plants that I stopped and stared before walking out onto the unstable mat of sphagnum moss. The bog at Devil's Elbow lies on top of a plateau at twenty-two hundred feet of elevation. It supports round-leaved sundews, rare orchids, several species of sedges, rhododendrons, bog laurel, and coniferous and deciduous trees.

The flowers of the pitcher plants dangled at the ends of tall, upright stems, reminding me of ornate desk lamps with mauve-colored shades. Bog cotton spangled the bog, a pale galaxy of white seedheads suspended a foot or two above the damp mat and stretching from one end of the wetland to the other. In the surrounding woods, the feathery needles of white pines and the blackish green boughs of hemlocks stood out against the paler leaves of hardwood trees, including American beech, black cherry, black and yellow birches, and red and sugar maples.

I squatted down, my rubber boots sinking slowly into the sphagnum, bubbles of pungent gas popping on the surface of the quaking mat. I took in the rich color palette, the many shades of green and red merging like an intricate tapestry, set off by the barkless trunks and branches of standing dead trees turned silvery by weather and time. At my feet, the large, round fruits of wild cranberry were turning pink. I picked and ate a couple of bog dewberries, black and seedy and sweet, which hung from trailing thorny vines decked with toothed, green leaves slowly turning red.

Between two velvety clumps of sphagnum grew several sundew plants. Sundews are thought to have a southern, perhaps even a near-tropical, origin: they grow slowly during the cool temperatures of spring and fall, but in summer the bright sun stimulates them into rapid expansion. Today the sky's milky light caused the sundews' pinkish leaves to glow subtly. Each

In late summer, the fluffy seedheads of bog cotton spangle the ground at Devil's Elbow Natural Area.

leaf—there were ten to a dozen or more per plant—resembled an inch-long tennis racket covered with little spikes, each spike ending in a blob of bright pink liquid. The liquid has a subtly sweet smell, and the deceptive perfume—along with the flower-mimicking color—lures in insects. The insects get stuck in the liquid, which is as viscous as tar. Then the plant goes into action. It folds tentaclelike hairs around the insect's body. The tentacles don't actually move; rather, they grow swiftly, with fast cell division commencing less than two minutes after prey becomes ensnared. A tentacle can completely lasso a struggling insect in half an hour.

As the plant holds the creature in an ever-more-intimate embrace, shorter hairs on the leaves' inner surfaces release anesthetizing compounds and digestive enzymes. The enzymes dissolve the insect's flesh, which the leaf takes in and later distributes to other parts of the plant. When all that remains of the prey are shards of indigestible chitin, the leaf unfurls and the spikes stick out again: the trap is reset. A leaf can repeat this sequence several times during one growing season. Sundews do not require animal protein to survive and grow, but the plants do a better job at both if they manage to snare a few midges or mosquitoes.

In not too many nights, when the first frost settled on the low, boggy land, the leaves of the sundews would shrivel. The plants would stay hun-

The carnivorous pitcher plant turns a deep rich maroon in autumn.

kered down in the sphagnum moss, living roots and hibernating leaf buds waiting to put forth new growth in spring. Hunkered down myself on the bog, I knew that the leaves were only a temporary part of the plant—yet I could not bring myself to rise and strike off across the wetland, fearing I would trample the vegetation. Instead, I studied the sundews through my magnifying lens and used binoculars to scan the beds of pitcher plants.

TO GET THERE. From Main and Water Streets in the Bradford County village of Grover, south of Canton on PA Route 14, go east on the Grover-Wheelerville Road (SR 3012) 0.3 mile to two white churches. Between the churches, which are catercorner to one another, turn right on Ellenton Mountain Road, SR 3003. After 4.6 miles, there is a parking area on the right for the natural area. To begin your hike, cross the road from the parking area and enter at the metal gate.

Request the free map for the Old Loggers Path and Hawkeye Cross Country Ski Trails from the Tiadaghton State Forest district office or the Bureau of Forestry in Harrisburg. Sand Springs Trail, a 3-mile loop, circles around the four small bogs at Devil's Elbow Natural Area. The southern and eastern parts of the trail are on an old railroad grade, and the path is excellent for cross-country skiing.

The name Devil's Elbow refers to a sharp turn in the road southeast of the bog.

46   LEBO RED PINE

124 ACRES, TIADAGHTON STATE FOREST, LYCOMING COUNTY

Most of the red pines I have seen in Pennsylvania were growing in rows: plantations started by the Bureau of Forestry during the first half of the twentieth century to reforest woodlands that were logged by private companies and abandoned to repeated scourging by wildfires.

These red pines were different.

They grew on a north-facing slope that was steep enough, in places, to force me to haul myself about by holding onto mountain laurel boughs. Branch stubs studded the tall, straight trunks of the red pines, starting about two-thirds of the way up. The trunks tapered slightly as they mounted to where the crowns hung in the air like dark clouds. The upper portions of the trunks and the thick, twisted branches caught the light and gave off a telltale reddish orange color: the color of its bark earns the red pine its name. At ground level, where the trunks were about eighteen inches in diameter, the bark consisted of large gray-brown plates. Many of the plates had flaked off between the shallow furrows, revealing a ruddy or orangish layer beneath. The bark of a nearby white pine looked almost black by comparison.

Red pines are not common in Pennsylvania. *Pinus resinosa* is a species of the north. In Canada, it grows from Newfoundland to Manitoba. Red pine occurs in Minnesota, Wisconsin, and Michigan, surrounding the northern shores of the Great Lakes; on canoe trips in the Boundary Waters Wilderness of northern Minnesota, I have pitched my tent in mixed groves of white and red pines, smelled their clean, astringent scent, and been serenaded by the breeze in the boughs mingling high overhead. In the East, the red pine's range comes as far south in the mountains as north-central Pennsylvania and West Virginia. I have seen red pines decorating the campus of Penn State University and growing in monotonous cropfield rows on the flat land surrounding the lake at Black Moshannon State Park in Centre County.

These Lycoming County specimens were red pines planted by nature rather than by man. It is thought that two centuries in the past (for that is how old the trees proved to be, when foresters took corings a few years ago), a tree-gobbling fire swept up the slope above the First Big Fork of Trout Run—which was not then known as the First Big Fork of Trout Run, because European settlement hadn't yet penetrated into this wild, mountainous region. After the fire, red pine seeds drifted in: *Pinus resinosa* produces large quantities of lightweight, winged seeds that are blown about by the wind. The north-facing slope proved to be a hospitable place. The trees are not massive, but they are considered to be old-growth, and I found it impressive how they reared their crowns above lesser hardwoods in the stand.

A deer trail slanted downhill, and I followed it. On the trail lay several piles of coyote scat, along with many red pinecones. The cones were chestnut brown and a little larger than a Ping-Pong ball,

Red pine, a rare tree in Pennsylvania, can be identified by its distinctive bark. A grove of old-growth red pines stands at Lebo Red Pine Natural Area.

with a trim, slightly elongated shape. The cones carry the tree's seeds. Red pine seeds need open, sunny places in which to germinate and grow. The only seedlings beneath the Lebo red pines were eastern hemlock and white pine, which are more tolerant of shady conditions. However, on the powerline right-of-way that gives access to the natural area (and which, unfortunately, split the stand when it was put in during the 1960s), I found several young red pines. They gave me a close-up look at the needles: dark green, slender, limber, four to six inches long, and bound in clusters of two. In contrast, the needles of the more common white pine are two and a half to five inches long and packaged in bundles of five.

On that muggy morning in August, I spent several hours exploring the natural area. Other trees in the stand included red and chestnut oaks, black and paper birches, and red maples. I heard a pileated woodpecker calling from somewhere in the canopy, a raven's far-off croaking, and a chipmunk scurrying through the leaves. I met a young hermit thrush hunting for insects in a small spring seep on the slope; it flitted away, then perched to watch me as I picked my way among the rocks and through the mountain laurel.

The mature red pines looked healthy, with only a few of them fallen or standing dead. Would hardwoods someday overtop them? Except for the red oaks, the hardwood species in the stand would not be very tall at maturity. Would a slowly warming climate cause the pines to die out? Perhaps the red pines will prove to be a barometer of tree response to global warming. It is for such purposes—as well as providing a place for sitting quietly and listening to wind and rodent scufflings and sweet birdcalls—that conservationists set aside the state forest natural areas.

> **TO GET THERE.** From the bridge in Waterville, in western Lycoming County, drive north on PA Route 44. After 6.7 miles, turn right in Haneyville. Continue beyond Haneyville another 3.6 miles on Route 44, then turn right on Lebo Road. After 2.4 miles, you come to a powerline right-of-way. Park on the left in a grassy area next to a service road.
>
> Walk on the service road as far as the steep drop into the hollow containing the First Big Fork of Trout Run; where the service road swings to the left, leave it and go to the right, crossing the right-of-way through huckleberry and sweetfern. (Watch out for snakes.) The red pines are on the north side of the right-of-way just below where the slope drops off from the relatively flat tableland. The natural area is marked "Red Pine N.A." on the Tiadaghton State Forest public-use map. It is in the southeast corner of the Slate Run, Pennsylvania, topographic quadrangle, near where the Slate Run, Cammal, Glen Union, and Jersey Mills quadrangles come together.

47   MILLER RUN

4,987 ACRES, TIADAGHTON STATE FOREST, LYCOMING COUNTY

Miller Run Natural Area is so large that it could easily qualify as a state forest wild area. A wild area is an extensive tract of state land where, according to a Bureau of Forestry description, people can enjoy "such activities as hiking, hunting, fishing, and the pursuit of peace and solitude." The five thousand acres of Miller Run Natural Area encompass four small stream drainages: Miller Run (with three tributaries, each a half mile to a mile long), Solomon Run, Shanty Run, and McClure Run. The streams flow in a northeasterly direction, draining into Pine Creek between the villages of Cammal and Jersey Mills. The area is rocky and remote, with plenty of ups and downs, in summer a pure unbroken green.

Many routes lead into and through Miller Run Natural Area—or so the Tiadaghton State Forest public-use map implies. Before going there, I spoke with forester Charlie Schwartz. I wondered if I might make a loop hike starting from Lebo Road and descending Sam Carson Trail to Miller Run, then trekking west up the run to another footpath, marked Poff Trail on the public-use map, and ascending on Poff Trail to Lebo Road, and then back to my car. In theory, it could be done. But, Schwartz admitted, he hadn't been down the Poff Trail in years, and he wasn't sure it was still passable. The route I'd suggested would require stamina, map-reading skills, and perhaps more time than the single August afternoon I could spend.

I decided to hike down the Carson Trail and, when I reached Miller Run, make a decision about where to head then.

Leaving Lebo Road, I walked cautiously through waist-high huckleberry and between patches of mountain laurel, advancing my wooden hiking staff in front of my feet and listening for that sudden warning buzz: this first section of trail led me through what looked like a prime habitat for timber rattlesnakes. On either hand grew areas of bear oak, a low, straggling oak species that's more of a shrub than a tree, mixed in with sweet and bracken ferns. The trail passed white, red, and chestnut oaks, with here and there a gaunt-looking pitch pine, one of whose cones I picked up from the path. The cone was about two and a half inches long, and it had a prickly feel to it, caused by a small burr on the lower tip of each cone scale.

As the path descended, the oak forest gave way to northern hardwoods. A few paper birches held up their white branches, and I began seeing white ash, yellow and black birches, American basswood, and red maple. Beneath the trees, deep green Christmas ferns grew in clumps. American beech trees had smooth, pale gray bark. The northern hardwoods show a different green than the oak forest, paler and more metallic looking. The pale green provided a greater contrast with the dark green of the hemlocks standing along the dry streambed. Throughout the woods were old white pine stumps left by long-ago loggers, slowly breaking down into reddish dust.

The trail became indistinct. However, if I kept walking down the streambed, I knew I would eventually come to Miller Run, a thousand feet in elevation below where I'd started my walk. The lack of a trail, and the intact patches of ferns through which I picked my way, made me wonder if I was the first person to walk down the hollow all summer.

A strange plant brought me up short. Since it was no longer in flower, it took some time for me to find it in *Newcomb's Wildflower Guide*. The leaves were divided into wide-spreading leaflets with toothed edges. A thick, blood red stalk bore the fruit, a dozen silken white berries, each with a prominent purplish dot on the end. White baneberry, *Newcomb's* told me, is also known as "doll's eyes" for its conspicuous pale fruit. The plant is poisonous, particularly its roots and berries. As few as six berries can bring on diarrhea, vomiting, dizziness, and delirium, and the roots contain a violent purgative.

An hour's steady hiking brought me to Miller Run. There I found several clearings, the remains of an old logging camp. A century ago, a logging railroad extended up the hollow; logs were carried on flatbed cars to the mouth of the run, then splashed into Pine Creek and floated to the huge steel-chain boom that spanned the Susquehanna at Williamsport, there to be sorted and taken to the lumbermill. Now the clearings were grown with Queen Anne's lace, mosses, and small white pines. White snakeroot was blooming, and bumblebees visited the abundant white wood asters. The orange flowers of jewelweed nodded on their stems, and on the bank of Miller Run, bee balm shed its raggedy scarlet petals into the water.

A short walk convinced me that an unimproved trail led up Miller Run. I decided not to take it, and instead to walk downstream toward Pine Creek rather than risking not being able to locate Poff Trail a mile and more upstream.

Now the walking was easy. Depressions lay where wooden ties had rotted away on the broad, flat railroad grade. Beech nutlets, still encased in their prickly burs, littered the ground. Bald-faced hornets hunted for insects around my boots; their buzzing was the only sound save for the melodic tinkling of Miller Run.

The stream had carved out a fluted passageway through reddish moss-covered rocks, with rivulets separating quiet pools, one of which was deep enough to allow a tired walker to take a cooling swim. A small waterfall fed the pool, and ferns and vines cloaked the surrounding rock walls.

Eventually I turned and retraced my steps. A tough two hours later, I emerged at the head of Sam Carson Trail. In the dusk, I came face-to-face with a gray fox padding along on Lebo Road. The fox swapped ends and dashed off into the scrub oak—for me, a satisfying ending to a day spent in a superb wild place.

TO GET THERE. For the hike I have described, drive north on PA Route 44 from the bridge in Waterville. After 6.7 miles, turn right in Haneyville. Continue beyond Haneyville another 3.6 miles on Route 44, then turn right on Lebo Road. After 2.2 miles, look sharp for a small grassy parking spot on the left, large enough for one car; if you come to a powerline, you have gone about 100 yards too far. Across from the parking spot is a pitch pine with a severe wound where someone hacked a blaze into its bark.

Sam Carson Trail begins just to the left of the pitch pine. The path dwindles soon after leaving the plateau in its descent toward Miller Run, which is around 1.4 miles away and, at 900 feet of elevation, about 1,000 feet lower than where you parked. Turn left (east) on Miller Run to find several pools along a pleasant trail leading to Pine Creek. Retrace your route up Sam Carson Trail to return to your car. Consult the state forest public-use map and the Cammal, Pennsylvania, topographic quadrangle. Be sure to carry the topo map and a compass.

Miller Run can also be reached by crossing Pine Creek during low water in summer.

Most of Miller Run Natural Area is second-growth forest, but patches of old-growth trees remain along Solomon Run and Shanty Run, white pines and hemlocks two feet and larger in diameter. Near Sinking Springs Road, in the southern part of the natural area, an insect pest called the oak leaf roller devastated many acres, which were later burned by a forest fire.

Lebo Road bounds the natural area to the north. It ends at Lebo Vista, with a lookout over Pine Creek and the mountains cradling the great stream; unfortunately, several powerlines mar the view. From Sinking Springs Road, on the southern boundary of the natural area, a spur road (for four-wheel-drive vehicles) leads north to another overlook with glimpses into the burned section of the natural area.

48   TORBERT ISLAND

18 ACRES, TIADAGHTON STATE FOREST, LYCOMING COUNTY

The mink crouched on the edge of the ice. It did a sudden nosedive into Pine Creek and disappeared beneath the swift, dark water, only to emerge again, swimming downstream along the frozen fringe that extended out from the shore toward Torbert Island.

The mink—a large weasel with a long, sinuous body that appeared dark brown in the dirty light—kept hauling itself out onto the ice, looking around, and then diving into the creek again. It swam strongly, in agile bursts, frequently ducking its head underwater. Perhaps it was hunting for crayfish, a favorite prey, among stones in the stream bottom. Finally the mink swam across the channel and emerged on the ice rimming tree-covered Torbert Island. When open water freezes over—a condition toward which Pine Creek was rapidly progressing during this uncommonly cold December—

minks may abandon their streamside habitats and spend more time in woodlands, where they often den in woodchuck or rabbit burrows. Torbert Island
was an excellent place for a mink to find both food and shelter.

I was kicking myself for not visiting the island earlier in the year. In
summer, I could have waded to it in sneakers and a swimsuit: the current in
the west channel is gentle during low water conditions. I had contemplated
a canoe trip leading to a thorough exploration, but with the year winding
down and ice starting to seal off Pine Creek, launching a boat was now out
of the question.

So I was reduced to inspecting Torbert Island using binoculars. The
mink, now slipping along on the shore of the island, insinuating its body
between stranded logs and patches of brush, was a huge bonus, an exciting,
seldom-seen predator, much more than I'd expected to witness.

Many houses and summer camps stand on both sides of Pine Creek
near Torbert Island. Farmland extends down to the water in places. The
island is less than a hundred yards wide and not quite half a mile long. It is
a rich habitat used by many amphibians, reptiles, birds, and mammals. As
forester Charlie Schwartz told me, "We don't have much riparian forest
growing on state forest land, and that's why Torbert Island was made a natural area." *Riparian* comes from the Latin *riparius,* or "bank," and is used to
describe things growing on, living along, or pertaining to the banks of a
natural course of water.

Schwartz had mentioned sugar maple, river birch, sycamore, and basswood growing on Torbert Island, trees that I could easily identify from
where I now stood, a wide spot on the snow-covered road elevated above
Pine Creek's west bank. A host of plants grow in the damp, silty bottomland soil blanketing the island, including large specimens of jack-in-the-pulpit and its less common relative, dragon arum. Invasive non-native plants,
particularly Japanese knotweed and dame's rocket, flourish on the island,
crowding out some native species.

Winter, however, was not a good time to observe plants. Fortunately, I
found plenty of birds to focus my binoculars on.

Right around me, and trading back and forth with the island fifty yards
off, was a mix of winter species, the birds all ignoring me as they searched
intently for food. Male cardinals were splashes of scarlet against the grays
and browns of the brushy woods; female cardinals were more muted, their
olive plumage accented with touches of red on the head crest and the tail,
their thick, seed-cracking beaks standing out as red-orange triangles. A

brown creeper—dull brown and only five inches long from the end of its curving bill to the tip of its stiff tail—crept in a spiral pattern up the bark of a black cherry, probing between plates of bark to find insects. A hairy woodpecker, a flicker, and a red-bellied woodpecker all shared the same black birch tree, snapping up the frost-gray berries on a poison ivy vine that coiled up the tree's trunk. On sloping ground nearer the stream, dark-eyed juncos and song sparrows gleaned fallen seeds.

Blue jays, white-breasted nuthatches, and American robins augmented the feeding flock. Crows flapped overhead, descending quickly to land in the trees on Torbert Island, where they began ranting at a red-tailed hawk; the hawk flew upstream on pale wings, the crows tagging along after it.

TO GET THERE. Between the towns of Avis and Jersey Shore, take the PA Route 44 exit off U.S. Route 220. Go north on Route 44 less than 0.2 mile, and turn left before the highway crosses Pine Creek on a bridge. Drive along the west shore of Pine Creek, with the water on your right, for 0.25 mile to a stop sign. Continue straight through at the sign. After another 1.0 mile, the road curves left and heads up the hollow: you turn right, crossing a small bridge near several houses. The road ascends, then curves back toward Pine Creek, and Torbert Island lies below the road less than 100 yards away. After 0.5 mile, there is a wide area where you can park and look out over the island. If you continue another 0.2 mile, you reach a sign for state forest land near the island's north end.

For a canoe trip, take along a friend and leave one vehicle at Torbert Access Area, on Route 44, 1.8 miles upstream from where the highway crosses Pine Creek; then drive, with partner and canoe, in a second vehicle to the Ramsey Access Area 7.2 miles upstream from the highway bridge. The float down Pine Creek takes you past Pine Breeze Island, which the state is in the process of acquiring for possible addition to the natural area system, and then Torbert Island. Both the Torbert and Ramsey Access Areas are on state forest lands.

---

49   CRANBERRY SWAMP

144 ACRES, SPROUL STATE FOREST, CLINTON COUNTY

I sloshed through the narrow, black-water stream and stepped onto the pine island in the middle of the swamp. White pines and pitch pines. The humid, midsummer heat and the breeze soughing through the conifers' crowns brought South Florida to my mind: there, the damp, grassy savannas are dotted with hammocks, rises of land sometimes colonized by yellow pine, through whose long and limber needles the southern breeze whispers.

It was a distinctly northern bird, however, on which I had trained my binoculars. The black-capped chickadee hung upside down from a pine branch, scolding me. Beyond the chickadee, a black-and-white warbler hitched itself up a tree's trunk, shifting from side to side with each hop as it searched for insects and spiders. Hermit thrushes sang from the shadows— desultorily, on this hot day in early August; Pennsylvania is about as far south as these birds breed in the East, and hermit thrushes are often found in damp coniferous woods. A few steps farther on, I spotted a small fly-catcher, which, before I could even try to identify it, flitted off in pursuit of some insect that I couldn't see. And a solitary vireo—with white eye rings and throat set off by a slate blue head—gave me a good minute of observation time as it caught and ate a caterpillar.

While standing quietly, absorbed by the birds, I noticed a black shape moving through the swamp. The bear was about the size of a Labrador retriever. It was biting off the seed heads of sedges and stopping to turn over rotten logs to look for insects. I could see the bear clearly for a while, then only the grasses swaying, then a patch of moving black, then the level line of the bear's back as it fed past me thirty yards away. I was fairly sure the bear was on its own, but I kept still and watched out for a sow, which did not appear.

After a while, the bear worked its way into the stream of my scent. It rose slowly on its hind legs and stood there limp-wristed, head high, nose twitching, trying to figure out where I was. Apparently its mother had taught it well, for it dropped to all fours (rather than falling over backward, as did a young bruin that my wife had watched a few weeks earlier) and quickly padded away.

Cranberry Swamp Natural Area, the headwaters of Cranberry Run, fills a basin between low ridges. The surrounding forest is mostly oak, with scattered red maples, black cherries, and birches. The swamp itself is about half a mile long and a few hundred yards wide; it was drier than I had fore-seen (I wore rubber knee-boots, which were necessary in only a few places), its surface covered with rushes, sedges, cattails, and grasses. Old pine stumps showed where great trees had stood before loggers took them around 1915. At the northwestern or upstream end of the wetland, broad beds of spirea—also known as hardhack and steeplebush—held high their steeple-shaped clusters of bright, rose pink flowers. Among the grasses, I spotted song sparrows and scared a pair of yellowthroats off their nest.

Less than a minute after I saw the bear, a big doe fed toward me. I happened to be positioned so that a pine stump stood between me and the deer. I was making a certain amount of noise, jotting down my observations of the birds and the bear, but the doe didn't run—she just watched me, her head raised high on a sleek, slender neck, her ears aimed in my direction. When I waved my notepad at her, she actually took a few steps toward me.

"Hello there," I said, which sent her veering off through the huckleberry and provoked a loud snort from another deer I hadn't seen. It was late in the day, and I couldn't stay much longer. I wondered what might have come past—walking, stalking, slithering, crawling, fluttering—had I sat in that one prolific spot all day.

TO GET THERE. From the village of Moshannon, west of the Snow Shoe exit off I-80, travel north on PA Route 144, the Ridge Road, 22.2 miles and turn right on Petes Run Road. After 2.6 miles, turn right on Benjamin Run Road. Continue another 0.5 mile and park next to a woods road descending to the right. (If you come to a gas well, you have missed the parking spot; turn around on Benjamin Run Road and come back.) Hike downhill, immediately crossing a gas pipeline right-of-way. Where a camp lane bears to the right, keep to the left, remaining on the main woods road. About half a mile from where you parked, you come to a second pipeline right-of-way with a chain-link fence. Turn right and follow the right-of-way into the upper end of Cranberry Swamp.

The Chuck Keiper Trail crosses Cranberry Run over a wooden footbridge at the south end of the wetland. The Renovo East and Howard Northwest topographic quadrangles bracket the natural area. The Sproul State Forest public-use map shows a trail on the west side of the area, but that footpath is faint and pretty rough going. The trail along the east side of the swamp, although not marked, is well used and easy to follow.

---

50 EAST BRANCH SWAMP

186 ACRES, SPROUL STATE FOREST, CLINTON COUNTY

On the night of May 31, 1985, a powerful storm swept through the Northeast. Its frontal edge stretched from Ohio to Ontario. The storm spawned six tornadoes, one of which touched down near Parker Dam State Park in Clearfield County. With wind speeds of nearly three hundred miles per hour, the tornado tracked eastward through the Quehanna region of the Moshannon State Forest, crossed the West Branch of the Susquehanna, and churned into the Sproul State Forest. For fifty miles it carved a swath

Huge weathered stumps mark where old-growth white pines stood before loggers cut the trees around 1900.

through the woods varying in width from one-half mile to two miles. I remember the near-constant thunder and lightning of that appalling night; later I found book pages, family photographs, and a business ledger from a store in a town in western Pennsylvania, all scattered through our woods, twenty-five miles south of the tornado's path.

The storm left its mark on the East Branch Swamp Natural Area. East Branch Trail, part of the Chuck Keiper Trail system, winds through an area denuded by the storm, brushy and tangled, with uprooted trees, leaning trees, trees snapped off halfway up their trunks. The *Atlas of Pennsylvania* lists East Branch Swamp as an example of a mixed-hardwood swamp, a closed-canopy wetland that generally occurs on mineral soils, mud, or muck, but not on peat. The part of the wetland I had so far traversed did not have a closed canopy of trees; the tornado had taken care of that.

Phoebes, myrtle warblers, and rufous-sided towhees foraged in the brush along the trail's edge. I found a grouse's breast feather—white barred with dark brown—lying on the path. I stopped when I heard a rustling in the brush: a large buck with a wide eight-point rack, bulbous and covered with velvet, came browsing slowly along. As I watched him through my binoculars, I felt the breeze shift to the back of my neck. It didn't take the buck long to catch my scent. When he did, he departed without fanfare: took a few steps, faded into the thicket, was gone.

The orange-blazed trail became a tunnel through rhododendrons and mountain laurel, shrubby hemlocks and pines, white oaks, red maples, yellow birches, and mountain ashes. In the middle of the path lay a mound of bear droppings so voluminous a horse would have shied at it. It was old enough to be covered with mold, so I didn't feel too jittery, following the only easy route through the blowdown for both man and beast.

Soon the forest opened up, and the sun shone down on the trail. Grasses, rushes, sedges, and goldenrod grew between scattered wind-damaged trees. Leaving the trail, I followed a feeder stream west into the swamp, though sedge meadows and mats of spongy sphagnum moss colored green and red. The green variety of sphagnum favors damper parts of a wetland, and the red species prospers in drier zones.

Alders and red maples grew in the saturated soil. Cotton grasses had begun putting out their soft, fluffy flowers, which look like small tufts of cotton; the flowers are wind-pollinated, and their seeds also disperse on the wind in autumn. The feathery flower heads of wool grass, *Scirpus cyperinus,* waved in the breeze, along with their slender, leafy bracts.

On the unshaded wetland, the August sun was hot and glaring. Heat waves rose from the grass. A raven passing high overhead gave a whimsical snoring call. Bees buzzed softly. A gentle breeze caressed the plants of the marsh and whistled in the tops of hemlocks and pines. How different from that hellish night fifteen years past.

TO GET THERE. From the village of Moshannon, just west of the Snow Shoe exit off I-80, go north on PA Route 144 (also known as the Ridge Road) for 21.6 miles to an area known as State Camp, where several hunting camps stand near the highway. Look for a double orange paint blaze on a small tamarack tree, marking where the Chuck Keiper Trail crosses the road. Park on the south side of the highway. Hike southeast on the trail, which takes you across a gas pipeline right-of-way and then along the east edge of East Branch Swamp. Return via the same route. Request a copy of the Chuck Keiper Trail map from the Bureau of Forestry.

51 TAMARACK SWAMP

86 ACRES, SPROUL STATE FOREST, CLINTON COUNTY

At Tamarack Swamp on a sunny December day, I remembered that Donald Peattie, in *A Natural History of Trees,* described the tamarack tree in winter as "the deadest looking vegetation on the globe."

Tamarack *(Larix laricina)*, also called larch, is an uncommon tree in Pennsylvania. It grows mainly in bogs such as Tamarack Swamp in the northern part of the state. It is our only deciduous conifer: our only cone-producing, needle-leaved tree to drop all of its foliage in the fall in much the same way that an oak or a maple or a hickory sheds its leaves.

Tamaracks dotted the broad basin of the snow-covered swamp. They jutted up above the highbush blueberry and bog rosemary and among the patches of low gnarled alders. Without their needles, the tamaracks looked lifeless indeed. In the ruddy light, their crowns were pyramids of naked, grayish twigs that seemed to hover insubstantially above the reddish brown trunks.

The tamarack grows farther north than any other American tree, spanning the continent from Labrador to Alaska. In the East, it extends south as far as the mountains of northern West Virginia. The tree grows slowly, particularly in the nutrient-poor environment of a bog. According to Hal Borland in *A Countryman's Woods,* a tamarack may take 250 years to achieve a trunk diameter of twenty inches.

In spring, tamaracks put forth needles that are about an inch long, triangular in cross section, and clustered in little tufts all over the twigs and branches. The new needles shine a bright pale green—"like a rime of light and life," wrote Peattie. Some that I've seen have been a handsome frosty blue-green. But five long months would have to pass before the skeletal trees at Tamarack Swamp would send forth new needles. Many of the tamaracks were thick with cones, small, pale brown ovals about three-quarters of an inch long. Tamarack cones look somewhat like hemlock cones, except that tamaracks bear their cones on the upper surfaces of their twigs instead of dangling them, hemlock-fashion, at the tips of branchlets. In the West, blue and spruce grouses feed on needles and buds of tamaracks—do our ruffed grouse ever sample this fare?—and red crossbills occasionally eat the small, winged seeds. Porcupines go after the trees' bark.

Butch Davey, the local district forester, advised me that parts of Tamarack Swamp are extremely thick and treacherous. "It's a good environment to study plants and animals," he said, "but it's not a place to go if you're looking for an afternoon hike." I'm certain that is excellent advice during spring, summer, and fall; but on this winter day, with the bog frozen solid, I was free to wander throughout the wetland.

Along the bog's edge, ruffed grouse tracks pottered here and there among the alders. I found where one bird had taken to the air, each wingtip carving dainty, fanlike marks in the snow. Farther on, a brown creature sud-

Tamarack, or larch, trees turn yellow in fall, then shed their needles before winter.

denly darted out at my feet, its white tail flashing: the rabbit sped across the ground, dodging this way and that between the hummocks, and soon vanished from sight. I backtracked and found where the cottontail had bedded in a sheltered spot beneath a small, wind-toppled black spruce. Like the tamarack, the black spruce is another northern tree, rare in Pennsylvania, that finds Tamarack Swamp a congenial place. A third boreal tree in the natural area is balsam fir.

A band of dark-eyed juncos hopped about in the snow, feeding on the seeds of grasses or sedges, while overhead a hairy woodpecker chiseled out a grub from an aspen stub. I struck some fox tracks and followed them until the straight line of neat prints vanished where deer had milled about. Crows cawed angrily in a copse of dense hemlocks; a large, brown bird with broad wings and a short neck, almost surely a great horned owl, went gliding out of the conifers before I could get close.

The noted ornithologist Francis R. Cope described a June 1900 visit to Tamarack Swamp for the birding journal *Cassinia*. After tramping through mile after depressing mile of logged-off old-growth forest, Cope and his companion, Stewardson Brown, arrived at the swamp, which Cope likened to "a little oasis in the desert. . . . The dense growth of hemlocks, spruces, balsams and other heavy foliaged forest trees keeps out the hot rays of the summer sun and affords a cool retreat both for birds and plants." Cope observed "many birds typical of the Canadian fauna"—Swainson's thrush, brown creeper, winter wren, olive-sided flycatcher, crossbills, and various wood-warblers, including Blackburnian, magnolia, Canada, black-throated blue, and black-throated green.

Soon after 1900, however, logging began in the wetland. In 1947 Edward J. Reimann described Tamarack Swamp as "a ghost of what Cope and Brown had observed. Of the tamaracks remaining, scarcely a dozen of them were over 25 feet high." Wrote Reimann, "There was no dense, cool primeval forest, in fact, there was no shade to be found." The bird species he noted were usual for more open woods and drier areas.

Like many sites abused by humans, Tamarack Swamp is making a comeback. Some of the spruce, fir, and larch remained after the logging, and they and their descendents are maturing, providing an increasingly attractive habitat for northern birds. In June 2000, a century after Cope and Brown ventured there, my friends Nick Bolgiano and Clark Shiffer visited Tamarack Swamp. Bolgiano is a birder (he showed me around Bear Meadows Natural Area; see page 67) and Shiffer an odonatologist. Their trip was a brief one, but Bolgiano spotted a number of birds, including a northern harrier (also known as the marsh hawk), sharp-shinned hawk, alder flycatcher, hermit thrush, swamp sparrow, blue-headed vireo, and these wood-warblers: golden-winged, Nashville, chestnut-sided, Blackburnian, black-and-white, and ovenbird. Shiffer netted several unusual dragonflies.

Tamarack Swamp is not without scars. A natural gas pipeline was laid across the bog, fragmenting and destroying some of the habitat. The Bureau of Forestry controls about a third of the wetland, and in 1998 the Western Pennsylvania Conservancy bought 351 acres there, a purchase that protects another third of the swamp. When conservancy staff members conducted a biological inventory, they found two plants currently classified as endangered in Pennsylvania: small floating manna grass and Hooker's orchid, which has intricately shaped, yellow-green flowers. Wild calla lily, wood lily, creeping snowberry, and soft-leaved sedge grow in the swamp, along with two carnivorous species, pitcher plant and sundew.

In this wet habitat thrive four rare dragonflies that live only in sphagnum moss bogs fed by pure, unpolluted spring water. One of the four is the Michigan bog skimmer. "If this aerial insect predator is present," commented Charles Bier, a zoologist who directs the Western Pennsylvania Conservancy's natural heritage program, "we have an indication that the ecosystem is healthy."

TO GET THERE. In the village of Tamarack on PA Route 144, turn north at a small white church onto Steward Hill Road. Drive approximately 0.9 mile to a wide pipeline right-of-way with a parking area on the right. Walk east (downhill) on the pipeline. After about 100 yards, pick up a forest road on the right or southern edge of the right-of-way and follow it through a stand of pines. Stay on the road as far as a steel gate (private property lies beyond the gate), then bear right and head south down the gentle drainage to the swamp.

   The wetlands and natural area are covered by the Tamarack, Pennsylvania, topographic quadrangle.

---

52   BUCKTAIL

16,433 ACRES, SPROUL AND ELK STATE FORESTS, CLINTON AND CAMERON COUNTIES

The canoe drifted with the current. Rocks on the bottom—gray, greenish, rust red, tan, visible in great detail through the clear water—seemed to move slowly past beneath the boat. Trout slipped past, too, streamlined shapes that finned, steadied, and suddenly darted away. It was an unusually hot day in early May. I was drowsing off when Gary, my canoeing partner, whispered: "On the bank."

The bull elk looked black in the hazy light. He stood poised on the edge of Round Island in Sinnemahoning Creek. His antlers were surprisingly large for so early in the year: almost four feet long, thick, branching, and covered with velvet. He had his head up, and his eyes were fixed on us. In the stern, Gary dipped his paddle to rudder us toward shore. The canoe drew closer to the elk. He turned and cantered up the bank, revealing a yellow radio collar around his neck. He stopped and stared. Finally, as we closed to within twenty yards, the big bull trotted off into the woods.

Elk are but one of the attractions of the Bucktail Natural Area, the largest natural area designated by the Bureau of Forestry and unique in

A bull elk makes his exit on Round Island in Sinnemahoning Creek, part of the seventy-mile-long Bucktail Natural Area.

consisting of a series of state-owned tracts separated by private inholdings. The Bucktail contains 16,433 acres in forty parcels ranging in size from 20 to 2,400 acres. It stretches for nearly seventy miles between Lock Haven and Emporium, following Pennsylvania Route 120. The landscape there is mostly up-and-down: steep mountains jumbled together on the Allegheny High Plateau, separated by streams flowing down canyonlike valleys. Almost all of the land is forested, save for a few cleared areas near the highway and around the infrequent small towns. Visitors can drive through the Bucktail Natural Area, or, as Gary and I had chosen, they can canoe through it on Sinnemahoning Creek and the West Branch of the Susquehanna.

We began our trip at Driftwood, a hamlet where Bennett's Branch meets Driftwood Branch of the Sinnemahoning to form Sinnemahoning Creek proper. We had launched our canoe within view of a monument topped by a statue of a rifle-toting man. The monument was dedicated to Civil War volunteers who, at Driftwood on April 27, 1861, according to the marker's text, "embarked upon four rafts for Harrisburg, where they were mustered into the service and formed the nucleus about which the Bucktail Regiment of the Pennsylvania Reserve Corps was organized." The men were loggers, woodsmen, and hunters. To maintain their identity in the Army of the Potomac, and perhaps to remind themselves of home, those up-country Pennsylvanians—mainly from Elk, Cameron, and McKean Counties—pinned the snowy tails of white-tailed deer to their hats and forage caps.

At Driftwood, the Sinnemahoning was about a hundred yards wide and had a fairly brisk current. Bank swallows swooped over the canoe, catching flying insects. A kingfisher looped across the stream, calling in rattling tones. Three common mergansers—a male with a green-black head and two females with crested ruddy heads—ran splashing across the water's surface before taking off, white-banded wings flashing. They banked and rocketed past us. With necks extended in front of their bodies, they looked very purposeful in their flight. Kingfishers and mergansers both eat fish, and their presence testified to the Sinnemahoning's clarity and productivity. Common mergansers were once rare birds in the state, but their population has risen dramatically over the last twenty years, with pairs breeding on many streams in northern Pennsylvania.

Sinnemahoning comes from an Indian word meaning "stony lick." No doubt "lick" refers to a place where deer and elk came to lick salt; and obviously the creek is a stony waterway, its long, smooth sections punctuated by rapids. According to Edward Gertler in his book *Keystone Canoeing,* canoeists should avoid the Sinnemahoning in summer, when the waterway becomes "relentlessly shallow, and you may thus find yourself taking a canoe hike." There was enough flow for Gary and me to scrape through in most places; only twice did we have to jump out, raising the canoe enough to float it through a particularly shallow stretch. We heard the rushing sound of the rapids well in advance, giving us time to avoid the boulders and ledges lurking below the surface.

A spot of red on a shady cliff caught my eye: columbines, their lantern-shaped, red-and-yellow flowers borne on thin, pliant stems. The columbines waved in the breeze—a breeze that, as it turned out, was in our faces for much of the day, so that we had to paddle to make reasonable progress even though we were floating downstream. A hemlock grew out of the bluff, its gnarled trunk bending out and then up from a crack in the rocks. On a bare lower branch sat an eastern phoebe, its head crest held erect and wagging its tail. Rock faces are favorite places for phoebes to anchor their nests, woven out of weeds, grasses, and plant fibers held together with mud.

Just past the rocks, we were startled by a snake. It was not a water snake, per se, but a black racer, and obviously not at all out of its element in the middle of Sinnemahoning Creek. With its pale chin tipped up and its head held above the water, the racer swam with S-shaped movements across the current. When it gained the far bank, it vanished among the rocks.

A great blue heron stood immobile, waiting for prey in the shallows. A green heron gave a squawk, flew down the creek, and landed in a sycamore.

A black duck raced overhead, flying with quick, shallow wingbeats, the white linings of its wings catching the light. Pairs of Canada geese guarded small islands.

I spent a lot of time just looking at the landscape. The hardwoods were leafing out, and their bright, citron green foliage thinly cloaked the abrupt hills. Hemlocks were swatches of darker green, and white pines lifted their airy crowns above the rest of the forest. Scattered through the lower level of the woods, the flowering dogwoods looked like white puffs of smoke. Above the mountains, migrating turkey vultures were the size of pepper grains.

We ate lunch on a big rock on the east side of the Sinnemahoning opposite where Wycoff Run flows into the creek. Fixed to the rock was a massive, rusty iron eyebolt with a huge link attached to it, through which smaller chains had once been secured. The bolt and link were a remnant of the logging era, when white pine spars, cut from great stands of virgin timber in what was then known as the Black Forest of Pennsylvania, were tied into rafts and floated down the Susquehanna to mills at Williamsport and points farther south. I wondered if the village here, called Jericho—even tinier and sleepier than Driftwood—had been an important stopping point for the timber rafts.

Under way again, we scared up a spotted sandpiper. It fled across the stream on short, rapid wingbeats, its wings working stiffly and held below the horizontal. It landed on a small rock. Teetering up and down, it began to search through the pebbles for insects and snails. This small sandpiper—brownish, with a white breast that is strongly spotted in the spring breeding plumage—is known as a "tip-up" for its incessant bobbing habit. It breeds along rivers, streams, and creeks across Pennsylvania.

Considering the number of trout we saw in the creek, I was surprised we encountered no fishermen. Route 120 closely parallels the Sinnemahoning on one side, and railroad tracks follow it on the other side. A few cars and trucks passed, as did two freight trains. There is something about traveling in a canoe: several people waved at us from their cars, and a train engineer hallooed us with his air horn.

It was midafternoon when we reached Round Island and spotted the elk. After he ran back onto the island, we beached the canoe. As we climbed onto the flat, Gary glimpsed the bull sneaking off into the brush. We crept about looking for more elk, but didn't see any. Probably we weren't creeping stealthily enough: the blackflies were swarming, there out of the wind, and they soon drove us, muttering and slapping, back to the boat and onto the stream.

Before European settlement, elk lived in great numbers in the Alleghenies. According to Philip Tome in *Pioneer Life; or, Thirty Years a Hunter,* in the late 1700s and early 1800s, when Tome was living on the frontier of northern Pennsylvania, elk were exceedingly plentiful along Young Woman's, Kettle, and Sinnemahoning Creeks—"the greatest elk country known," he wrote. But the elk vanished along with the virgin timber, the mountain lion, the gray wolf, and the moose—all wiped out in the name of "progress," which so often is synonymous with "profit" and "greed." Historians believe that the last native elk in Pennsylvania survived along Bennett's Branch in what are now Cameron and Elk Counties. In 1867, a lone bull was shot by an Indian, Jim Jacobs, along the headwaters of the Clarion River—and the species was extinguished in the state.

Between 1913 and 1926, the Pennsylvania Game Commission took 177 Rocky Mountain elk from Yellowstone National Park and released them in scattered sites in north-central Pennsylvania. The population fluctuated for years, dwindling to fewer than forty in the 1970s. Lately, the herd has rebounded to around five hundred animals; most of them live near St. Marys and Benezette in Elk County. In the late 1990s, the game commission began capturing elk—darting and sedating them, outfitting them with radio collars, and trucking them to release sites in the Kettle Creek drainage in northwestern Clinton County, both to start a new herd there and to relieve crowding in the core range farther west. Elk being peripatetic creatures, others have moved on their own from Bennett's Branch into the Quehanna region of Clearfield and Centre Counties.

When I got home, I phoned Rawley Cogan, elk biologist for the game commission. He said that the yellow collar identified the bull as having wandered up from Quehanna. I asked Cogan where in the Bucktail Natural Area one could expect to see elk. "You'd have a chance of seeing them anywhere from Sterling Run to Westport," he said. "They like Round Island, the area around Keating, and the flats near the mouth of Jerry Run."

As impressive as the elk had been, I found myself even more astonished by the toads. I am certain that far more biomass—more living matter, by weight—is tied up in the small, warty amphibians that were abandoning themselves to the spring breeding frenzy on that hot May day. Toads squatted on rocks and treaded water in the shallows of the Sinnemahoning. We canoed to within inches of males that sat in full view, trying to call in females. On the throat of each male, an air sac swelled like a bubble; the toad then let out a monotonic trill that joined with the trills of hundreds of other toads, each pitched slightly differently, filling the air with a sweet warbling.

We had paddled for six hours by the time we reached the settlement of Keating, where the Sinnemahoning joins the larger West Branch of the Susquehanna. Now the water flowed deep as well as broad. The West Branch has a true wilderness feeling to it; in a long stretch above Keating, no roads follow the river, and where we joined it, the lightly traveled Route 120 remains hidden behind trees. Cliffs stud the steep slopes. The writer Bil Gilbert has called the West Branch "a river of great integrity," and indeed, it has an aspect of serenity and power all its own.

TO GET THERE. Follow PA Route 120 north from Lock Haven along the West Branch of the Susquehanna. The Bucktail Natural Area begins about 7 miles north of Lock Haven. Numerous forest roads and trails lead from the river into the natural area and to other state forest lands. At Keating, the Bucktail Natural Area continues north along Sinnemahoning Creek to Emporium.

---

53   JOHNSON RUN

216 ACRES, ELK STATE FOREST, CAMERON COUNTY

Shaded, cool, quiet, and with a level of humidity approaching 100 percent: Johnson Run on a summer afternoon. A high frustration level, as well. Do not fail to mention the gnats, very bothersome, in ears, eyes, nose. Or the footing, uneven at best.

No trail leads up Johnson Run. The hiker must find a way over slippery rocks that are either naked and sweating or skinned with damp moss. Dead hemlocks lie jackstrawed in the tight hollow. The slope above the run is only marginally easier to negotiate: ankle-turning steep, with assorted deadfalls.

Some impressively large hemlocks and pines stand above the run, in which I found water barely trickling on August 8, 2000. I ventured into the drainage carrying with me the admonition of an old woman living in a mobile home at the mouth of the hollow (she sat on the porch reading a magazine and listening to the television, which was on inside the dwelling). She gave me permission to cross her land en route to the natural area, saying, "Watch out for rattlesnakes. Get a good stick, and kill any snake you see, no matter how big or small." I wasn't about to kill a snake, which I felt had more right to the inner sanctum of Johnson Run than I did. On the other hand, I did not look forward to being surprised by one.

The walking was difficult, and the rewards were few. I saw a tall, perfectly straight tuliptree. A few yards farther on, a tiny, dark bird went scuttling along on the ground. It was a winter wren, and very likely it had nested or was the result of a nesting along Johnson Run, which represents an ideal habitat for this uncommon species. The *Atlas of Breeding Birds in Pennsylvania* states that one is most likely to find winter wrens "in dense hemlock stands on steep slopes." Wrote the noted ornithologist A. C. Bent, "Shade and dampness produce the conditions that the Winter Wren seems to require." I heard the bird give its *kip-kip* call. It was past the season when males of the species broadcast their song, which features long, musical trills.

The wren flicked its barred wings and flicked its stubby tail. It looked like a small rodent as it scurried among the massed fallen branches and across the leaf-strewn, fern-blanketed ground. Winter wrens eat spiders, millipedes, bugs, ants, and snails. They are also rodentlike when it comes to nesting, choosing recesses among the roots of downed trees, cracks in rotten stumps, and holes in streambanks. The little bird moved almost constantly, overturning the leaf litter with its bill, combing through the sopping twigs, darting through the dense vegetation—then took a wing-flapping leap in under the stream's overhanging bank, where a fallen hemlock leaned, and thereby disappeared.

TO GET THERE. Drive 1.8 miles north from Driftwood on PA Route 120 to the vicinity of the natural area. It is difficult to find a place to park along the highway. A natural gas pipeline right-of-way, which crosses a narrow strip of private land and then enters the state forest, provides the best access.

Walk northeast on the grassy right-of-way, with hemlock-lined Johnson Run downhill to your left. The pipeline climbs and then descends; within half a mile, it crosses Johnson Run and heads steeply uphill on private land. Stay along the run, and remain in the natural area by angling off slightly to the right, on a northeast heading. Johnson Run forms the northern border of both the natural area and the state forest land; white paint blazes on trees delineate the boundary.

A marked hiking trail, the Bucktail Path, passes through forested terrain on the eastern edge of the natural area, which straddles the edges of the Driftwood and Sinnemahoning topographic quadrangles.

54 LOWER JERRY RUN

892 ACRES, ELK STATE FOREST, CAMERON AND CLINTON COUNTIES

Where the two tributaries of Lower Jerry Run came together, Gary and I climbed the slope to a rock formation. The many-layered slabs stood in a broken, irregular overhang, with frost-heaved chunks lying at the base of the outcropping. The sky was a pure, deep blue, and the autumn sun, riding low in the east, cast a golden light on the rocks and on the mountains bordering the deep valley. The air was chilly, but as we sat in the shelter of the overhang, the sun warmed us. My friend and I presumed that this formation—and others like it, jutting from the steep slopes above Lower Jerry Run—provided basking and hibernating sites for timber rattlesnakes. In spring, after leaving their winter dens in deep crevices, the snakes lie on rocks while the sun slowly warms their bodies. I kept an eye peeled for any serpent that might be returning to the den or intent on catching a few last rays before slithering down a crack into its hibernaculum.

We were startled—not by a sinuous shape or buzzing rattles, but by a large bird that flew past thirty feet away. The ruffed grouse banked abruptly, displaying rounded wings, rich brown feathering on its back, and a chestnut brown tail marked with a gray-edged black band. The grouse pitched down among some small pines just around the rocky prow. While hiking down the run, we had heard three other grouse as they flushed unseen among dense hemlocks on the west-facing slope.

As a grouse hunter, I could not restrain myself, and tiptoed around the promontory. But I couldn't get close to it: the grouse took off on whirring wings, scattering dry leaves that slowly drifted down in its wake. It rocketed across the narrow hollow and vanished among the trees.

From our perch, Gary and I could look far down Lower Jerry Run, which flows northward and drains into Sinnemahoning Creek. Sunlight glinted off the slick bark of black birch trees. It lit up the dainty, green needles of the hemlocks. It made the steep mountains glow. Above us, a patch of old-growth hemlocks and white pines occupied the high ground on the wedge of land separating the two branches of Lower Jerry Run.

Gary is a longtime hiking and canoeing partner of mine. For safety's sake, I had asked him to go with me to this steep, isolated natural area, which is known for having many timber rattlesnakes. It is not the kind of easy, accessible place where one feels totally comfortable hiking alone.

We edged our way down the rocky slope and resumed our journey. A dogwood growing near the stream held clusters of red berries; husks beneath the tree showed where songbirds had been feeding on the fruit. Teaberry, a small, ground-hugging evergreen plant, bore scarlet berries; I picked a couple, popped them into my mouth, and enjoyed their fresh, bright taste. Bare ground scored by claws, and dry leaves scuffed and scratched aside, showed us where turkeys had searched for acorns. Above our heads, the chestnut and red oaks had dropped almost all of their leaves, and red maples and white birches raised leafless boughs.

Lower Jerry Run is a pristine stream in a deep mountain valley in north-central Pennsylvania.

Farther down its gorge, Lower Jerry Run picked up more flow from the trickles and streamlets coming in from narrow side hollows. The stream flowed cold and clear; it fell, bubbling over rocks and logs. Since there was no trail, Gary and I shifted from one side of the stream to the other, wherever the footing was best. This would be a wet hike in the spring, or after a heavy rain, since Lower Jerry Run twists back and forth repeatedly in the narrow valley.

As we lost elevation, the forest changed from mixed-oak uplands to northern hardwoods: yellow birch, American beech, basswood. The beeches still held their bronze leaves, and sugar maples and tuliptrees wore sparse cloaks of yellow. Descending, not only did we move from one forest type into another, but we seemingly turned back the calendar of days, regressing from early winter to late autumn.

Brook trout flashed in the ten-foot-wide stream. The run flowed head-on into a huge boulder, danced left, and gushed on past. The rock was as large as a dump truck, and it was plastered all over with lichens, including many specimens of rock tripe.

American beech trees along Lower Jerry Run turn bronze-yellow in autumn.

Rock tripe consists of a thallus, or plant body, a thin, leathery, oblong pancake three or four inches across, held to the rock by a stout cord. The thallus is fairly smooth and grayish brown in color, often with a tint of green. It has a crinkly edge, and the drier the weather becomes, the more this edge curls up, exposing black undersurfaces. The plant is called rock tripe because in the past, people sometimes ate it, particularly hunters, trappers, and explorers in Canada and Alaska.

A band of dark-eyed juncos scratched in the leaf duff for seeds, spiders, and insects. Juncos are sparrow-size birds with slate gray wings, backs, and heads; white bellies; and white outer tailfeathers—which showed as the birds flicked their tails open and shut while hopping about on the ground. Juncos breed in the forested mountains of northern Pennsylvania. Starting in September, some of our local breeders depart and shift southward. As fall progresses, other juncos arrive from the north. Many remain as winter residents in the state, and I marvel that they can eke out a living when snow covers the ground to depths of two and three feet in places such as Lower Jerry Run.

Bob Martin, retired district forester in Elk State Forest, found evidence of juncos breeding at Lower Jerry Run Natural Area when he surveyed the valley during the 1980s for the *Atlas of Breeding Birds in Pennsylvania*. He also documented the expected suite of deep-woods species, including downy and hairy woodpeckers, northern flickers, eastern wood-pewees, least flycatchers, eastern phoebes, hermit and wood thrushes, solitary and red-eyed vireos, eight warbler species (including chestnut-sided, black-throated blue, black-throated green, Blackburnian, and black-and-white), scarlet tanagers, and rose-breasted grosbeaks. Bobcats, coyotes, and black bears inhabit the natural area, as well as more common mammals such as deer, squirrels, chipmunks, and smaller rodents.

Gary called me over to a witch hazel. One of the shrub's thick, upright stems had been scarred deeply: the bark torn lengthwise, the cuts digging down through the inner bark into the pale sapwood. Scuff marks reached seven feet up on the trunk. Twists of bark lay on the ground beneath the hazel. At first I thought a bear had done the damage, but there was no reason for a bruin to climb into a witch hazel, no food to be gotten at the ends of those springy branches. We were only a mile from the Sinnemahoning. Apparently an elk had wandered up the drainage and, using its teeth, scraped the bark off to eat it.

As we climbed out of Lower Jerry Run, the light began to dim, the sky became a deeper blue, and shadows filled the hollow. The forest shifted back to black birch, red maple, and chestnut oak, the trees all winter-bare. We smelled the fine cured scent of the fallen leaves. It can be hard to separate a place from the quality of the light and the quality of the weather on the day you went there. But I don't think the splendidness of that late October day biased me unduly: Lower Jerry Run is a superb and dramatic natural place.

TO GET THERE. From the bridge across the West Branch of the Susquehanna in the village of Karthaus, drive west 1.6 miles on PA Route 879 to a stop sign. Turn right onto the Quehanna Highway; proceed through Piper, and after 6.6 miles, turn right on Three Runs Road. After 5.6 miles, where Sand Rock Road goes to the right, Three Runs Road becomes Dutchmans Road. Altogether, drive 6.4 miles on Three Runs Road/Dutchmans Road to an electric transmission line. Park and hike west along the powerline, descending gradually to a hunting camp road; turn right and hike to the camp, then proceed down Lower Jerry Run.

Gary and I followed the stream as far as Smoke Draft, a prominent side hollow that descends from the southeast. We hiked up Smoke Draft, bushwhacked out to Jerry Ridge Road, turned south, and walked to Dutchmans Road. A right on Dutchmans Road took us back to the powerline and the truck. We completed the loop, a bit over six miles, in seven and a half hours. (A car shuttle would have shortened the hike by a couple miles.) This rugged, strenuous trek commences at approximately 2,000 feet of elevation, descends to 900 feet, and climbs back up to 2,000 feet. Essentials: a compass, a copy of the Sinnemahoning, Pennsylvania, topographic quadrangle, and the Elk State Forest public-use map.

In some years, deer ticks are pestiferous along Lower Jerry Run.

---

55   PINE TREE TRAIL

276 ACRES, ELK STATE FOREST, ELK COUNTY

Sitting on the old foundation, my son Will and I tried to re-create the time line of what had happened in this place over the last century and a half.

In the mid–1800s, loggers had come to this part of northern Pennsylvania, known as the Black Forest, because of the great, dark cloak of old-growth pines and hemlocks that covered the rugged, mountainous land. How tall were the original pines? A good 150 feet, and maybe taller, thick and straight, often with the first 80 feet of the trunk free of any branches.

With sharp-bitted axes and six-foot crosscut saws, logging crews felled the virgin pines. White pine lumber is soft, even-textured, and easy to work. The wood could have ended up as ship masts or roof shingles or the trim for a fine house in Philadelphia.

We had walked through the forest among stumps left from that first cutting: pitch-impregnated, they had resisted the elements and now stood jagged-topped and reddish, some of them with pine and hemlock seedlings growing from their tops.

After the pines were taken, successive waves of logging removed hemlocks and hardwoods, whose stumps had long since crumbled to dust. At some point, settlers arrived; on the sun-bathed soil between the scattered stumps, they planted crops and pastured livestock. And someone built a tiny house on the site where Will and I now sat. The old chimney lay in a pile, rudely shaped stones covered with moss. Grasses, ferns, the glossy leaves of partridgeberry, and cherry and maple seedlings grew where the dwelling had stood. Had there been a spring, under those ferns and fallen leaves, near that red oak growing so straight and tall? Had children been born in the house? Had elders died there?

It's not known how long the settlers stayed. Perhaps not even for a single generation, since their lives would have been harsh, their existence marginal, on this out-of-the-way mountaintop site. When the people left, the wind blew in small, winged seeds released by cones on nearby white pines. In the full sun, the seedlings grew swiftly, dominating the site and shading out competing trees.

Today, if you walk through the area without having any background knowledge, you might think it had been forest all along. The pines are impressive, for being only 150 years old. According to the brochure describing Pine Tree Trail Natural Area, the white pine stand occupies about twelve acres and averages over fourteen thousand board feet of timber per acre; most of the trees contain between five and six sixteen-foot logs. The pines are not now the equal of the old-growth trees, but some day, a century or more in the future, they may achieve a similar loft and girth.

When we started up the trail—perhaps it had been a logging slide, a road to the farm, or both—Will and I spotted four young hermit thrushes, with their prominently speckled breasts and reddish rumps, feeding actively in the crowns of low trees. A red squirrel came bounding down the path, saw us, and leaped abruptly into a hemlock, where it vanished among the deep green boughs. On the forest floor, the red fruiting capsule of a large-flowered trillium stood on a stalk; in autumn, it would release its seeds, which require two winters in the soil before sprouting.

The trail angled gradually up the hill, which lies between the East Branch and West Branch of Hicks Run. Youth Conservation Corps workers built the path between 1977 and 1979; later, the Bureau of Forestry converted it into an interpretive trail to educate visitors on forest ecology. It starts in a damp site stocked with northern hardwoods, including American beech and northern red oak, then climbs to a drier mixed-oak stand.

Toward the top of the ridge, the forest became denser, with oaks, maples, and black cherries mixing with the tall pines. It would be a pretty hike in the fall, with the ferns gone yellow underfoot and the many different species of trees changing colors, all set against the conifers' steadfast green. However, Will and I had chosen for our outing an August day that my son rhymed out as "hot, muggy, humid, and buggy."

The woods were somnolent in the heat. No breeze. I listened hard but didn't hear a bird. As we stared into the motionless green crown of a pine, a pileated woodpecker landed with an audible thump on the tree's trunk. The bird had a bright red head crest and a long, lean, black-and-white body. It held its neck in an S shape. With herky-jerky movements, the great woodpecker hitched itself up the thick trunk, stopped, and looked down at us, sixty feet below.

TO GET THERE. From the village of Dents Run, go east on PA Route 555 about 0.6 mile to Hicks Run Road, just beyond the Cameron County–Elk County line. Go 2.1 miles and turn left again onto West Hicks Road and, after crossing a bridge, make an immediate left turn and park at Hicks Run Camping Area. The trail is across the road from the state forest campground, heading uphill.

Before visiting the natural area, contact Elk State Forest headquarters and request the five-page handout on Pine Tree Trail. The trail is blazed with orange paint; numbered markers point out nineteen different trees, including lesser-known species such as slippery elm, Juneberry, and hornbeam. The trail surface is even and suitable for walking shoes. A leisurely hike takes about two hours.

56 WYCOFF RUN

1,215 ACRES, ELK STATE FOREST, CAMERON COUNTY

When the snow is too skimpy for skiing in Bald Eagle Valley, we head for the Allegheny Plateau, which, several hundred feet higher and a few score miles farther north, often has enough snow to let us glide easily over the rocks and on the trails.

Wycoff Run Natural Area sits on the rolling, wooded Allegheny Plateau at around two thousand feet of elevation, at the headwaters of Wycoff Run, which drains northeastward into Sinnemahoning Creek. On a map, the natural area looks like a misshapen bull's-eye at the center of the Quehanna Wild Area, a 48,186-acre polygon with sixteen sides approximating a circle in its overall shape. In the 1950s, the commonwealth of Pennsylvania, by decision of the legislature and Gov. George Leader, turned this area over to Curtiss-Wright, a private corporation. Public access was restricted, and the state cleared out 212 hunting camps on land leased from the Bureau of Forestry. The intent was to establish an isolated industrial area where Curtiss-Wright could test jet engines and develop a nuclear-powered airplane, and where the people of this depressed region could find jobs. Like most such schemes, this one fell apart when Curtiss-Wright pulled out, leaving behind nuclear and toxic wastes, and a name: Quehanna, apparently derived from the last three syllables of Susquehanna, the river whose West Branch cuts through the Allegheny Plateau and receives the waters of Sinnemahoning Creek and many other drainages.

My friend Gary and I were reminded of those strange Cold War doings when we skied through Wycoff Run Natural Area on an overcast, snow-flurrying day in February. Old Hoover Trail led us past a concrete bunker where engineers had once tested jet engines. The inside of the building was littered with trash and broken glass and covered with fantastic, rather sinister graffiti—skulls, devils' faces, and unintelligible symbols. Neither of us felt like staying inside very long, and I know that my own mental Geiger counter was ticking like mad as I squeezed back out through the rubble-choked entry and clamped my skis back on.

The trail tunneled through dense mountain laurel. Away from the highway, the only sound we heard was the wind sighing through the crowns of hemlocks and pines and making the other forest trees creak and moan. We skied past gray, paper, and black birch; white, chestnut, and red oak; red maple; and sassafras trees.

We listened to the *hiss-hiss* of our skis, the crunch of our ski poles, and our panting breath. A raven gave its rattling call overhead. Two deer stood up silently from where they had been bedded in the snow and watched us pass. Friends report seeing black bears, wild turkeys, coyotes, bobcats, elk, and timber rattlesnakes in the natural area and in its vicinity. The Quehanna Wild Area as a whole is listed as a Pennsylvania Important Bird Area by the state Audubon Society, and many species that require extensive, unbroken forested tracts nest in this lonely wooded realm.

The natural area also commemorates Maurice K. Goddard, who in 1955 became head of the Pennsylvania Department of Forests and Waters, which evolved into today's Department of Conservation and Natural Resources. Goddard directed the department for twenty-four years, under six governors. During his tenure, he added forty-five state parks and 130,000 acres of state forest to Pennsylvania's public lands network. I have my own fond memories of Dr. Goddard, a tall, lanky, outspoken, forthright man who was perhaps the greatest conservationist Pennsylvania has ever known.

In February, the Quehanna does not appear to be a particularly productive or a pretty forest. It is a place that humans have treated harshly, through logging, mining, and other means of exploitation. Gypsy moth and oak leaf roller infestations have killed many trees, and on May 31, 1985, a powerful tornado mowed down a broad swath of timber through the wild area. The region's ecological and human history is detailed in *Great Buffaloe Swamp, A Trail Guide and Historical Record for the Quehanna Plateau and the Moshannon State Forest,* by Ralph Seeley, a retired Penn State engineer who has constructed many trails through this wild, wooded sector. The softbound publication is sold by the Quehanna Area Trails Club, HC1, Karthaus, PA 16845, telephone (814) 263-4286. A Quehanna Trail map, showing cross-country ski trails as well as hiking routes, is available free from the Pennsylvania Bureau of Forestry.

I'm inclined to visit the Quehanna during winter, because at other times of the year deer ticks are active, and Lyme disease has been reported from the area. In spring, summer, and fall, take precautions: tuck your pants into your socks, and use rubber bands to seal the seam. Insect repellents that contain DEET don't work well against ticks; instead, use clothing sprays containing permethrin.

TO GET THERE. From Karthaus, in northern Centre County, drive north 1.6 miles on PA Route 879. At the stop sign, turn right on SR 1011, the Quehanna Highway. Go 8.5 miles to where Wycoff Run Road forks off to the right. Park in the small lot at this junction. Old Hoover Trail, marked by blue blazes, goes north from the parking area. The Quehanna Trail map, distributed by the Bureau of Forestry, is based on USGS topographic cartography; use it in combination with a compass for getting about in this remote, out-of-the way area.

57 FORREST H. DUTLINGER

1,521 ACRES, SUSQUEHANNOCK STATE FOREST, CLINTON COUNTY

Thank God for inexact surveying, cautious lumber companies (the penalty for cutting another firm's trees during the logging era in Pennsylvania was triple compensation), and early state foresters who, as the twentieth century opened, bought thousands of acres of logged-over land and then spared what few trifles of old-growth timber remained.

My son Will and I trudged toward a stand of old hemlocks at Forrest H. Dutlinger Natural Area along the Clinton County–Potter County line. It was a hot, humid day in August as we climbed Beech Bottom Hollow Trail, scaring up wood thrushes, ovenbirds, and dark-eyed juncos that flew off into the surrounding forest.

The red-spotted newts were about: every few paces, we stepped around one of these salamanders as it crept ponderously along the trail. All the newts we saw seemed to be traveling away from the water, moving upslope from Beech Bottom Run, which tinkled in its stony bed twenty feet below the path. All of the salamanders were adults, mustard-olive in color, with black-encircled red dots on their backs, much duller than the striking overall red of the smaller juveniles, known as red efts. In general, adult newts are aquatic; however, in some populations, the adults spend the winter on land, squirming down into sheltered nooks beneath logs, rocks, and leaf litter. They do their traveling when the air is damp, so that their amphibian skins remain moist, an aid in absorbing oxygen. As Will and I kept climbing, passing so many newts that they soon failed to draw our attention, our own skins were damp with the sweat running down our foreheads and soaking through our shirts.

The trail followed an old skid road. After loggers felled the old-growth trees, they would cut the limbs and tops off and buck the trunks into shorter, more manageable lengths. Using horses, they would skid the logs down inclines cut into the mountains. At the bottom of the hollow, the logs would have been loaded on railcars, then taken to a mill in a nearby boom town. Like much of Penn's Woods, Beech Bottom Hollow was logged off in the early 1900s. Now, set aside as a state forest natural area, it will never be cut again.

The natural area bears the name of Forrest Dutlinger, a 1908 graduate of the Pennsylvania State Forest Academy at Mont Alto and the first professional forester assigned to the newly acquired state holdings in Clinton County, 180,000 acres of remote, cut-over land that made up the core of today's Sproul State Forest.

My feet skidded on something round and hard. Scattered over the trail were many hard, green fruits, each about a third of an inch in diameter. I trained my binoculars overhead: in the tops of the basswood trees hung more of the fruits, nutlets that ripen in autumn and send winged seeds fluttering to the ground. Apparently a crown-thrashing storm had passed through the hollow, knocking down thousands of the unripened nutlets. As well as the basswoods, white ash, yellow and sweet birch, red maple, and American beech trees (the namesake species for Beech Bottom Hollow) grew near the skid road. Along the stream, the dark green boughs of hemlocks swept almost to the ground—but they were not the ancient trees toward which we were expectantly walking.

Gnats whined in our faces and came crashing into our ears. We ran into little puffs of breeze blowing down the hollow, which temporarily baffled the gnats and raised our spirits. Cream-colored coral fungi tufted the ground. Gnaw marks made by feeding porcupines showed as white patches on tree trunks. A small spring trickled its waters across the path; we each dipped a cupful.

The trail curved to the left, and the forest understory began opening up. A tall hemlock stood beside the path, a sentry guarding the perimeter of the old-growth stand, which contains about 160 acres. When last measured, the largest tree in the grove was forty-three inches in diameter at breast height and stood 112 feet tall. Many other hemlocks range from thirty-two to forty inches in diameter.

Each time I walk through a grove of old hemlocks, I am silenced and somewhat baffled by living things that are so much older and larger than I.

At Forrest H. Dutlinger Natural Area, a trail climbs up Beech Bottom Hollow to a 160-acre stand of old-growth hemlock.

Blind, anchored in place, the trees stand in contrast to the small, assertive bipeds that slew so many of them, so carelessly, in the name of profit and progress. Some people suggest that we subliminally structure our sacred buildings and houses of worship to resemble woodland settings, either to place us back in the habitat that we as a species shunned when we left the forest for an agricultural existence, or maybe even as a gesture of atonement.

In the old-growth stand at Forrest Dutlinger, a trail book sat in a metal box inside a small, roofed wooden structure. I paged through the journal.

A woman recorded that her boyfriend, surrounded by the big trees in the cathedral setting, proposed marriage; she accepted.

A visitor wrote of seeing "a beautiful tan coyote."

Another person jotted: " . . . lots of flies but they taste good if you're hungry."

"Had several heart attacks on the way up. The flies are wicked."

"Bugs don't bother my husband, because he already smells like Nature and then some."

"We don't have hills like these in Kansas."

"The trees are so beautiful. We should let more get this old."

"We're lucky that some places were saved here and there. It looks so inviolable, yet so much of its kind was demolished."

At Forrest Dutlinger Natural Area, Will and I found stumps of white pine intermixed with the hemlocks, showing that an early wave of logging had taken out the more valuable pine. I wondered what the place looked like when the ancients of both clans stood shoulder to shoulder.

TO GET THERE. On PA Route 144, 4.4 miles south of the village of Cross Fork, turn right (north) on Hammersley Fork Avenue. Follow this gravel road, on the east side of the stream, for about half a mile, and park just short of where the road fords the Hammersley Fork. You can cross the stream on a "footbridge" about a hundred yards upstream (two cables, one for your feet and the other for your hands, are strung between trees on opposite banks). Or take off your boots, roll up your pant legs, and wade.

Across the stream, turn right on a jeep road and hike for almost a mile past several hunting camps. After the stone chimney of a ruined cabin, take the first major hollow to the left (west). An exposed rock formation marks the mouth of Beech Bottom Hollow. The stand of virgin hemlocks is about 1 mile up the hollow on a gradually ascending trail.

The natural area is on the Hammersley Fork, Pennsylvania, topographic quadrangle. The publication *Forrest H. Dutlinger Natural Area* includes a trail map; request it from the Susquehannock State Forest district office or from Bureau of Forestry headquarters in Harrisburg.

58   BLACK ASH SWAMP

308 ACRES, TIOGA STATE FOREST, TIOGA COUNTY

If Will hadn't been along, I never would have seen the little gold-colored frog that hopped off the trail as we passed. Will cupped it in his hands, and we knelt to study it through the lens. The frog was about the size of a raspberry, with a faint, wavery X marking its back. Long legs stuck out from its bulbous body. The attenuated toes were tipped with round suction pads—which helped the creature hold on as it escaped from my son's grip and went clambering and hopping over our arms, shirts, binoculars.

It was a spring peeper. Probably it had hatched at nearby Black Ash Swamp. I could well imagine how the peeping calls of hundreds of these tiny amphibians had, in springtime, enlivened the upland bog that we could now see, off through the trees, gleaming a dull, polished silver under the hazy July sun.

After breeding in the shallows of ponds, lakes, and swamps, spring peepers take up a land existence. They hunt for insects—ants, beetles, flies, caterpillars, and the like—and gobble up spiders, springtails, mites, ticks, and snails. Their toe pads help them climb around in grasses, ferns, and brush. Peepers don't travel very far: a study in Michigan found that most individuals covered from 20 to 130 feet per day.

The peeper wasn't the only amphibian that my sharp-eyed son managed to catch. He grabbed a pickerel frog out of the trickle of a stream that we crossed on our way to the swamp. And he snatched a frog out of a water-filled rut in the woods road we were following. We identified the latter as a green frog by the two raised lines of skin—called dorsolateral ridges—that ran from the frog's head most of the way back to its tail. Its body was about two inches long, leading me to believe that it was a year old: it looked too big to have metamorphosed from a tadpole to a froglet this summer. Or maybe it had overwintered in the tadpole stage and had changed into its adult form this past spring.

A trail, used recently by horses, led from the road toward the swamp. We passed through a woods well stocked with tall, straight black cherry trees and sturdy sugar maples—a stand of timber characterized, in a report I'd read in the Bureau of Forestry files in Harrisburg, as "the best representative in a Natural Area of the high-quality, second-growth northern hardwood stands typical of state ownership on the high plateau." A young buck deer, his forked antlers still in velvet, fed slowly through the woods nearby; we froze, and he never saw us. Will stopped to catch yet another amphibian: an American toad no bigger than my thumbnail. The hand lens revealed tiny red dots on the toadlet's dark brown, warty back.

At the south edge of the swamp, beavers had built a low dam. Adult male green frogs called from sedges and reeds rimming the pond: their cries sounded like plucked banjo strings or tight rubber bands. As Will and I crept along the perimeter, one green frog after another gave a sharp yelp, abandoned his breeding territory, leaped with a splash into the pond, and hid among stems or dug down into the mucky bottom.

The beaver lodge looked like a gray igloo on the far side of the pond. A red-winged blackbird, his shoulder epaulets a vivid red, flew up from the cattails and scolded us with sharp *chack* calls. A great blue heron lifted up, seemingly out of nowhere, and flew around the swamp in a big, slow circle, calling harshly. Cedar waxwings and tree swallows chased flying insects above the pond.

Dragonflies flew erratically above the water, dipping their abdomens to its glassy surface. They were laying eggs; the eggs would hatch into water-dwelling nymphs, mud-colored larvae that would later crawl up onto a stem, shed their armored skins, and take to the air as nimble, maneuverable adults. A damselfly with an emerald body and jet black wings windmilled past. A red-bodied dragonfly landed on a sedge, his wings giving off a bronze reflection. A dozen or more big *Anax junius*—the Latin name translates loosely as "Lord and Master of June"—hawked above the marsh, sashaying, darting, almost stalling in slow flight, then zooming off in pursuit of insects.

On the western edge of the pond, Will and I scared up another heron-like bird. It was stout-bodied, an overall dull brown with darker wingtips. It dropped out of sight among the cattails in the middle of the swamp. I'm fairly certain it was an American bittern, a rare, secretive bird that I have spotted only twice before, in marshes near my Centre County home. In 1928, in a treatise on the birds of northwestern Pennsylvania, George Miksch Sutton wrote that local folk called the bittern "Bum Chuck," the name being a fair imitation of the bird's weird courtship call. In the last century, the population of the American bittern has dwindled dangerously in Pennsylvania, because people have drained and polluted thousands of acres of wetlands. Today the bittern is considered endangered in the state.

Black Ash Swamp is a key remaining habitat for bitterns, which prey on fish, frogs, tadpoles, aquatic insects, and snakes. It would be worthwhile to visit this rich wetland on an April night, to listen to the peepers in their shrill vernal chorus and perhaps to hear the queer booming call of breeding bitterns.

TO GET THERE. From Wellsboro, go north and then west on U.S. Route 6, watching out for a sign marking the turn to the village of Asaph. Turn right at the sign, go to the stop sign, turn left, and continue on to the intersection with Asaph Road, 0.7 mile after leaving Route 6. Turn right onto Asaph Road and go 2.6 miles to Asaph Picnic Area. Bear right on narrow Right Asaph Road and go another 3.1 miles to the signs, on the left, for Cross Trail and Asaph Wild Area. Park here and walk.

Cross Trail heads roughly southwest, going downhill, with a logged-off area on the left. At the bottom of the hollow, turn right, following blue paint blazes. Cross a shallow stream (rubber boots are useful here and will let you do some bog exploring later) and continue on a logging road, which bears west. Soon the pond will show itself through the mature forest on your right.

Take along a compass and the Asaph, Pennsylvania, topographic quadrangle.

---

59   PINE CREEK GORGE

12,163 ACRES, TIOGA STATE FOREST, TIOGA COUNTY

The best way to see Pine Creek Gorge Natural Area is on foot. Barbour Rocks Trail winds through a mature forest of red oak, black cherry, American beech, and yellow birch trees. Moosewood—also known as striped maple, for its green-striped bark—grows in the understory. Amid the dense greenery, clumps of white birches catch and hold the eye.

After walking half a mile, I sensed blueness in the offing, a pale light filtering through the leaves. I quit looking at the trees, the stop-sign red mushrooms, the waxen white Indian pipes pushing up through pool-table green moss. The singing of wood thrushes and red-eyed vireos receded in my consciousness as I approached the ever-brighter light.

The valley was forested and thoroughly green, steep, deep, with a curving creek occupying most of its narrow floor. The Owassee rapids muttered eight hundred feet below me. Trees on the rim bent their branches out into

Visitors can hike along the canyon rim, canoe the waters of Pine Creek, or ride on horseback or bicycle along an old railroad grade through Pennsylvania's "grand canyon."

the canyon to catch the light. I sat on a rock and let my mind dangle quietly out over Pine Creek Gorge like those tree branches. People call it the Grand Canyon of Pennsylvania. I remember, years ago, at an overlook above the other Grand Canyon, the one in Arizona carved out by the Colorado River, sitting on a red rock in the clear sunlight and the dry air, when two people walked casually up to the abyss, a middle-aged man and a woman, and looked into it. A cigarette dangled in the corner of the man's mouth. After a while, he said to the woman, "It ain't very green"; presently they turned and went back to their car. On the back of his blue nylon jacket, I read a script slogan for somebody's bar and grill, Johnstown, Pennsylvania. I am not about to make comparisons between that grand canyon and this grand canyon, but I must acknowledge, looking out over Pine Creek Gorge, that I, too, am a Pennsylvanian, imbued with a green-tinged, eastern point of view.

You could also say the best way to enjoy Pine Creek Gorge Natural Area is on a horse—especially if it's an Icelandic horse. My wife and I own two Icelandics, small, sturdy, sure-footed equines with a gait called the tölt, an amazingly comfortable run-walk that carries you efficiently across the miles.

We tacked up at a parking area north of Ansonia; we rode south, crossing beneath a bridge for U.S. Route 6 and entering the gorge. Pine Creek Trail follows an old railroad grade on the east bank of the creek. The graveled portion of the trail is for bicycles, and horses may travel on a packed-dirt surface next to the bike path: a perfect place to tölt.

You sit with your spine aligned vertically above the horse's spine and get the animal's head up with a shake of the reins; then you shift your weight back slightly, and the horse collects itself, hind legs underneath its body, back level and steady, and goes high-stepping down the trail. The tölt can be fast or slow. It feels like sitting in a chair on a rug while someone pulls the rug across a waxed floor. The tölt is very much a shared enterprise, a dialogue between rider and horse.

On that cool morning in July, my wife's mare, Gæska, and my gelding, Birkir, tölted along next to the creek.

A phoebe sat on a branch above a ledge, flipping its tail up and down. Young crows, attended by their parents, sounded squally, nasal "feed me" caws. A kingfisher flew just above the water, its red-banded breast almost touching the surface as it dipped in flight. A gaggle of young common mergansers, about thirty birds, all juveniles, with gray bodies and rusty red heads, swam in a tight formation, veering this way and that, then finally fleeing into the shallows.

Dazzling orange and black-spotted flowers of turk's-cap lily dangled from tall stems along the bank. Yellow woodland sunflowers and white daisies starred the grass. The four-beat gait of our horses echoed from rock walls where purple-flowering raspberry grew above shoals of orange jewelweed.

Another "best" way to travel through Pine Creek Gorge is in a canoe. Philip Tome grew up along the creek in the late 1700s. He reported in a book, *Pioneer Life; or, Thirty Years a Hunter,* that rattlesnakes were so plentiful that travelers would spend the nights in their canoes, anchored in midstream. Tome was a market hunter who killed elk, bears, and deer—up to 130 of these large animals in a single season. In canoes that could carry four thousand pounds, Tome and his brother and father freighted fish and wild game to settlements near the mouth of Pine Creek, where they traded for wheat, corn, rye, salt, leather, and other necessities. As they drifted downstream, they hunted, leaving a trail of offal for the bears and wolves that followed.

Edward Gertler, in the modern book *Keystone Canoeing,* describes the stretch from Ansonia to Blackwell as "the prime section, the filet, the heart of Pine." It is a popular stream, flowing between abrupt and scenic mountains; the gorge is a mile wide and a thousand feet deep in places. In late spring and early summer, Pine Creek attracts hordes of boaters, from Boy Scouts and fishermen in aluminum canoes, to canoe clubbers in the latest Kevlar designs, to tourists in rubber rafts.

A note penciled into my dog-eared copy of Gertler's book: "4/13/92. Canoed Tiadaghton to Blackwell w. Gary Thornbloom, Tom Serfass, &

Arnie Hayden. Saw bald eagle, mink, many mergansers, plus otter sign. Creek was fast and high—staff gauge at Waterville was 3', at Blackwell $1^1/2$'." The eagle, a mature bird with a snowy head and tail, sat perched on a dead limb in a tall streamside pine, watching imperiously as we floated past. Tom Serfass is a wildlife biologist; at the time, he was working to reintroduce the river otter to Pine Creek and several other Pennsylvania drainages. That day, he pointed out otter signs for us, including droppings loaded with fish scales deposited on prominent streamside rocks; haul-outs, areas of beaten-down grass where otters habitually left the water; and slides where the animals had played, skidding on their bellies down mud-slick inclines to splash headlong into the creek.

I remember, even farther in the past, before the rail line through the canyon was removed, canoe-camping along Pine Creek and being wrenched from sleep several times each night by the trains that came roaring, clashing, pounding past less than fifty feet away—there being but little room between the creek and the tracks to pitch a tent.

May is a good month to canoe Pine Creek. Water levels are generally adequate but not dangerously high. (The river dwindles and becomes unrunnable after around mid-June.) Boaters will encounter one serious stretch of whitewater in the seventeen miles from Ansonia to Blackwell: Owassee Rapids, which lie below Barbour Rocks, about three miles south of the state-maintained Big Meadows access area at Ansonia. Owassee is rated a class two to three drop, depending on water level, and during high flows it can easily swamp an open boat. Gertler, a veteran canoeist, calls Owassee "a nothing rapid." He concedes, however, that "so many inept boaters travel Pine Creek and blunder needlessly down the right side of this rip, where all the rocks lie exposed at low water and all the big waves and holes wait at high water, that Owassee probably has a more fearsome and bloodier reputation than most of the real rapids of the Grand Canyon of the Colorado."

Pine Creek Gorge, at 12,163 acres, is the second-largest Bureau of Forestry Natural Area (Bucktail Natural Area contains 16,433 acres) and is actually larger than thirteen of the fourteen state-designated wild areas. It runs between Ansonia and Blackwell, a corridor roughly two miles wide covering the creek. Private inholdings lie within the gorge, particularly around the village of Tiadaghton, and some of them are posted and off-limits to the public. In 1968, Pine Creek Gorge received recognition as a registered national natural landmark.

The natural area surrounds the Leonard Harrison and Colton Point State Parks, opposite each other on the east and west rims. It also includes the Bradley Wales Picnic Area; the West Rim Trail; and numerous vistas from the mostly gravel roads to the west of Pine Creek Gorge. The views are particularly fine from Colton Point and Leonard Harrison. From the visitors' center at Leonard Harrison, the rugged Turkey Path descends one mile to the bottom of the gorge, switchbacking through the woods past observation decks and waterfalls on Little Four Mile Run. If Pine Creek is low, hikers can ford the stream and ascend, still on the Turkey Path, to Colton Point on the other rim.

Four Mile Run, Little Slate Run, Campbell Run, and Pine Island Run are side streams with pretty waterfalls. Old-growth hemlocks and hardwoods stand along Four Mile Run.

The state forest surrounding Pine Creek consists of mixed-oak and northern hardwoods, mainly beeches, birches, and maples. In autumn, the foliage astounds in fiery oranges, deep reds, and lambent yellows. At that time, it's hard to imagine any place in the world—including that deep, arid, immense, and colorful chasm in Arizona—surpassing the intimate beauty of Pine Creek Gorge.

TO GET THERE. Contact the Tioga State Forest district headquarters for a public-use map and information packet. For a guidebook and maps for the 30.4-mile West Rim Trail, contact Pine Creek Outfitters, RR 4 Box 130B, Wellsboro, PA 16901, telephone (570) 724-3003, website www.pinecrk.com. *Pennsylvania's Grand Canyon: A Natural and Human History,* by Chuck Dillon, photography by Curt Weinhold, is also available from Pine Creek Outfitters. It has information on geology, Native Americans, the lumbering era, and wildlife and plants. Pine Creek Outfitters can arrange canoe, raft, backpacking, and bicycling trips. Their free *Outdoor Adventure Guide* covers a range of outdoor activities.

To reach Leonard Harrison State Park, take PA Route 660 west from Wellsboro. The highway dead-ends at the park. Colton Point State Park is 6 miles south of U.S. Route 6 and Ansonia via a paved forest road.

60   REYNOLDS SPRING

1,302 ACRES, TIOGA STATE FOREST,
TIOGA COUNTY

I followed where a bear had trod, between deep green shrubs of sweet fern and through the glossy, ground-hugging leaves of dewberry. Speckled alders pushed up in patches next to narrow Morris Run on my left. Gray, barkless pine stumps stood among the ferns, remains of huge trees that had darkened the shallow basin before falling to the woodsman's ax a century earlier.

The bear had fed as it walked: clipped-off stems of blueberries showed where the bruin had gobbled down clusters of fruit. I, too, paused to pick and eat handfuls of ripe berries. The bear's trail also was marked by crushed sedges, their green tips pointing ahead toward the high mountain bog that is Reynolds Spring Natural Area's most outstanding feature and the reason for its designation as a national natural landmark.

I watched for my black-coated predecessor, but neither hide nor hair of him did I see. A gray catbird flew out of a clump of mountain ash and red maple and circled me warily, keeping to the brush and never making a sound. Probably it had a nest and didn't want to advertise the fact: since it was well into July, I assumed the bird was working on its second brood. A towhee scratched for food on the ground in a patch of oaks bordering the meadow, while above it a scarlet tanager flew from one branch to another in the canopy. From where I stood, forest stretched in all directions, broken by occasional openings such as Reynolds Spring bog, a wet meadow believed to be a series of old beaver dams that subsequently silted in.

I had also visited Reynolds Spring earlier in the summer, joining a group of plant enthusiasts led by Dr. Carl Keener, professor emeritus of botany at Penn State University and an expert on Pennsylvania's native plants. Keener had handed out a list of the species he had identified in the natural area, which included twelve different sedges, grasslike herbs that often grow in bogs. Other shrubs and herbaceous plants at Reynolds Spring include mountain holly, wild raisin, northern jack-in-the-pulpit, wild calla lily, bog aster, bunchberry, wood horsetail, false hellebore (whose poisonous root can cause death by respiratory paralysis and asphyxiation), marsh marigold, and marsh blue violet. Keener had shown us three species of rare

Pitcher plants and sundews, rare bog plants that capture and digest insects, grow at Reynolds Spring Natural Area, along with many other wetlands plants.

Insects enter the mouths of the water-filled leaves of the pitcher plant and drown; the plant digests them, procuring food in the nutrient-poor bog environment.

orchids, as well as those remarkable bog-dwelling carnivores, the round-leaved sundew and pitcher plant.

The black bear's footmarks—depressions in the sphagnum moss now filled with water—led me into the center of the bog. White pines and pitch pines stood on drier spots, where their roots had found purchase. The low-growing wiry shrub known as leatherleaf grew abundantly. Between the glossy, yellowish green humps of the leatherleaf, pale green sphagnum moss covered the surface of the bog.

Sphagnum mosses are hardy plants that survive in, and help perpetuate, the acidic environment of the bog. Notes Charles W. Johnson in his book *Bogs of the Northeast,* "Sphagnum plants have a fascinating growth habit: they grow from the top and die from the bottom." The decomposing dead parts sink slowly to the bottom of the bog, where they become layers of peat. In some wetlands, the peat builds up to depths of ten or more feet. Removed from the bog and dried, peat can be burned for fuel; absorbent and naturally sterile, it has been used as surgical dressings for wounds and as baby diapers. The peat moss sold in garden supply stores is mined from bogs, mainly in the Canadian province of New Brunswick.

I bent over and, using my hands, pushed aside the sphagnums until I had separated a single sphagnum plant from the bog carpet. The top of a sphagnum supports buds, stems, and pliant, leaf-covered branches. Some of the branches lie along the plant's stem, while others spread outward. The branches are only a few cells across, and the leaves are but a single cell thick. In the leaves, large, hollow cells store water and release it slowly during drought; smaller cells contain molecules of chlorophyll that manufacture food for the plant and, in the case of the sphagnum I was examining, color it a glowing green. Other sphagnum species are red, brown, or yellow.

Different species grow in different parts of the bog basin. Some thrive in low, saturated areas; others flourish in drier zones. The mat of interwoven sphagnum supports plants ranging from tall trees, like the pines, to tiny ones such as the sundew I spied tucked into the edge of the bank along a dark-water stream trickling through the bog.

The sundew had small, rounded leaves covered with pinkish red hairs. At the end of each hair, a bead of sticky fluid caught the sun like a ruby. The flower-bright hairs attract insects; should an insect brush against a hair, the creature is ensnared. The hair then acts like a tentacle, growing with astonishing speed, folding itself around the prey. The plant slowly releases enzymes and digests its victim.

Like the sundew, the pitcher plant is carnivorous; and it, too, lies in wait. The plant's gracefully curved leaves are shaped like pitchers, and like pitchers, they hold water. The leaves, four to ten inches tall, stand in clusters on the sphagnum at Reynolds Spring. I happened to look into one just as a daddy longlegs spider chose to enter.

On its outsize legs, the daddy longlegs walked tentatively into the leaf's open mouth. It may have been attracted by sweet-smelling nectar or the leaf's purple-colored veins, or perhaps it had come in search of its own prey.

I knelt to watch, heedless of the wet that soaked my trousers. The daddy longlegs stopped and waved a frontal pair of legs, like feelers. It edged deeper into the leaf. The inside of the flared leaf had hundreds of downward-pointing spikes, protrusions that make it almost impossible for a creature to turn around after it gets inside. The daddy longlegs kept walking. Where the pitcher constricted to a narrow necklike zone, the spider encountered a band of cells: sticky, easily dislodged. The spider flailed its legs. It skidded downward. It pitched into the smooth-sided bowl, half filled with rainwater. There it joined two other daddy longlegs, both still alive, although moving feebly, and a floating midge, dead.

The spiders were a jumble of jointed legs and dark, elliptical bodies. The recent victim tried to climb by standing on the abdomens of its fellows. It got partway up, but when its feet slid on the recurved walls, it fell back down. The daddy longlegs struggled in this manner for several minutes, but there was no way out. The spider would eventually drown. It would sink to the leaf's next zone, where enzymes and bacteria would begin decomposing its body. Over time, the corpse would drift down to yet a deeper zone, in the leaf's long, narrow stalk, from where vascular tissues would carry the animal protein to the rest of the plant.

A bumblebee sped noisily past, waking me to my surroundings. It was a glorious summer's day, with puffy clouds waltzing across a pure blue sky. Farther into the bog I went. Sinking to my ankles with each step, I felt the chill of the water through my rubber boots.

A great crested flycatcher called from the surrounding forest, and a veery gave its liquid, down-trending song. But the plants seemed to be the real presence at Reynolds Spring bog. Breast-high cinnamon ferns. Wild cranberries sprawling over the sphagnum, with white berries that would turn red in autumn. I detoured around more pitcher plants than I'd encountered in almost any other place. I saw grass pink orchids with showy magenta-and-yellow flowers. Another pink orchid, rose pogonia—sometimes called snake-mouth—showed a crested, fringed lip.

The sedges were many, and of many different species. Dr. Keener had said there were more species in the sedges, around three thousand, than in any other botanical family. Most sedges have triangular stems, and there is a memory jogger that goes "Rushes are round, sedges have edges, grasses have joints from their tops to the ground." Much of the life in a bog is tied up in the shallow, entwining roots and underground stems of sedges. Sedges are sometimes called "marsh hay," and people have traditionally pastured animals in bogs.

In that vegetative riot, one plant stuck out for me. It was a common thing, beautiful in its simplicity. Keener had identified it as white beak-sedge, a species found in the Old World as well as the New World. It grew thickly in the damp places, waving in the breeze. A foot tall, it had grasslike leaves and slender stems holding up delicate tufted flowers that blazed a tawny white, like bleached hay under the brilliant sun. The effect was of a heaven full of stars brought down to earth.

> **TO GET THERE.** From the general store in Slate Run, drive north on PA Route 414 for 3.9 miles to Gamble Run Road. Turn left and ascend past Algerine Lane (at 2.1 miles) and Buskirk Trail (at 2.3 miles); pass the sign for Algerine Swamp Natural Area on the left (at 3.0 miles beyond Route 414) and continue 0.9 mile to a fork in the road. Take Reynolds Spring Road to the left and go another 0.8 mile to a small parking area on the left. Cross the road and hike northeast along Morris Run to the bog.
>
> The only trail in the natural area is Little Morris Run Trail, which follows Little Morris Run through mixed-oak forest. Reynolds Spring Trail forms the eastern and northern boundaries of the natural area, included in the Lee Fire Tower and Cedar Run topographic quadrangles.

61 ANDERS RUN

96 ACRES, CORNPLANTER STATE FOREST, WARREN COUNTY

Snow fell softly in the woods. The flakes settled on three inches of powder already covering the ground. The unmarred surface made it plain that no one had walked the trail through the natural area for several days.

The pines on each side of the path reached into the snow-filled sky. Sometime during the first two decades of the nineteenth century, the forest in this valley fell to the ax. The Allegheny River, into which Anders Run flows a half mile east of the natural area, was a highway for explorers and soldiers, then for the lumberjacks and settlers who followed. The white pines now reigning in the narrow valley must have grown from seeds blown by the wind into the newly created clearing.

It was December 19, 2000, and Anders Run was the last of the sixty-one natural areas I visited. I had seen hundreds of big trees in some of those other sixty places, but that didn't lessen my wonder at these giants.

In 1987, Ted Grisez, a retired forest scientist living in nearby Warren, measured ten of the tallest pines at Anders Run and found that their heights ranged from 126 to 146 feet; Grisez made his measurements using a clinometer, an optical device that compares slope to a known distance, thus revealing the height of something that can't easily be measured. By now, thirteen years later, no doubt the trees were somewhat taller. According to the local district forester, a white pine 180 feet tall recently blew down during a storm.

In the snow-filled light of the winter morning, the bark on the Anders Run pines showed as a dull grayish brown. Some of the trees stood perpendicular, and others leaned away at a slight angle from the vertical. Their trunks were straight, and for a long way up they had no branches. The crowns of the pines made up the top third of the trees. The crowns were green and soft and feathery looking, their boughs held out and away from the trunks by massive branches, some of the branches straight and some of them curved like brawny arms. Snow capped the upper surfaces of the branches. The pines' crowns did not quite merge, as if each tree maintained its own individual space, its own thousand square feet of forest canopy.

Below the trees, Anders Run gushed down its bed. A car came driving down a road through the woods; at first the intrusion of the machine bothered me, but after the car had gone, silence descended again, and the road seemed of little importance.

Standing before one of the pines, I took off my gloves. I tried to get a grip on the trunk by spreading my arms and sinking my fingertips into valleys between the bark ridges. My palms rested on the bark, which somehow felt soft and rough at the same time. My arms went halfway around the trunk. I stood there, leaning against the solidity of the giant pine. I decided I must look a little odd. However, I've never considered "tree hugger" to be much of an insult.

In 1963, the pines at Anders Run were slated to be cut by the National Forge Company, which owned the property. When the Northern Allegheny Conservation Association—a group of local citizens involved in protecting places of scenic and biological interest—heard about the logging, they asked National Forge to spare the giant pines. The company, based in Warren, agreed. In 1987, the Western Pennsylvania Conservancy joined with the Northern Allegheny Conservation Association and the DeFrees Family Foundation, another local entity, to buy the land from National Forge at a much-reduced price. The ninety-six acres were turned over to the Bureau of Forestry and given protection as a natural area.

Today a 1.8-mile trail winds between the large pines and a smaller number of equally impressive hemlocks, along with red and white oak, American beech, black cherry, black gum, sugar maple, shagbark hickory, yellow birch, tuliptree, basswood, and eastern hornbeam trees. Since it was winter, I did not see any ground plants, but the rich soil supports many wildflowers, including hepatica, painted and red trillium, pink lady's slip-

In winter, large hemlocks and white pines at Anders Run Natural Area stand blanketed with snow.

per, wild ginger, white clintonia, Solomon's seal, wild geranium, Indian cucumber root, bunchberry, foamflower, and several species of violets. Along the stream grow New York, sensitive, Christmas, cinnamon, and maidenhair ferns.

I walked on the soft, quiet snow. Deer, fox, and squirrel tracks slowly filled in with the falling flakes. A white-breasted nuthatch gave its *yank-yank* call, but the only birds I actually saw were a small band of black-capped chickadees.

Some of the pines had deep wounds, places where branches had broken away, leaving vertical slits that their bark was slowly closing over. The ball-shaped bark nest of a red squirrel sat halfway out on one branch, snow-capped. The trees did not move at all as the snow continued to cover them. The hemlocks held great loads of snow on their dense, short needles; on the ground beneath them, the snow depth was much less than beneath the pines. Seen from the slope and at a distance, the pines showed tiers of branches, one above the other, spreading outward and slightly down from the main trunk, then tipping up over their last quarter.

The pines at Anders Run will not always be present. A climax forest is a stable, self-perpetuating ecosystem. White pines need direct light to prosper. Beneath the giant pines, hemlock and beech seedlings grew—both shade-tolerant species—but no young pines. Some day, hundreds of years hence, if we keep our forests healthy, the hemlocks and beeches will take over from the pines, which, having reached the ends of their natural lives, will die and become hollow and perhaps stand as barkless hulks for decades and then come crashing down to lie upon the earth and decompose and release their nutrients to feed other trees, in a forest capable of regenerating itself.

I hoped Pennsylvanians would come and take notice.

TO GET THERE. From U.S. Route 6 west of Warren, take the PA Route 62 exit toward Tidioute. About 0.1 mile after exiting, before you reach the Allegheny River bridge, turn right at a sign for the Buckaloons Recreation Area and the USDA Forest Sciences Laboratory. Continue 0.7 mile and turn left onto Dunns Eddy River Road. Go 1.0 mile to the natural area. On the left is a parking area with a sign depicting the 1.8-mile loop trail.

ACKNOWLEDGMENTS

I would like to thank the many people who helped in the making of this book. They include Will Fergus, Nancy Marie Brown, Gary Thornbloom, Ed Dix, Jim Nelson, Bob Hill, Nick Bolgiano, John McGonigle, Mike Silvestri, Mike McMenamin, John Miller, Duke Hobaugh, Merlin Benner, Kurt Carr, Mike Kusko, Tim Maret, Bob Beleski, Jerry Hassinger, Greg Grove, Robert Gruver, Marcia Bonta, Bruce Bonta, Carl Keener, Les Johnson, Tom Thwaites, James Conner, Tim Ladner, Jeff Stuffle, Butch Davey, Charlie Schwartz, Clark Shiffer, Dean Lapp, Rick Wardrop, Tommy Wardrop, Bill Jordan, Doug Gross, Allen Schweinsberg, and Cindy Dunn. A special thanks also goes to the many other Bureau of Forestry employees who provided guidance and information.

RESOURCES

REFERENCES

Almost as important to a naturalist as hiking boots and binoculars are *books*: field guides, texts, and other references. The following volumes are good resources for anyone interested in getting the most out of visits to Pennsylvania's Bureau of Forestry Natural Areas.

Pennsylvania Outdoors

Outbound Journeys in Pennsylvania and *More Outbound Journeys in Pennsylvania,* by Marcia Bonta (Penn State Press, University Park, PA). Marcia Bonte is an excellent naturalist, and I enjoyed her observations of twenty of the state forest natural areas, shared between her two books, which also cover a selection of state parks, private nature preserves, wildlife sanctuaries, and arboretums and gardens.

50 Hikes in Western Pennsylvania, 50 Hikes in Central Pennsylvania, and *50 Hikes in Eastern Pennsylvania,* by Tom Thwaites (Countryman Press, Woodstock, VT). These three hiking guides include detailed maps and descriptions of hikes in and passing through a number of state forest natural areas.

Wildlife

Atlas of Breeding Birds in Pennsylvania, edited by Daniel W. Brauning, (University of Pittsburgh Press, Pittsburgh, PA). This reference book includes maps showing the breeding ranges of all the bird species in the state.

The Birds of Pennsylvania, by Gerald M. McWilliams and Daniel W. Brauning (Cornell University Press, Ithaca, NY). A thorough and accurate guide to our state's birds in all seasons.

I rely on two old friends for bird identification: *A Field Guide to the Birds,* by Roger Tory Peterson (Houghton Mifflin, Boston, MA), and *Birds of North America,* by Chandler S. Robbins, Bertel Bruun, and Herbert S. Zim (Golden Press, New York, NY). A newer field guide is *The Sibley Guide to Birds,* by David Allen Sibley (Alfred A. Knopf, New York, NY).

A Guide to Amphibians and Reptiles, by Thomas F. Tyning (Little, Brown, Boston, MA). Life history information on many of the commonly seen reptile and amphibian species.

Wildlife of Pennsylvania and the Northeast, by Charles Fergus (Stackpole Books, Mechanicsburg, PA), takes up where field guides leave off: it presents the natural histories of all the state's mammals, birds, reptiles, and amphibians. Illustrations by Amelia Hansen.

Plants

For trees, the two best field guides are *Eastern Trees,* by George A. Petrides (Houghton Mifflin, Boston, MA), and *The Audubon Society Field Guide to North American Trees, Eastern Region,* by Elbert L. Little (Alfred Knopf, New York, NY).

An easy-to-use wildflower identification book is *Newcomb's Wildflower Guide,* by Lawrence Newcomb (Little, Brown, Boston, MA).

After identifying a tree, shrub, or wildflower, learn about it from *The Book of Forest and Thicket* and *The Book of Swamp and Bog,* by John Eastman, illustrated by Amelia Hansen (Stackpole Books, Mechanicsburg, PA).

General

Eastern Old-Growth Forests, edited by Mary Byrd Davis (Island Press, Washington, D.C.), presents essays by leading experts examing the ecology and characteristics of eastern old growth.

Bogs of the Northeast, by Charles W. Johnson (University Press of New England, Hanover, NH), explores the ecology of these strange and dwindling habitats. (Many of the Pennsylvania state forest natural areas preserve bogs and related wetlands.)

Mountains of the Heart, by Scott Weidensaul (Fulcrum Publishing, Golden, CO), is a readable and informative natural history of the Appalachians, in which a majority of our state's natural areas are located.

Outdoor Skills

Using a Map & Compass, by Don Geary (Stackpole Books, Mechanicsburg, PA), teaches the basics of map-reading and orienteering.

NOLS Wilderness First Aid, by Tod Schimelpfenig and Linda Lindsey (Stackpole Books, Mechanicsburg, PA), is a good primer with many helpful illustrations.

STATE FOREST DISTRICT OFFICES

Bald Eagle Forest District Office
P.O. Box 147
Laurelton, PA 17835
570-922-3344

Buchanan Forest District Office
440 Buchanan Trail
McConnellsburg, PA 17233
717-485-3148

Cornplanter Forest District Office
323 North State Street
North Warren, PA 16365
814-723-0262

Delaware Forest District Office
HC 1, Box 95A
Swiftwater, PA 18370-9723
570-895-4000

Elk Forest District Office
R.R. 4, Box 212 – Suite 1
Emporium, PA 15834
814-486-3353

Forbes Forest District Office
P.O. Box 519
Laughlintown, PA 15655
724-238-1200

Gallitzin Forest District Office
P.O. Box 506
Ebensburg, PA 15931
814-472-1862

Kittanning Forest District Office
158 South Second Avenue
Clarion, PA 16214
814-226-1901

Lackawanna Forest District Office
401 Samters Bldg., 101 Penn Avenue
Scranton, PA 18503
570-963-4561

Michaux Forest District Office
10099 Lincoln Way East
Fayetteville, PA 17222
717-352-2211

Moshannon Forest District Office
R.R. 1, Box 184
Penfield, PA 15849
814-765-0821

Rothrock Forest District Office
P.O. Box 403
Rothrock Lane
Huntingdon, PA 16652
814-643-2340

Sproul Forest District Office
HCR 62, Box 90
Renovo, PA 17764
570-923-6011

Susquehannock Forest District Office
P.O. Box 673
Coudersport, PA 16915-0673
814-274-3600

Tiadaghton Forest District Office
423 East Central Avenue
South Williamsport, PA 17702
570-327-3450

Tioga Forest District Office
One Nessmuk Lane
Wellsboro, PA 16901
570-724-2868

Tuscarora Forest District Office
R.R. 1, Box 42-A
Blain, PA 17006
717-536-3191

Valley Forge Forest District Office
845 Park Road
Elverson, PA 19520-9523
610-582-9660

Weiser Forest District Office
P.O. Box 99
Cressona, PA 17929
570-385-7800

Wyoming Forest District Office
274 Arbutus Park Road
Bloomsburg, PA 17815
570-387-4255